D1155270

WITH BENEFIT OF ARCHITECT

Edward X Tuttle, Jr., A.I.A.

WITH BENEFIT OF ARCHITECT

A MANUAL FOR THOSE ABOUT TO BUILD

THE MACMILLAN COMPANY, NEW YORK

Library of Congress Catalog Card Number: 68-19826
First Printing

The Macmillan Company, New York
Collier-Macmillan Canada Ltd., Toronto, Ontario

Printed in the United States of America

Acknowledgments

Many valuable suggestions, which I have adopted, were made by people who read this book in manuscript form. Cecil A. Scott, a distinguished editor, first encouraged me to write the book, then roundly and soundly criticized the results. Betty F. Tuttle, my mother, represented the intelligent layman in her criticism and also saved me from many solecisms. Edward X Tuttle, Sr., my father, is an architect with twice my experience and, like my friend Thomas E. M. Wheat, also an architect, represented the profession in his criticism. I thank each for his help but remind the reader that any remaining errors are the sole responsibility of the author.

CONTENTS

WITH BENEFIT OF ARCHITECT

A SMALL BUILDUP

This book is not for architects; it is for their clients, present and future. You may wish a house built to your own requirements. You may be a businessman who will need a new or enlarged store, shopping center, hotel, bank, factory, warehouse, garage, or other commercial building. You may be a member of a church, hospital, or other building committee. You may be a member of a school board or a university trustee, partly responsible for the shape of new schools. You may serve the government in a position that involves the building of federal, state, or municipal buildings, or you may work for a corporation in connection with private construction. You may be a real estate investor, whose activities might include construction of almost any type of building. Some of you are frequently involved in building, but most of you will be involved only once. In the latter case, you will have to accept or share responsibility for investing a lot of money, in a single venture, without prior experience.

This book is an attempt to provide some substitute for that experience. It traces the course of events in which you will be participating from the beginning of a building to the day it is finished and occupied. Although most of the examples used here are taken from houses, the problems discussed and recommendations given apply to all types of buildings, ranging from simple sheds to complex laboratories. A house, however, is ideal for illustrative purposes not only because it is familiar to all readers, but because it combines the features of a restaurant, bus station, hotel, recreation building, warehouse, and so forth.

This book, then, is not about architecture, architects, contractors, or building construction. All of these matters come in for a certain amount of discussion here, but the real subject of this book is how you, the client, can handle client-architect-contractor relations to obtain a building of maximum value at minimum cost. So far as I can determine, no other such book as this exists.

There are two significant omissions in what follows: construction financing, and property values. The architect understands costs of construction and requirements of site; but sources of money and land, their value, and problems of their acquisition, should be dealt with by experts in other fields.

Looking back on any large venture we usually find it impossible to label the exact point of beginning. In the case of a new building the beginning is certainly not the groundbreaking, nor is it the hiring of an architect to make plans. Perhaps the beginning occurs when you decide to build. Yet the form the building will take depends on ideas and attitudes that have been developing in you all your life. A review of such ideas therefore seems to be the best way to begin this book.

After that we shall consider how buildings affect their occupants. Only after deciding what effects are wanted from a building can it be designed to produce them. Then you will either hire an architect or decide that one is unnecessary. To make this decision, you should know something about architects in general, and how to choose one. The rest of the book takes up matters in roughly chronological order to the completion of construction.

Almost everyone knows a lot about how buildings work, but few really know very much about how architects and the construction industry work. This ignorance hurts. Some people, for instance, seem to think that contractors are generally employed by architects, but that is as wrong as to believe that prosecuting attorneys are employed by judges. Others believe that architects run up the cost of construction (to get higher fees, presumably), and design monuments to themselves. Some think that architects "bid" on jobs. All these notions are naive; they are caused by certain faults of a few architects. They can lead to bad relations among owner, architect, and contractor, and may even cause the contractor to retaliate at the owner's expense.

It is possible to hire an architect and learn about the problems of building as you go along, but is much better to know them in advance, and let them sink in before actually having to deal with architects and contractors. There is also value in simply knowing what to expect as events unwind. The unexpected, even if harmless, tends to be worrisome.

You can play a part in the shaping of a new building that is broader and more decisive than many people realize. This book should help you, in a positive sense, to act that part so as to serve your own best interests, and in a negative sense, to avoid damaging mistakes. If the path seems too difficult, you can place yourself in the hands of a competent architect and simply follow his advice, even as you might in the case of a doctor or lawyer, but any advance familiarity with the problems of building will tend to improve the quality of the results. An informed client may spell the difference between architecture and great architecture.

Chapter 1

APPROACHES TO ARCHITECTURE

Most of us spend most of our lives inside buildings. When not inside them we are usually surrounded by them as we travel from one to another. Buildings affect our thoughts and our physical comfort. They hinder or facilitate our actions. They offer means of making money or going bankrupt. They can maintain us in health today, or collapse and kill us tomorrow. They can fascinate, awe, depress, delight, or bore us. They are so much with us that sometimes familiarity breeds contempt.

The total value of buildings in the United States is about 700 billion dollars: over one-third of our nation's tangible wealth. In all the world only other human beings affect us more constantly and deeply than buildings.

When a new building is stitched into the fabric of our environment it reflects conscious and unconscious beliefs about art, economics, sociology, and psychology; and about structural, mechanical, and electrical engineering. All buildings do this, but each building also reflects beliefs as to its own particular purpose, which is to benefit its occupants' family life, business, health, religion, or other human activities. Just as it is sometimes said that no one really knows enough to bring up children, so it can be said that no one really knows enough to conceive, design, and construct a new building. These considerations have little effect on the proliferation of either children or buildings, however, because we must have both, and the fact that our understanding is imperfect is no excuse for not using what knowledge we have. Just as it is wise to think carefully before investing a lifetime in marriage and children, so it is advisable to study and think carefully before investing several years' salary in a building. These investments, in family and building, are the largest most people ever make—one emotional, the other monetary—and few make them more than once. A great deal must be risked in both cases without benefit of personal experience. The man who plans to build must lean heavily on the knowledge and experience of others.

There is another complication where buildings are concerned. A building is a many-faceted thing, but we are a nation of specialists. Each of us has blind spots which prevent him from paying adequate attention to some aspects of buildings. A person sensitive to art is inclined to misconstrue the role of engineering in architecture; engineers tend to subordinate human convenience to the elegant layout of plumbing pipes, and so forth. A faulty stance thus characterizes both the future owners of buildings and the specialists who help build. In this situation an architect takes on additional value simply from his relative lack of specialization. Of all those concerned with building, he is least likely to have serious blind spots.

The architect has experience and breadth of knowledge that future owners of buildings lack, but hiring him is not enough. If you commission an architect to design a building, you must first tell him what you want, and this is harder than it sounds. After he starts work, he will periodically show you drawings and make suggestions, which you must either approve, modify, or disapprove. Your ability to "place your order" intelligently, and then evaluate the architect's response—as embodied in the drawings and recommendations he makes—is a fundamental factor in the success or failure of the building. How you do it depends not only on your knowledge of facts but also on your architectural outlook.

One's outlook or approach to architecture is usually a mixture of largely unconscious attitudes which appear to echo stages in the historical evolution of architecture. It seems worthwhile to explore different outlooks and try to understand them, because there may be attainable advantages in outlooks different from your own, and you may also discover inconsistencies among your own attitudes.

For most people the problem is simply the question of "traditional" versus "modern." Once most people have decided between these two possibilities, they seek an architect of like persuasion. For reasons that will appear later, both traditionalists and modernists can be viewed as having basically similar attitudes, which I shall call Imitative. Others think that the controversy between modernism and traditionalism misses the point.

Before we can build successfully, they say, we must critically examine the ways buildings are related to human activities; the modernists and traditionalists just emphasize the ways buildings are related to each other. As this second approach involves higher generalities, I shall call it Abstract. A third approach ignores both the modern-traditional controversy, and the broad relations of buildings to life. It focuses squarely on cost and physical utility. I shall call this approach Utilitarian.

Let us explore these three approaches to building and try to see their implications as well as their origin. Historically it is probable that the Utilitarian outlook is the earliest, with the Imitative next, and the Abstract coming last. We will discuss them in the same order. We will also attempt to illustrate different outlooks with photographs of buildings, but it must be remembered that we are considering mental approaches to building, not buildings themselves. It is quite possible for different attitudes to produce similar buildings, or for similar attitudes to produce different buildings. We can only say that certain buildings, or parts of them, appear consistent with certain approaches to architecture, and that certain approaches tend to produce certain characteristics in buildings.

UTILITARIAN APPROACH

Bird nests and beaver dams illustrate a Utilitarian approach to architecture. The caves and lean-tos of primitive man were Utilitarian, and so are most of the dams, powerhouses, undecorated sheds and barns, and many of the factories of modern man. The Utilitarian approach avoids ornament. More generally speaking, it ignores the psychological (including esthetic) effects buildings have on their occupants and viewers. In a positive sense, the Utilitarian approach is an attempt to acquire maximum physical utility at minimum cost.

In pursuing his important but limited objectives, the Utilitarian sometimes accidentally produces beauty: a psychological effect. Almost everyone can bring to mind some Utilitarian building—perhaps a log cabin or grain elevator, a dam or a bridge—that has struck him as being beautiful. The accidental beauty of some Utilitarian buildings complicates discussions of architecture: some people maintain that if buildings are simply stripped of non-Utilitarian artifice they will inevitably be beautiful. We do not, however, know what others mean by "beauty," and if we did, it is only one of many psychological aspects of buildings.

BUCKMINSTER FULLER

This railroad car repair and maintenance shop is one of a growing family of geodesic domes, simple and spare. If the activities to be housed benefit from a circular plan with increasing headroom toward the center, then structures like this are extremely economical; but their appearance, however handsome, arises from an elegant solution to mechanical problems, not from any attempt to create art or other psychological effects.

Some buildings, such as automated factories and power stations, perhaps invisible from public roads, are virtually unoccupied and unseen. In such cases the Utilitarian approach is usually pursued. As all buildings, nevertheless, are seen by somebody, sometime, there is still question whether ugliness is ever justifiable. But we can dodge the issue. It seems likely that if the problems of cost and physical utility are carefully considered in advance, and the building is intelligently planned to meet their requirements, it will exhibit several predictable qualities. First, there will be no waste: Every stick and stone will have definite purpose and meaningful arrangement. Second, there will be no inconsistencies of design tending to produce an inharmonious appearance. Third, there will be no artifice. It follows that a building designed from a strictly Utilitarian approach, although it may not be beautiful or psychologically "deft," will probably not be ugly either, because ugliness usually stems from waste, disharmony, and distasteful artifice.

The Utilitarian approach is justified when the psychological effects of the building are relatively unimportant, which is not the same as saying they are of no importance at all. The successful Utilitarian approach requires the designer to strive for a kind of "natural simplicity" in providing maximum physical usefulness for minimum cost. The architect must continually remind himself (or be reminded) that complicated, controlled psychological effects, in this case, are of negligible value to his client and to society.

IMITATIVE APPROACH

Like the Utilitarian, the Imitative approach includes the desire for physical utility and economy. It differs in adding a desire for the psychological effects obtainable by having new buildings, or parts of them, copy something else, usually other buildings. This desire for *resemblance* is the distinguishing mark of the Imitative approach.

The origin of Imitation is probably the magical beliefs of primitive man. When ideas about personal demons or family totems prevailed, it was believed that their beneficent presence could be invoked by erecting their sculptured likeness at the mouth of the cave, or hanging it from a tentpole. As in the practice of sticking pins in dolls, it was believed that the being or spirit actually resided in its effigy. Such belief is the cause of what I am calling the Imitative approach to architecture. Thus the traditionalist desires a house that imitates the house he lived in as a child, because for him it brings home the spirit of childhood security. Surprisingly the modernist is subject to the same feeling: for him a sense of freedom, or refreshing novelty, or something else pleasing, resides in "modernistic" buildings, and he imitates them in order to re-create this spirit.

Imitation is easily misunderstood because the impulse is usually unconscious and is afterward rationalized. Traditional shutters on houses, it may reasonably be argued, are interesting and ornamental, but if the person who insists on shutters cannot be convinced that any alternative can also be interesting and ornamental he fairly well demonstrates that his approach is Imitative. The same is true in the case of the modernist who blindly

WAYNE ANDREWS

BUILDING IMITATION: TRADITIONAL VARIETY

The modern house below is a current scion of the family whose ancestors are represented above by the Parson Capen house, Topsfield, Massachusetts, c. 1683. Notice that despite the over-all similarity, perceptible at a glance, the modern house is actually different in most details.

BUILDING IMITATION: MODERN VARIETY

The upper building, a theater in Germany, was built about 1955. The lower building, a metropolitan post office in the United States, was designed during 1958–59. The similarity between them may be coincidental, arising from the use of similar materials and methods in designing buildings whose masses have similar shapes. Only if the designer of the lower building admitted copying the upper (earlier) one could Imitation be conclusively proved.

ABOVE: ROBERT HAUSER

insists on some modern feature (level roof, picture window, or what have you) merely because it is modern and not because it is suitable for physical, psychological, and economic reasons. On the other hand there exist practical solutions to some of the problems of building, and many of these, at least temporarily, defy improvement. If, for this reason, the designer adopts an 8-foot ceiling height, or a double-loaded corridor, he is not Imitative: he is copying, not to evoke the spirit of the original, but to solve practical problems the best way he can. This illustrates the difficulty of inferring the designer's outlook from an inspection of his design. If the design includes definite vestiges of historical styles, however, it is almost certainly Imitative.

In the past the Imitator often demanded precise duplication of some admired building. After Thomas Jefferson had pondered the design of the Virginia State House, he decided that what this country needed to start out on the right architectural foot was a copy of the Roman temple of Fortuna Virilis at Nîmes, France. His object was to bring the spirit of Republican Rome over here, and drive back the spirit of aristocratic, Georgian England. Nowadays wholehearted reproduction of antique architecture is rare; it tends to be prohibitively expensive.

If psychological effect is really important in architecture, then Imitation is superior to Utilitarianism. Certainly it stands higher on the evolutionary scale: The birds and the bees are Utilitarian, but only man creates Imitative Architecture.

1. Building Imitation

So far we have discussed the Imitative approach as a desire to copy other buildings or details of them. We can call this Building Imitation, and it is just one of the possibilities for the Imitator. Also discernible are Whimsical Imitation, and Anti-Imitation.

2. Whimsical Imitation

Hot dog stands that look like hot dogs exemplify the approach of the Whimsical Imitator. There is a church that looks like an open book (no doubt a bible), and the office of a company manufacturing concrete sewer pipe that looks like an overgrown piece of concrete sewer pipe. The spirit of the commodity purveyed—hot dogs, fundamentalist religion, and sewer pipe, respectively—is bathetically effigized in the architecture.

WHIMSICAL IMITATION
The most intricate piece of concrete sewer pipe ever built.

Few people can take Whimsical Imitation seriously. It seems appropriate for only the most frivolous, temporary structures. I think it belongs only in carnivals and amusement parks, not by the roadside.

3. Anti-Imitation

It may seem odd to call this a form of Imitation. All varieties of Imitators have a common concern for *resemblance.* The Building Imitator desires resemblance to other buildings. The Whimsical Imitator desires resemblance to other objects. The Anti-Imitator desires resemblance to no other building or object. The Anti-Imitator characteristically judges architecture by exalting difference for its own sake. He rejects the level roof because it is modern, and the pitched roof because it is traditional. Thus he symbolically rejects his past and present cultural environment. He is sometimes called a futurist, but he is not one who takes a step forward: rather he steps, as it were, to the side.

Anti-Imitation, however, also appears in a different and more rational form. Sometimes there is a desire to create a unique building or style in order to instill a consciousness of "corporate image" or separate identity. This is not "difference for its own sake," and does not imply alienation

ANTI-IMITATION

The manager of this car wash told me that the method of constructing the central part of the building was too expensive to be extended the full length. When I asked why the building had an expensive central section, he said, "For looks."

The result, although exuberant, is uneconomical and lacks unity; hence it fails as architecture. The uniqueness of the central section, plus the inane pylons at the near end, must therefore be classified as "difference for its own sake."

from society; it is difference for the sake of individualism, or for advertising purposes, and implies merely that society is composed of distinct individuals. This form of Anti-Imitation is often pursued in connection with the Abstract approach.

ABSTRACT APPROACH

The Abstract outlook was stated two thousand years ago by Vitruvius, a Roman architect-engineer. He said, in Wotton's translation, "Well building hath three qualities . . . commoditie, firmnesse, and delight." Today we would say usefulness, durability, and beauty; or, in the jargon of art critics: function, structure, and expression. Today we would also add a fourth quality: economy.

These notions can be simplified. We have used the phrase *psychological effect* to include art and beauty, and used *physical utility* as a substitute for *usefulness*. For a building to be economical it must go on being a building, that is it must not fall down or wear out before producing the desired return on the investment. So durability and strength can be thought of as included in the idea of economy. The definition of the Abstract outlook can now be worded thus: a good building is one that economically provides physical and psychological utility.

The Abstract outlook differs from the Utilitarian by adding the requirement of psychological utility. It differs from the Imitative outlook by omitting any requirement concerning resemblance to other buildings or objects. Where the Imitator copies old (or not so old) buildings, the Abstractionist invents new ones. The Imitator wants to learn what former architects have done; the Abstractionist wants to learn why they did it. The Abstractionist tries to survey all of architectural history and then rise above it.

To appreciate buildings designed from the Abstract approach, a person needs to know (or intuitively realize) a lot of facts about nature and civilization, and then discover how the designer has used these facts to produce a good building. Here is a small sample of the reasoning that might occur in the course of designing a building. None of the following is necessarily true in general, but any or all of it might be true for some proposed building somewhere.

Assuming they are not for display, how large should the windows be? With air-conditioning, the cost of offsetting heat loss and gain through windows is so great that, even though solid wall has a higher first cost, it is cheaper in the long run to omit windows. Nor are windows in an air-conditioned building used for ventilation. As enough lights must be installed for nighttime use, windows will not reduce initial lighting costs. Windows will save some electricity by permitting lights to be turned off on sunny days. Windows have some value for escape in an emergency, but perhaps their greatest value is in permitting occupants to see out: to rest their eyes on a distant view, and to observe the weather. Then windows must extend high and low enough for standing or seated occupants to view the horizon. The further away from them the occupants will normally be, the wider the windows should be; that is wide windows for deep rooms. The size of windows must also take into account manufacturers' standard sizes; spacing depends on location of the building's partitions and structural elements. Now the designer, by sketching alternative façades, must find an arrangement of windows that not only satisfies all of the foregoing conditions but is also "beautiful" (or handsome, or good looking, or visually pleasing, or harmonious, or what you will).

ABSTRACT APPROACH

The visitor to this art museum elevators up and then, while strolling easily down a spiral ramp, views paintings and sculpture along the wall toplighted by glazing in the "grooves" visible on the outside. There is a large central skylight in the top of the "drum." The drum diminishes in diameter as the ramp descends. Thus lower levels are drawn in under the central skylight and less shadowed by the upper reaches of the ramp. The visitor on the ramp has not only a close view of paintings on the adjacent wall but also a contrasting distant view of paintings across the central light well.

The appearance of the building thus arises from the reality of its physical arrangements. It also seems obvious to me that the architect gave no consideration whatsoever to resemblances or differences between this building and any other building or object.

WAYNE ANDREWS

The foregoing is oversimplified but it may be enough to show that the Abstract approach is to take a great deal into account in arriving at rational decisions. An understanding of the reasoning is often a prerequisite for appreciating the resulting architecture. Shown the sketch of the façade, however, the hardened Traditional Imitator will probably say: "I don't like it! Make it look like the Flatiron Building. There's *real* architecture!"

The advantage of the Abstract outlook is that it eases the adaptation of each building to the peculiarities of its site, current costs and construction practices, availability and characteristics of building materials; and to the number, age, sex, and activities of its occupants. If the new building must also resemble other buildings, this last requirement has to be added to the others, and the more requirements there are, the greater the likelihood that some of them will have to be seriously compromised.

If resemblance to other buildings is not a requirement, then the new building may look strange. This is a disadvantage, because some people just don't like anything new or unfamiliar. To these people the Abstractionist

points out that the Greeks had their problems, and incidental to solving them, produced one kind of beauty; the medieval French had different problems and produced a different kind of beauty, and so forth. Today we have still different problems—of materials, methods, and human activities—and incidental to solving them, are producing a still different kind of beauty, even if it is not immediately recognizable as such by everyone. The reservoir of beautiful shapes did not run dry in 1850.

There is also a physical disadvantage of the Abstract approach. New materials and methods of construction are usually tested separately. When several are combined for the first time in a building, their conjunction may produce unforeseen problems. This is an inevitable price of change.

These disadvantages are not too serious. After all, women welcome innovation in the design of their clothing, and new designs in automobiles are accepted annually, even though new cars, like new buildings, often have "bugs" in them. Both clothing and automobiles are like architecture in that they are forms of shelter and can be labeled "good" when they economically provide physical and psychological utility. The fact that buildings are looked to for a sense of permanence and stability, however, makes them different from cars and clothes. About all one can say is that the radical designs of ten years ago do not look radical today, and the radical designs of today will not look radical ten years from now.

The conflict between the Abstract and Imitative outlooks in architecture is paralleled in the other arts. Creative painters are "Abstract" and reject Imitation, as do creative Modern authors, choreographers, and composers. New outlooks are always difficult for the nonspecialist to understand and enjoy, unless he possesses a natural sensitivity, or thoroughly studies the subject, or accepts the product on faith.

The outlooks we have discussed can be summarized as follows:

A. *Utilitarian:* Aims to achieve economical physical utility.
B. *Imitative:* Aims to achieve resemblance plus economical physical and psychological utility.
   1. *Building Imitation:* Resemblance is to other buildings.
      A *Traditional:* Resemblance is to historical buildings.
      B *Modern:* Resemblance is to modern buildings.
   2. *Whimsical Imitation:* Resemblance is to something other than buildings.
   3. *Anti-Imitation:* Resemblance is to no buildings or other things. "Difference" is sought.
C. *Abstract:* Aims to achieve physical and psychological utility economically. Resemblance is not a consideration.

This system of classification should not be granted more importance than it deserves. It is a handy framework for discussing "how we shape our buildings." If you ask an architect whether he is an Imitator or an Abstractionist, he won't quite know what you mean unless he happens to have read this book.

COMBINED OUTLOOKS

It should again be emphasized that only people, not buildings, have outlooks. If we say that a building is Imitative we mean only that its designer appears to have adopted an Imitative approach. Furthermore, a designer rarely sticks exclusively to one outlook. It is common to employ a Utilitarian approach to the invisible parts of a building, an Imitative ap-

operation. Both costs must be reckoned and compared with predicted return, or else building is no better than gambling.

Many people are oddly reluctant to consider problems of upkeep and maintenance costs. When an architect tries to explain why double-glazing is, or is not, economically justified, they seem to fall into reveries of "magic casements opening on the foam. . . ." When he advises that 4 inches of insulation will cost *X* dollars more than 3 inches of insulation and will save *Y* dollars per year in air-conditioning cost, thus producing a return of *Z* per cent on the investment, they often act as if *he,* not they, were day-dreaming, and that first cost is all that matters.

When data are available, economic effects can be analyzed as in the following example. Brick veneer may cost about one dollar per square foot. Wood siding, a common alternative, may cost about thirty cents per square foot, but must be repainted at a cost of about six cents per square foot every four or five years, depending on climate and severity of exposure. The problem is to make a valid comparison between the cost of brick and the cost of wood: Brick has a higher first cost but a lower "operating" cost because it need not be painted. We can see that the seventy cents saved on the first cost of wood will pay for almost twelve repaintings. If only this many repaintings are required during the useful life of the building, the effective cost of wood and brick may appear to be the same. Yet if the money initially saved by using wood were invested at 4 per cent interest, the return ($0.028 per square foot per year, or $0.132 per square foot every four years) would equal twice the cost of quadrennial repainting. A more careful analysis would consider additional factors, such as relative insurance rates, tax deductibility, and so forth. Economic effects, of course, are just that and no more: They do not include, in this case, the visual attractions or other *psychological utility* of brick compared with wood siding.

The operating costs of buildings include all future payments for fuel, electricity, water, and sewage; and for equipment maintenance, repair, and replacement. They also include costs of cleaning, redecorating, and replacing any building materials that get dirty or wear out. The useful life of some new materials cannot be predicted with assurance, but there is reliable data on air-conditioning operating costs, cost of maintaining conventional materials, and many other operating costs. It would be unreasonable to ignore them. First costs combined with predicted operating costs should affect choice of equipment, materials, and their arrangement, which is to say, all architectural decisions.

PHYSICAL EFFECTS

Most of the physical effects of buildings are accurately predictable. The amount of space required for various human activities is known, and so is the amount required for installation of equipment of known size. Temperature, humidity, and freshness of air for comfort can be accurately calculated. A large amount of data has been gathered from observation of housewives and applied to increasing the efficiency of kitchens and the rest of the house. Architecture shapes industry's output, and so information gathered from time and motion studies is applied to architectural design to effect greater operating efficiency.

The dollar value of comfort and utility cannot always be determined, but intelligent decisions can usually be made nevertheless. Here is an example.

If you were the client in the following case would you decide in favor of the more expensive refrigerative air conditioning or the cheaper evaporative cooling? (The following, incidentally, is a good example of what goes on between architects and their clients. The architect has made calculations, produced a recommendation, and presented it with an explanation. The client is thus equipped to make a decision.)

The problem was to decide, for a building in the Near East, between refrigerative and evaporative systems for the cooling stage of an air-conditioning system. Evaporative cooling works well in hot weather if the outdoor air is dry, but fails to produce comfort when the outdoor air is humid; evaporative cooling also costs less, both to install and operate, than refrigerative cooling. Having studied the seasonal variations in the local weather, and estimated construction and operating costs of the alternate systems, the architect addressed the following memorandum to his client:

> The first cost of evaporative cooling will be about $100,000 less than refrigerative cooling—an amount equal to 2% of the total building construction cost. Evaporative cooling, however, while substantially cheaper than refrigerative cooling, and adequate during the 5 hot, dry months of the year, will fail to produce comfort during the 3½ hot, humid months of the year. Refrigerative cooling, on the other hand, will produce comfort all year, thus increasing the comfort period from 8½ to 12 months, an increase of 40%. It seems to the architect that increasing building cost 2% in order to increase comfort time 40% is justified.

The operating cost of evaporative cooling will be about $8,000 per year lower than refrigerative cooling—an amount about equal to the wages of one of the 200 employees the building is designed to house. It seems to the architect that for the same total operating cost it would be better to have 199 employees who are comfortable all year than 200 employees who are comfortable only 8½ months of the year.

The problem of the physical effects of buildings is simple in the sense that it deals with tangible factors, most of which can be evaluated and numerically compared. Psychological effects, the intangibles, present a different picture.

PSYCHOLOGICAL EFFECTS

Here are knotty problems. No one really knows how buildings shape our thoughts and emotions, nor how important these effects are. Was any part of Shakespeare's genius attributable to the architecture of his surroundings? Did beautiful churches ever make anyone more holy? Would Lincoln have been greater if a handsome mansion had been substituted for the ramshackle house of his youth?

Do filthy streets and dilapidated buildings foster juvenile delinquency? Probably, but only as part of a degenerative process in which physical decay, poverty, and lack of education reinforce each other. The elimination of decay (which in part means architectural renewal) will not correct the situation unless poverty is also eliminated, and neither poverty nor decay can be eliminated unless the occupants of the neighborhood are educated to sustain themselves at a higher socio-economic level. It appears then that inadequacy of architecture has bad psychological effects, but architectural improvement by itself is not enough to reverse them.

A business firm or institution hires an architect to help analyze corporate activities and then design a building carefully adapted to need. Do the psychological effects of the resulting architecture increase the prosperity of the firm or institution? In many cases, yes. One president of a corporation said "since we moved into new offices, I notice our female employees dress better," a small matter perhaps, but indicative of improved morale, which should result in higher employee output, lower turnover, and fewer complaints.

It is possible to overlook the psychological effects of architecture partly because our social environment has much stronger psychological effects. The actions of parents, relatives, teachers, friends, and business associates are what predominantly shape us. But this means that insofar as buildings affect our relations with other people they have important indirect psychological effects upon us.

The effect of architecture on privacy is one example. Everyone sometimes desires visual privacy, and architecture must provide it. Acoustic privacy is also frequently desirable. Often rooms must be designed to permit private conversations and conferences. Lack of acoustic privacy in bathrooms can cause constipation. According to Dr. N. Balfour Slonim (in a letter to the author, August 13, 1962), lack of acoustic privacy between parents' and children's bath-bedroom suites may even be a factor in producing psychoneurosis.

Another way that buildings affect personal contacts is in the size and relative location of private offices in a business firm. Truly a vice president is shaped by the number of square feet of glass and carpet devoted to him, and these affect his influence in the firm.

These examples have involved the shaping of relations between people, but there is also the matter of direct psychological effects on individuals, including the effect called "esthetic." Although these effects may be less important, they can be powerful. For example, a deep-seated need for a particular psychological effect characterizes the Imitative approach to architecture. The Imitator is shaped by the spirits architecture evokes. Probably he derives from them a feeling of security which permits relaxation and something like psychological regeneration. No doubt the Abstractionist experiences the same need, but he chooses a different means of satisfying it. He will argue that feelings of security spring from a recognition of real security. He thinks, for example, that if a building displays its structural elements, the viewer can sense at a glance that the building is really strong. This is the sort of thing the Abstractionist has in mind when he urges "integrity" in buildings, or "honest" architecture. Buildings should be strong, comfortable, useful, temperate, and clean, in order to perform their physical functions; and it is partly by exposing these qualities to view that buildings perform their psychological functions. In short, buildings should both be good (for physical effect) and look like what they really are (for psychological effect).

The value of psychological regeneration and a sense of safety cannot be measured, but their importance can be indirectly gauged by the strength of emotion they engender. I think every architect who designs houses has had some woman weep in his office over the problems presented by the psychological effects of buildings.

There are more specific psychological effects than inducing general feelings of security. A restaurant owner had a problem with patrons who lingered over their coffee while others waited impatiently to be seated. For some unknown reason repainting the dining room walls a subdued orange markedly reduced the lingering and increased business. (I don't know the exact shade used, and slight variation may be important. If you have this problem and try this solution, don't blame me if it fails.)

Buildings can be entertaining, a theory that is entertainingly developed in *Here of All Places* by Osbert Lancaster (Houghton Mifflin Company, Boston, 1958). Entertainment is a common quality of all art, of course, but unfortunately the ability of buildings to entertain is lessened by the attention we pay to their physical utility—and to other aspects of their psychological utility. The hot dog stand that looks like a hot dog is blatant entertainment, an obvious fact, even to those who find such buildings repulsive.

Buildings communicate information about their owners and occupants, thus serving a public relations or advertising role in the case of commercial architecture, and a status-defining role in the case of residences. This is a very important quality of buildings, but a complex problem for the designer. The message communicated by a building depends on the attitudes and education of the viewer. Unusual design or materials may mislead some viewers into supposing that a cheap building is expensive, or vice versa. If a building looks expensive (whether it is or not), the viewer may feel that its owner is rich, hence powerful and important; or the viewer may feel that the owner is merely ostentatious. It is difficult, in budgeting a commercial building, to decide explicitly on the dollar value of architecture as advertising.

Buildings can furnish their occupants valuable variety. Everyone sometimes appreciates being able to change his surroundings, not because there is something wrong with the space he occupies, but merely because he has been in it too long. It can be pleasant and refreshing to move from a small room to a large one, or vice versa; or from bright to dim surroundings, and so forth. Variety in architecture is more than just "the spice of life." It is part of "change of scene"; it provides the same advantages sought from "getting away from it all": It promotes psychological regeneration. Going into the other room is like taking a little vacation.

It may be argued that architecture is psychologically important only when we are paying conscious attention to it, and that most of the time our attention is elsewhere. On the contrary, there is reason to believe that architecture is most important when we are *not* conscious of it. In the normal course of events we observe our surroundings from time to time, and then proceed with other activities. The impressions we get from these observations, however, linger in our subconscious, and color all we do. Our first impressions of many people, for example, are acquired from architecture, not from the people themselves. A man's office, or his house, if viewed before we meet him, partly dictate our initial attitude toward him. The architecture of a commercial establishment affects, to some extent, our behavior toward its personnel. Even when we are traveling, especially by car, we seem constantly to be evaluating the relative "friendliness" of the passing scene, perhaps in order to act in an appropriate way if our transportation breaks down. Our reaction to the architecture of a church often affects our reactions as we listen to a sermon preached there. It appears, then, that we act upon architectural impressions of which we are, to a large extent, unaware; and that the effects of architecture can be profoundly soothing or disturbing.

The effects of art in architecture, as stated earlier, are among the psychological effects. Art is the subject of infinitely varied shades of opinion. Most people don't know anything about art, but they "know what they like." Others know—or think they know—a great deal about art, but they don't know what they like. These two groups are unable to converse, but have spent many a sad and bloody hour in controversy.

Let us come right out and say that a person can lead a full and happy life without knowing anything about art. There is no absolute need to talk of Michelangelo, and pretensions in this area are pathetic, like a tone-deaf man at a concert.

As for me, I agree in general with Suzanne K. Langer, and recommend her *Feeling and Form* (Charles Scribner's Sons, New York, 1954) to anyone who wants to think about the nature of art, including architecture. She says "art is the creation of forms symbolic of human feeling." Why create forms symbolic of human feeling? In order to understand those feelings. Art interprets the universe, and this helps us to act appropriately in the face of nature, man, and God.

> The architect creates the image of a culture . . . a physically present environment that expresses the characteristic rhythmic functional patterns which constitute a culture . . . patterns such as alternations of sleep and waking, venture and safety, emotion and calm, austerity and abandon; the tempo, and the smoothness or abruptness of life (Langer: *op. cit.*).

The problems of art are only what you make them. They should either be mastered, or left to the architect. The alternative, all too frequently chosen, is pretentiousness.

CONCLUSION

The architect should try to design buildings that will have the desired economic, physical, and psychological effects on their owners and occupants. His job is to find specific solutions to the problems discussed here in a general way. As his client you play a cooperative role. You are in charge, and have the privilege not only of giving the architect his initial instructions but also of approving or disapproving his work in the light of those instructions. I hope that this and the preceding chapter will help you play your part in the genesis of buildings.

Chapter 3

THE ARCHITECT AND HIS SERVICES

The architect's primary responsibility is to spend his clients' money wisely.

—SHERLEY W. MORGAN, Former Dean,
Princeton University
School of Architecture

ONE of the earliest known architects is Imhotep. He lived about 2860 B.C. in Egypt, during the Third Dynasty, and designed the great stepped pyramid and surrounding temples at Saqqara. He was also a physician, sage, scribe, and vizier to Pharaoh Zoser. Imhotep's talents and wisdom were so widely revered that after death he was regarded as a demigod. Temples were erected to him in Egypt and Nubia. Twenty-five hundred years later, during the Ptolemaic period, Imhotep was promoted to full godhood.

In the centuries that have lapsed since then, however, not all architects have managed to live up to the high standard of Imhotep's career. Indeed, if you comb the annals of crime, you will undoubtedly find many celebrated scalawags who were also architects. (Curiously I can find no record of an architect who was hung as a horse thief. It may be simply that when and where the theft of horses was common, the professional design of buildings was not.) In direct contrast to Imhotep, for example, consider Stanford

White, possibly the most famous architect of his day. In 1906 he was shot and killed for adultery with Evelyn Nesbitt by her outraged husband, Harry Thaw.

Of course it is unlikely that any architect you hire will possess the outstanding professional talents of either Imhotep or Stanford White, but on the other hand today's architect is also unlikely to be shockingly adulterous or disconcertingly divine. He will probably be courteous and businesslike. He may belong to Rotary or Kiwanis.

Architects, like any group of comparable size, exhibit varying degrees of competence and integrity. Certainly some practitioners are bad architects, bad by any standard you care to apply. Some will cheat you. Others will be careless of your interests, which it is their duty to further. Some are relatively ignorant of one or more important aspects of their profession. Others simply lack talent. The next chapter contains what information I can give to help you separate the sheep from the goats, but a great deal will inevitably depend on your own ability to judge character.

Assuming now, as I will for the most part throughout this book, that your architect is reasonably honest, competent, intelligent, and talented; you may still not have a clear idea of precisely what he will try to do for you. To say that everyone knows all about what doctors and lawyers do, but no one knows anything about what architects do is no doubt an exaggeration, but contains more than a grain of truth. There are so many novels, there is so much television time, devoted to the medical and legal professions that the typical American has acquired a detailed, relatively accurate picture of them. When books or television deal with architects, however, they usually tell us little more than that architects

> Draw straight lines on very large sheets of paper, indicate which way doors open by a clever device, and hope in time to get taken on as a partner and be allowed a crack at the new Town Hall. There is more in architecture than this, of course, but that seems to me a good general idea of the public notion of an architect, of the picture he conjures up.

The foregoing, by H. F. Ellis, appeared in *Punch,* December 2, 1959, and was reprinted in the *A.I.A. Journal,* March, 1960. Harold Burson, a public relations consultant, writing in *Architectural Forum,* February, 1960, adds:

> The public may be dimly aware of the participation of an architect in the building process, but they are apt to regard the few lines he draws on a few sheets of paper as pretty much of a routine function compared to the really substantial work performed by others. They can see the stonework, the roof, the electrical outlets and the plumbing—they know the roof is good if it

doesn't leak or that the plumbing job is satisfactory if there is abundant hot water. They are, unfortunately, unable to visualize that those lines on a few sheets of paper could have made living more enjoyable if some lines had gone in other directions.

Do architects just draw a few lines on a few sheets of paper and accomplish merely a routine function? Let me try to answer by starting with a consideration of what the architect is trained to do, that is, his professional education. Next I will outline the services he normally provides, and conclude with a consideration of some of his limitations and obligations.

THE ARCHITECT'S TRAINING

Most courses leading to a Bachelor's degree in architecture take five years, and the bulk of the college curriculum is split between the two fields of Liberal Arts and Engineering. In Engineering the first half is devoted to the sciences: Mathematics, Chemistry, and Physics. The latter half concerns the "mechanics" of buildings: construction methods, building materials; and structural, mechanical, and electrical engineering. In the field of Liberal Arts the first half is devoted to English, History, Economics, and Electives. The other half is spent practicing architectural design, which is the utilization of all the other subject matter to solve the problems of designing complete buildings.

1. Art vs. Engineering

The problem of utilizing both art and engineering in building seems to have special significance. So far as I know, no other vocation deals equally in both fields. We tend to think of art as imaginative and insubstantial, and of engineering as practical and materialistic. They seem poles apart. A person who tries to join them together may look like a freak with his head in the clouds and his feet on the ground. The client, who controls architecture, must therefore either appreciate the importance of both art and engineering or else at least avoid obstructing the architect in one field or the other. If you, as client, adopt the Utilitarian approach, you will ignore the psychological effects of buildings, which is all right. At the same time the architect, without violating Utilitarian criteria, may succeed in producing a psychologically pleasing building. You should realize, in this case, that you have nothing to gain by preventing him from doing so. On the other hand, if you are primarily interested in art, try not to limit yourself to a single esthetic idea. If a hundred good architects tackle the same design problem, they will produce a hundred good solutions—all different. Give your architect freedom to produce a good design that is also consistent with the engineering requirements of the building.

The intricate and varied ways that art and engineering are related is hard for any of us to understand. The subject is too complex to be covered here, but it may be helpful to assert that (1) it is not enough to "engineer" a building and then "decorate" it, and (2) it is equally unsatisfactory to dream up an "artistic" creation and then insert beams, toilets, and so forth. The building as a whole, and each visible part of it, arises from and exhibits both art and engineering. Therefore the architect must simultaneously apply his knowledge of both as he designs.

2. Post-Graduation

If the architecture student fails to learn how to synthesize art and engineering while he is still in school he may never learn how. Before licensing he is required by law, in most states, to acquire three or four years of experience working in established architectural firms. He will probably be a draftsman, working out details of building construction rather than designing buildings as a whole. He should also be learning to write specifications, deal with contractors, handle some legal aspects of building, cooperate with engineers and clients, and face the ethical and business problems of architectural practice. This period corresponds to a doctor's internship and residency. During it the architect also learns how far, in his own case, academic ideals may have to be compromised in practice.

When this "apprenticeship" is over the architectural graduate can take the three- or four-day state examination, which will cover most of the subjects he has learned. Probably more candidates pass than fail, but many fail. Some fail parts of the examination year after year. Only when all parts have been passed can a person legitimately style himself "Architect."

The newly registered architect may go into business for himself, but chances are he will work a while longer in an established firm to increase his experience; many architects never enter private practice in the sense of starting their own firm.

THE ARCHITECT'S SERVICES

The three leading actors in the production of new buildings are the owner, the architect, and the contractor. The "owner" is you, the client of the architect. The architect transforms your requirements into a detailed, explicit guide for construction (drawings and specifications) contingent upon your approval. The contractor follows this guide to build the building. The architect observes the contractor's work as it proceeds. Although our concern here is the general capabilities and limitations of architects, the following will also serve to introduce the more detailed discussions in later chapters.

1. Building Program

Before he designs anything, the architect needs a complete knowledge of the requirements of the new building. These requirements are usually written down and the result is called the *program*. It is jointly produced by you and and the architect. The contribution each makes depends on circumstances. Ordinarily you simply explain what you want, then the architect asks questions to clear up doubtful points. Often he will suggest revisions to the requirements based on his own experience. Someone like a school superintendent, experienced with both architects and the physical problems of schools, may produce an excellent, complete building program by himself. In other cases the client may lean heavily on the architect. A retired salesman, for example, who decides to build and run a motel, may have relatively few convictions about the requirements of the building and follow the architect's initiative in programming. In any case, good programming pools all pertinent knowledge and judgment possessed by both client and architect. Gaps that may remain should be corrected by investigation and research.

2. Preliminary Design

Using the program as a guide, the architect starts thinking out the form of the building and sketching plans and other views until he finds a design that satisfies the program. Here is where genius, if available, plays its part; where art and engineering are wedded, and where creative imagination gets a workout. The architect then shows you the sketches. You will ponder them, listen to the architect's explanations; check them against the program, and then either approve them, suggest modifications, or if they are unsatisfactory, reject them. If you approve the program, however, it is very unlikely that you will reject a preliminary design which conforms to it.

3. Cost Estimate

It is still too early to predict construction costs with great accuracy, but the architect will normally keep you advised of the cost calculated as closely as the preliminary character of the design permits. Unless you hear otherwise, you can assume that construction cost will be within 10 percent of budgeted cost.

4. Working Drawings and Specifications

With the preliminary design approved by you, the architect now prepares thoroughly detailed drawings at larger scale. They are called working drawings because the contractor will use them to do the work of construction. Some of the information needed by the contractor, however, can more conveniently be presented in verbal form, so the drawings will be supplemented by specifications. These are written by the architect and furnished as a book or pamphlet. In the course of preparing working drawings and specifications—which will take several months—a few new problems will arise, which the architect will have to refer to you for a decision. For the most part, however, you will have nothing to do during this stage of the work.

5. Bids for Construction

When the working drawings and specifications have been completed and checked, and you have approved them, reproductions of them are made in quantity. Sets of reproductions are distributed to contractors who have agreed to bid on the job. A few weeks later the bids are submitted. Normally you will accept the lowest one. You and the low-bidder then execute the construction contract, whereby he agrees to build the building according to the drawings and specifications, and you agree to pay him the amount of his bid. Payments are usually made monthly and based on the amount of work he has completed.

6. Construction

As the work proceeds, the architect will periodically visit the site. He will observe the work of construction with the object of checking to see that the contractor understands and is correctly following the drawings and specifications. When the contractor applies for his monthly payment, the architect checks the application for accuracy. Eventually the work is done, the contractor receives final payment, and you can move into the completed building.

7. Note on Large Architectural Firms

In a large firm the "architect" to whom we have been referring will actually be several people, each specializing in one part of the "architect's" work. Your direct contact will be with a project manager. He will supervise the work of the firm's designers, draftsmen, engineers, specifications writers, and field men.

THE ARCHITECT'S LIMITATIONS

Architecture is a profession. The majority of architects subscribe to a code of ethics formulated by the American Institute of Architects (A.I.A.). Your knowledge of this code can help you in two ways. First, it completes your picture of the architect by stating things he will not do. Second, as clients are sometimes the recipients of unethical proposals by the rascals in any profession, you will have an advantage if you are able to recognize an ethical violation as such.

The complete code is printed as A.I.A. Document No. J-330, *The Standards of Professional Practice,* in four pages. Much of this document is discussion and commentary on the actual provisions. Almost any architect will mail you a copy if you call and ask.

Briefly, the architect's ethics can be divided into four sets of obligations: to his fellow professionals, to the public, to contractors, and to his clients. His clients, however, are affected by all of them.

1. Obligations to Fellow Professionals

Architects are prohibited from competing with each other on the basis of fees. They believe that substantial fee-reduction inevitably entails inadequate professional service. This provision therefore benefits clients and the public, as well as protecting the majority of architects, who feel bound to furnish either adequate service or none at all. Architects are also prohibited from attacking each other's reputations, and from using paid advertising.

2. Obligations to the Public

The architect has a general obligation not to subvert the public interest by designing fire traps, nuisances, menaces to public health, and so on. Most applications of this ethical provision are also covered by law in building codes, and an architect's license to practice can be revoked for attempts to violate them.

Many architects also feel an obligation to avoid cluttering the landscape with eyesores.

3. Obligations to Contractors

Ethics—and the construction contract itself—require the architect to treat the contractor fairly. During construction the architect may appear to be acting mainly in the owner's interest, but must carefully refrain from taking unfair advantage of the contractor. The architect must not demand that the contractor perform work that is not shown on the drawings or stated in the specifications, and must not demand that the contractor remedy—without charge—errors made by the architect.

4. Obligations to Clients

The architect must give his clients unbiased service and advice. He should never place himself in a position where he stands to gain from the success of any contractor or supplier of building materials. He may not engage in contracting himself, nor accept "rakeoffs" from those who do. In other words, to protect his clients, he must be in a position to insist that contractors rectify their occasional mistakes, even if it drives them into bankruptcy, which it sometimes does; and he must not accept bribes to specify materials or equipment whose use may not be in the best interests of his client.

The architect must not guarantee the work of contractors because this amounts to acting as a contractor himself. Contractors guarantee their own work.

The architect has one obligation to his clients that is often misunderstood: He is forbidden to render professional service without compensation. You may receive casual professional service from a friend or relative, who will be rewarded only by your regard or affection, but a comparative stranger offering free service most likely has some ulterior motive, and his advice cannot be considered unbiased.

Sometimes prospective clients, unaware of or insensitive to the implications of what they are doing, ask several architects to prepare free sketches of a proposed building to be used as a basis for final selection of the architect for the job. *Free sketches* means, in effect, the preliminary design, which ordinarily earns the architect about one-fourth of his total fee. How can he do them for nothing? Architects who do "free" work under these circumstances skimp their efforts; What they turn out is "quick and dirty." As their main objective is to get the rest of the commission, *not* to design well, they fill the sketches with superficially pleasing elements, exaggerate the size of the building and the age of the trees surrounding it, underestimate the cost of construction, suppress the chimney, and so forth. An architect who does "free" work for you has probably done it before for others without success. Now he will try to overcharge *you* to make up for time wasted on earlier "free" work, assuming you give him the job. The overcharge will naturally not appear as a raised fee: he will probably cut fees. It will appear in the form of plagiarism, incomplete drawings, and "bob-tailed" specifications. In effect, this type of architect turns over part of the design work to the contractor, who is not qualified to perform it and unlikely to try.

Unfortunately, it seems that the world will always contain a goodly supply of prospective clients who think they can get something for nothing.

SUMMARY

Becoming an architect requires eight or more years of training in school and offices. The architect attempts to furnish professional service to his clients while meeting his obligations to the public. His services include assistance in programming, complete design of buildings, and observation of construction. The architect does not build; he invents buildings. He sells a service, not a commodity.

Chapter 4

THE ARCHITECT: TO HAVE OR HAVE NOT

In most localities it is illegal to build unless the work is planned by a licensed architect or engineer. (In some cases, exceptions are made for private residences.) Because the state assumes a degree of responsibility for protecting its citizens, the state is also granted authority to make and enforce health and safety regulations. One of the ways the state protects its citizens is by requiring that buildings, which are potentially hazardous if improperly designed, be designed by licensed professionals, and at the same time, by requiring persons to pass tests demonstrating their knowledge of and ability to apply health and safety regulations to building design as a condition to licensing.

Enforcement of the "laws of building" is normally in the hands of a municipal agency called the *building department*, a branch of city or county government. Ordinarily, when a new building or alterations are planned, two sets of working drawings and specifications must be submitted to the building department, which first checks each set for an architect's seal and signature which signify design by a licensed professional. The department then usually reviews the design, or at least spot-checks it for conformity to local laws of building. When satisfied, the department issues a building permit, stamps both sets of prints and specifications, and returns one to be kept at the job site. During construction the building department sends its inspectors to visit the project and verify that construction is being performed in accordance with the approved documents. If the work is faulty, the inspector can order the contractor to revise it.

In practice the objectives of the foregoing process are sometimes subverted. Building inspectors may be lax or lenient. Through budget limitations the building department may not have enough personnel to do its job. Nor are such agencies always immune to bribery. There are also unscrupulous architects who will, for a small fee, put their seal on anyone's design, sometimes without careful study to insure that the design conforms to law. In such cases, if, for instance, the design involves long or complex structural calculations, the building department is unlikely to detect errors, and the result may be disastrous.

Building design is a specialized activity, and we live in a society of specialists. It is thus a reasonable as well as a legal requirement that buildings be designed by specialists. Yet Americans are not noted for a great propensity to abide by law, nor are we always reasonable. It might thus be suspected that many buildings get built entirely without benefit of architect.

In addition to illegal evasion of architectural services, there are other ways to acquire a building without first hiring an architect. Most are discused below, but first I want to point out that even if you don't hire an architect your building will probably still be designed by one. Ready-built houses are usually either built from some architect's design, or what amounts to the same thing, copied from a published design whose ultimate source is an architect. Prefabricated industrial buildings are built to standardized designs originated by an architect or engineer working for the building manufacturer. "Package builders" will design, construct, and sell you almost any type of building according to your stated requirements. Such firms have a staff of architects and engineers for the design work.

In these examples, however, the architect who designs the building is not working for you, the owner, but for whoever sells you the completed building. Your involvement with the architect in such cases is indirect. He is charged with directly furthering someone else's interests, not yours. It also works out in practice that indirect architectural services, besides being at least potentially unsatisfactory in themselves, are also usually incomplete. For illustration consider the common ways of acquiring a lawful building without using direct architectural services.

BUYING AN EXISTING BUILDING

If you buy an existing building, obviously any architectural service devoted to it was indirect because the architect worked for an earlier owner or the builder.

If the building appears to be in good condition, it was probably soundly constructed, but it is often a good idea to hire a building contractor, engineer, or architect to check it over for you.

An architect can be used to analyze your specific needs with respect to physical facilities before you buy, and then determine if the proposed building answers those needs or can be economically altered to suit them. If you are seeking a simple building, such as a warehouse, small office, store, or residence, then hiring an architect to determine if a particular existing building will suit your requirements may be superfluous or even downright silly. Still, there is something to be said for getting an outside opinion whether you are buying a house or a hat.

A divorced woman of my acquaintance, with children and housekeeper, offered to buy a house, and put down a $1,000 deposit. She then took some friends to see the house. After looking around they pointed out that in her enthusiastic reaction to the landscaping and several other amenities, she had apparently neglected to count bedrooms: there simply weren't enough to accommodate her household. She backed out of the deal, relinquishing her deposit in the process.

DESIGNING IT YOURSELF

Nobody knows exactly what qualities are required of successful architects, but there must be people with those qualities who have not chosen to become professional architects. If you are such a person, then aside from experience and technical knowledge, you may have what it takes to act as your own architect. Success is most likely if the project is your own house. You have a lifetime of experience with houses on which to draw, and much of the technical knowledge will either be known to you or widely available. Best of all you can spend months or years revising and polishing the design.

A danger in acting as your own architect may lie in the human tendency to fall in love with one's own creations, in this case the design you originate. Professional architects start life with the same failing, but constant criticism by their instructors, employers, and clients tends to teach architects to view their work dispassionately.

If you design your own building, consider hiring an architect for a couple of hundred dollars to review your design. He may spot some errors of inexperience that might otherwise have gone undetected and have led to major drawbacks in the building. His esthetic criticism will be worthless, however, unless you eschew false pride in your creation.

Once the design is established, the builder and building department will require detailed drawings, which will probably exceed your ability to produce. A cheap way to get them is to hire a "moonlight" draftsman, such as a junior architectural employee, who will charge from $100. Some builders and building materials suppliers also provide drafting service at similar rates, although the charge may be hidden in the cost of their other services.

BUILDERS' DESIGNS

Some potential architects wind up as building contractors. They may design or help you design your building, but will not attempt complex buildings unless they have architects on their staff, which makes their firm a package builder, discussed below.

Success as a building contractor requires abilities quite unlike those required for architectural design. There is no reason to suppose a builder has any design talent at all. In fact, the attention he must pay to the business of construction may blind him to considerations of habitability and efficient use. Asking a builder to design your building is the riskiest alternative I know.

STOCK PLANS

There are hundreds, maybe thousands, of stock plans for houses and vacation houses. Many magazines and newspapers publish them; by sending anywhere from $10 to $100 you can get the working drawings for any one of the published designs. Having the drawings you can then get bids from builders.

Consumer Reports 1961 Buying Guide, by the way, in the section entitled "Buying and Maintaining a House," says: "If you use stock plans, don't attempt radical revisions."

If you want to build a Howard Johnson's restaurant, a Texaco gasoline station, or any of a large number of commercial chain establishments, you will most likely end up with a standard design furnished by the parent company, and prepared by their architects. You or the company will have to seek some additional architectural service to adapt the stock plans to the peculiarities of the actual building site and to local laws.

The use of stock plans for public and governmental buildings is often debated. Stock plans for schools have been experimented with; architectural firms have been hired by state governments to prepare detailed designs for high schools, junior high schools, and so forth. When a local school board determined the need and floated the bonds for a new school, the state would trot out the appropriate plans from its files. A local architect would then be hired to adapt the stock plans to the local site and add or subtract standardized elements, such as classrooms and offices, to meet current local requirements. The amount of architectural work required to make these adaptations has proved to be a substantial fraction of the work that would have been required if each school had been designed from scratch. It has also turned out that changes in the economics of construction—materials and methods—and changes in educational programs made stock plans obsolete before they could pay off in a net reduction of architectural fees. To my knowledge no governmental body that has commissioned anything more complex than pumping station stock plans is still using them.

When adapting stock plans to specific sites, many problems arise, and in each case the best solution usually turns out to be merely the least of several evils. If the site slopes, for example, the stock-plan user must compromise between the cost of excavation and the costs—tangible and intangible—of underground rooms. As well as varying with respect to slope, sites also vary in shape, size, orientation; and in location of streets, views (either to exploit or avoid), acoustic nuisances, utilities, trees, rocks, prevailing winds, and so on. Only if a building is specially designed for a particular site is it likely to maximize the site's advantages and minimize its shortcomings.

Stock plans widely used would also tend to produce monotony. Imagine adjacent county seats, or a cluster of metropolitan suburbs, each exhibiting nearly identical schools, city halls, theaters, office buildings, fire stations, and so forth. On the other hand, vast numbers of people seem unmoved by such sameness: witness America's countless little Levittownlike developments. Their advocates are just as pleased if each new building, instead of being nobler than the last, is pretty much the same as the last.

PREFABRICATION

All buildings exhibit prefabrication to some degree. Bricks and doors, after all, are manufactured at some remote plant, not on the job site. A prefabricated building, however, means a complete, or almost complete, building sold as a package by a single manufacturer and requiring a minimum of on-site labor because most of the shaping and assembly was done at the factory. Houses, storage buildings, one-story retail and office buildings, and light manufacturing buildings are all available prefabricated. The only completely prefabricated building is the house trailer, or "mobile home."

Prefabricated buildings are shipped from the factory to be erected by local contractors, who also put in the foundations and make connections to the street mains. If you want a building that varies from the manufacturer's standard designs, you or he will have to obtain some additional architectural service.

In my experience prefabricated buildings have not been substantially different in cost from buildings of similar quality built on site. "Prefabs" are also rarely either ugly or attractive.

The manufacturers of prefabricated houses have managed to imitate all the currently popular residential styles, thus sacrificing much of the benefit of mass production, the opportunity for which was supposed to be the principal advantage of prefabrication in the first place. If the public did not appear to demand houses that could be labeled *colonial, ranch, tri-level,* and so forth, manufacturers could direct their architects to concentrate on problems of efficient layout, durable materials, simple appearance, easy transportation, and over-all general economy. In short, they could adopt the Abstract approach. The resulting houses might cost no more than half what one now pays for comparable facilities.

PACKAGE BUILDERS

Package builders combine the services of architects, engineers, and building contractors. Such firms build mostly industrial buildings but will usually take on almost anything in the $100,000-and-up class.

Package builders can be seen as a revival of the medieval "master builder," who both designed and constructed buildings. The Renaissance brought about specialization and the separation of the two functions.

Recently an architectural firm was hired to design a factory. The owner also asked a package builder, on speculation, to prepare an independent design and construction cost bid. Bids by other contractors on the architect's design, however, proved to be 10 percent lower than the package builder's bid on his own design. The architectural firm had more carefully analyzed the owner's requirements and produced a more efficient, economical design than had the package builder.

ARCHITECTS AND HOUSES

Alternatives to hiring an architect have been explored. Most of what was said applies to houses as well as to buildings in general, but as houses generate the widest interest, they deserve specific discussion. Much of the following, however, also applies to buildings in general.

The passage quoted from *Consumer Reports* also says "Build only if you can't find what you want in existing houses . . . For anything extraordinary or expensive, hire an architect, preferably to supervise the building as well as to prepare plans." That's good advice, provided you understand that *architecture* is always extraordinary. Ninety-nine houses out of a hundred, including many designed by architects, do not deserve to be called architecture. Such houses are largely Semiutilitarian structures, dolled up with a few Traditional Imitative features, and sold like automobiles or cattle. If you want architecture, you will have to find a good architect and build.

If you want a house that is neither extraordinary nor expensive, and you go to an architect for planning and supervision, here is how the results will probably compare with other houses.

The design will proceed from an analysis of your family living patterns. No such analysis is made by anyone else who produces houses.

The arrangement of rooms and circulation, and the relationships among street, driveway, doors, windows, and outdoor living areas will all tend to be convenient and economical. In short, the house will be better planned, inside and outside.

Hidden quality of construction will not knowingly be sacrificed. The speculative builder, by contrast, under pressure to keep first costs low for quick sale, may, for instance, elect to save $100 by using 1-inch instead of 3-inch wall insulation. He can still say the walls are insulated. What he hopes you won't realize is that with the thinner insulation your annual fuel bills may be $35 higher, so that after the first three years the house will cost you an extra $35 per year.

The speculative builder also realizes surprisingly large savings from building several nearly identical houses with the same crew. When building the first house the crew moves slowly and makes many mistakes that have to be rectified at a high cost in wages and materials. When they finish, however, they will have learned how to build that particular house and can erect copies of it at greatly reduced cost. Therefore the average cost of several identical houses is much less than the actual cost of building the first one. The house designed by an architect specifically for you is, of course, a "first"—and only—house. Its extra cost cannot be allocated among later, similar houses.

An architect's detailed, explicit drawings and specifications plus the bidders' knowledge that the architect will administer the construction contract enable you to obtain truly competitive construction cost bids. The spread between the high bid and the low bid you accept will usually be 10 to 15 percent, which strongly suggests that, in the absence of competitive bidding, your house would cost 10 to 15 percent more. Thus, by establishing true competition, the architect cuts construction cost by an amount about equal to his fee.

To sum up, the architect's fee is not a cost factor. If we assume that high-quality construction is worth what you pay for it then it is not a cost factor either. We are left with the extra cost of a "first" house to be balanced by the extra value of better design.

Regardless of the advantages of an architect most one-family houses will continue to be built without direct architectural service to the original occupants. Most people are unable to conceive of anything better than is currently being offered to them, and are hence unwilling to believe that an architect can do them much good. Bad design doesn't particularly bother them. They are so adaptable, they often don't notice many of the inconveniences and inefficiencies of the houses they inhabit. Someone has said that only zoos are well designed nowadays because if they aren't the animals don't adapt: they die.

Chapter 5

CHOOSING AN ARCHITECT

In the United States there are over twenty-five thousand licensed architects in roughly eleven thousand architectural firms, which also include thousands of engineers and draftsmen. The largest of these firms has about one thousand employees. Firms of from five to fifty employees are common, and there are thousands of one- or two-man firms.

What you will probably do is select a local architect whose work you have seen and liked. Your choice will also be influenced by your personal impression of him, and by his reputation. Selection on this basis is easy and fairly reliable, but complications may arise. Several choices may look equally good, or none may look good enough. You may wonder if some internationally famous architect, perhaps hundreds of miles away, is available and willing to take your job. Your job may have unique characteristics, raising the question of need for a specialist. In fact, many circumstances may indicate that you should carefully investigate several architects before settling on one. The usual way is to hold personal interviews.

Location of the interviews—your home ground or the architect's—is a matter of mutual convenience. The number of interviews naturally is limited by the number of available architects, and also by the time and energy you can muster. You may interview just one or two. School boards sometimes interview twenty or more. A one-hour meeting may be enough for each architect, but if the job is in the million-dollar-and-up class, you may spend more than a day on each interview and investigation.

BEGINNING THE PROCESS OF SELECTION

From recommendations by friends, buildings you have seen, and perhaps from photographs of buildings or other publicity, you should be able to compile a list of architects to interview. If the list seems too short, it can be augmented by asking a disinterested architectural firm to make recommendations. (A disinterested firm is one that is far too large or small to take on the job in question.) Another source of names of reputable architects is the nearest chapter office of the A.I.A. The classified telephone directory is a possible last resort.

An architect will usually appear for his interview with the following:

1. A written résumé of his past experience, including buildings he has designed, former employers, awards, and educational and biographical information.
2. A list of references.
3. A brochure showing photographs and drawings of buildings he and his firm have designed.
4. An invitation to accompany him on a visit to some of the buildings illustrated in the brochure.

During the interviews you will accumulate information and personal impressions. In reaching a final decision, the following discussion of factors may be helpful. None of them is conclusive, and you will have to determine for your own case how much weight to give to each.

FACTORS TO CONSIDER IN SELECTING AN ARCHITECT

1. Academic Grades

An architect's marks as a college student are hardly worth considering. The fact that he has passed the state registration examination is far more significant.

2. Specialization

It is hard to evaluate specialization. The specialized architect may just be "in a rut" for his own profit, or he may be able to furnish valuable extra service as a result of his speciality. There are architectural firms that specialize in hospitals, schools, banks, factories, or other building types. If a firm acquires a reputation for a particular kind of building it may, by limiting itself to that (or a closely similar) type, reduce its operating costs. It may then either charge slightly lower fees, or earn higher profits. Other firms specialize in order to master thoroughly the design of exceptionally complicated buildings. Hospitals and laboratories are examples. Usually, however, you yourself will be quite familiar with details of the activities to be carried on in your proposed building, so specialization of the architect will be unimportant. Your knowledge, plus the breadth of experience of the average architect, will be adequate.

In addition, a good architect can be depended on to evaluate his own capabilities. If one is hired, for example, to design a large restaurant, he may himself hire an outside professional consultant to advise on the kitchen design and layout. An architect will usually turn down a job he feels unqualified to perform even with outside help.

3. Size of Fee

The importance of the size of the fee is easily and frequently exaggerated. Fees are discussed in more detail in the next chapter. Here it should be enough to say that most architects charge about the same amount for the same service.

4. Prizewinning

Architectural design competitions are frequent. Some are government sponsored, and others are sponsored by manufacturers of building materials. Hundreds of architects enter them. Entries are judged by juries of other architects, businessmen, and sometimes politicians. If you know the members of a jury, or otherwise have reason to respect their judgment, then you have reason to respect the architects who win the competition.

Juries are not noticeably infallible. Several decades ago the great Eliel Saarinen placed only second in competition for the design of the Chicago *Tribune* Tower. The winning design for the Franklin D. Roosevelt memorial in Washington, D.C., chosen by a jury in 1960, was rejected by higher authority.

Winning a competition is not the same as furnishing complete architectural service. In competitions there are no working drawings, specifications, or field observation of construction. Nor is there any give and take between architect and client. Competitions test only part of an architect's required repertory.

5. Fellowship in the A.I.A.

The initials F.A.I.A. after an architect's name stand for *Fellow of the American Institute of Architects.* Fellowships are awarded for outstanding work in architectural design, public service, education, or service to the A.I.A. To evaluate how much a Fellowship means in your particular case, first find out for what it was awarded.

6. Fame

If you want what he appears to offer, don't hesitate to seek the services of any architect, no matter how imposing his image. Your job may be too small for his firm to handle efficiently, or he may have a discouragingly long waiting list, but there is no harm in asking. He may also charge higher fees than other architects, but not much higher, and you may decide he is worth the difference: Others have. Even if you don't hire him, he may give you helpful references to other architects.

7. Location

You and the architect will have to get together frequently in the early stages of the job. Time and transportation expense will be saved if his office is nearby. His visits to the job site will be even more frequent, however, so even more will be saved if his office is near the new building. A handy indicator for working proximity is one mile per $1,000 of construction cost. Applied to a $50,000 house, for example, it means that if the job is more than about fifty miles from the architect's office the cost of his travel becomes undesirably high when compared with the size of his fee. If you particularly want to employ some architect who is further away, it may be a good idea for him to find a colleague near the job site to handle the observation of construction. This procedure is neither impractical nor uncommon. The too-distant architect, if he is doing other work in the vicinity of your project, may also be able to combine visits and split costs.

8. Engineering Services

Hitherto "service of an architect" has tacitly included work actually performed by engineers. Although on many jobs costing about $50,000 or less, the architect will do the necessary engineering himself, on larger jobs he needs specialized help. The architect will then be the designer, and the coordinator of professional service, but he will be assisted closely by mechanical and electrical and sometimes structural and civil engineers. As engineering work amounts to anywhere from one-fourth to one-half of the total, the persons performing it ought to be investigated along with the architect.

In evaluating engineers, the same factors apply as when evaluating architects. Architects will explain their arrangements for engineering service, and may be accompanied to the interview by engineers who work with them.

When engineering services are needed, many architects associate with independent engineering firms. A common alternative is for an architectural firm to hire or retain engineers on a temporary basis. Some large architectural firms contain a full array of both architects and engineers all the time. It is not important to you which of these arrangements may exist as long as provision is made for availability of all required service. If the architect and his engineers have worked together successfully before, however, it is evidence that they can probably do so again.

9. Size of the Architectural Firm

An undersized firm is one that cannot accomplish your job in the available time, simply through lack of enough hands to manipulate pencils. An oversized firm is one whose largeness has led to complexity of organization that is inappropriate and inefficient when brought to bear on your "small" job. It is easy to see that a one-man firm is too small for a ten-million-dollar job, and most one-hundred-man firms will tactfully avoid the client with a fifty-thousand-dollar house. It is not difficult to eliminate firms that are far too large or far too small, but it *is* difficult to indicate the optimum range of size. Assuming nonspecialized firms furnishing complete architectural service, I recommend the following range:

(A) Minimum Size

Divide budgeted construction cost by $300,000, round off the quotient to the nearest whole number, and add one. The result is the minimum acceptable number of architectural personnel in the firm. (Architectural personnel includes all members of the firm who are architecturally trained. It excludes those with engineering training, and clerical-accounting personnel.) For a million-dollar job this calculation gives 4 (1,000,000/300,000 = 3⅓. Nearest whole number: 3. Adding 1 makes 4). A firm with slightly less than this number of architectural personnel would be acceptable if it agreed to hire some additional draftsmen before time to commence working drawings.

A one-man firm, by this calculation, can handle jobs costing up to $150,000. For larger jobs he should hire a draftsman. For jobs costing over $450,000 he needs two draftsmen, and so on.

To the calculated number of architectural personnel add one-fourth to one-half as many engineering personnel.

(B) Maximum Size

No matter how large the firm, it will not be too large for jobs costing over a million dollars. On jobs costing a million dollars or less, assume that the maximum size of the firm should be ten times the calculated minimum size. For a million-dollar job, then, the recommended maximum is 10 x 4, or 40 architectural personnel.

A firm larger than this maximum will probably possess wider experience and greater technical competence, but these qualities will be dispersed among employees, some of whom will have no contact with your job. In a large firm each project is performed by a team, composed of some fraction of the employees and headed by a project manager. The size of this team will about equal the size of an entire firm in the middle of the optimum range, and speed of performance will not be much different in either case, because the additional personnel will be draftsmen who can do no more than shorten the time required for preparation of working drawings by a few weeks: an amount not very significant in the total time.

One disadvantage of the large firm is that its teams tend to be ephemeral and so rarely attain the efficiency possible in smaller firms. There are also some fairly obvious advantages in choosing a small firm. "Small" means so small that to perform your job almost the entire firm is put on the team. Then the "project manager" will be the head of the firm, or a partner. He will have no higher-ups to please: only you, his client. He will tend to have a strong feeling of responsibility for the work. He will also have enough authority to adapt policy, modify procedures, or take such unconventional action as the peculiarities of your project suggest. He can "expedite," where a subordinate project manager in a larger firm is forced to "go through channels."

10. Buildings Designed by the Firm

You will naturally be attracted to an architect if he has designed a building you greatly admire. In fact, if your approach to architecture is wholly Imitative, and you can find an existing building to serve as a model for duplication, you need only hire its architect and have him turn out a copy. If he is dead, of course, you will have to make do with an imitation of him. But if you recognize that your proposed new building has some unique requirements, your approach is at least partly Abstract, and the problem of evaluating an architect on the basis of buildings he has designed becomes a little more complicated.

Buildings are the joint products of their owners, architects, and builders. For the building to be a success, each must do his work well, but if any one of them fails, so will the building. Therefore a good building implies a good architect, but as either the owner, architect, or builder alone can spoil the project an unsuccessful building does not necessarily imply a poor architect. Of course if you dislike almost all the buildings an architect has designed, chances are you should steer clear of him, but if you dislike only a few, the few can be ignored.

It is important to realize, however, that whether you like or dislike a building, such feeling often changes in time. Initial dislike may change to understanding, acceptance, and even high regard. Originality of architecture, in particular, takes some familiarity. On the other hand, a building that appeals at first sight may, with the passage of time, come to seem commonplace, or even repulsive: Novelty wears off, leaving only bad ornamentality. So it is best to avoid snap judgments. It will help if you let the architect explain the rationale and appearance of his buildings; careful judgment requires an understanding of relationships which may not be apparent at first sight.

11. References: Former Clients

Of all people, an architect's former clients with their problems, most nearly resemble you with your problems. Knowing what their experience was with the architect is invaluable. No matter how good an architect is, however, his relations with some of his clients will have been unsatisfactory. When you check his references be sure you talk to enough former clients to avoid being unduly influenced by a disgruntled minority.

12. References: Contractors

Those who have built buildings designed by an architect can give valuable information about him. You must allow for the fact that architects, to protect their clients, must sometimes oppose the interests of contractors, but both architect and contractor have a common desire to please the owner. If an architect habitually prepares drawings and specifications that are incomplete, full of mistakes, or deceptive, you will not want to hire him, and on this subject a contractor's opinion can be sought. Contractors can also say whether the architect visited the job site regularly, whether he was cooperative, and whether he was willing to be realistic about construction problems. In all these matters the architect should help, not obstruct, the contractor.

As with former clients, be sure to query enough contractors to get a representative sample.

13. References: Other Architects

After interviewing architects, and perhaps eliminating some, it is possible to consult a disinterested architect concerning the remainder. He should be offered a fee for consultation, but unless he knows all the candidates he should decline to give an opinion.

On relatively large jobs a better way to use a disinterested architect is to hire him to be present at the interviews. He can raise questions you might overlook, and is better able to evaluate some of the factors involved. Again, he should receive a fee for consultation, probably in the range of fifteen to forty dollars per hour.

14. Scheduling

Learn how soon the firm can start work on your job and the time they will require to finish. The "right-sized" firms may turn out to be too busy, and you will then have to consider "wrong-sized" firms.

15. The Architect's Approach to Architecture

Your architect should be willing and able to approach your project with an attitude consistent with your own. The problem is to determine what is consistent. By the very nature of his profession you can expect him to take a more Abstract view of architecture than you do. If your approach is Imitative, but you are open to Abstract reasoning, then any architect whose past work you admire can be assumed to have a satisfactory approach. If your approach is unquestioningly Imitative, however, you need an architect who is also Imitative from basic, personal conviction. The more Abstract your approach, the more important it is to distinguish between the architect who is also Abstract and the one who is merely a Modern Imitator: They may be hard to tell apart. Unless you are an avid fan of architecture, the buildings designed by the Modern Imitator may look original to you, when in fact they are copies of other buildings. If an architect shows you a "modern" building he designed, but is unable to furnish convincing reasons for its specific plan and appearance, he must be suspected of having copied it. If his reasons are good, however, the fact that it may not be entirely original doesn't matter.

CONCLUDING THE PROCESS OF SELECTION

Some architectural firms can be eliminated before the interviews: You can at least omit the too-distant and (tentatively) the wrong-sized. Checking references and visiting buildings can most conveniently be done after the interviews. During the interviews you will evaluate some or all of the other factors discussed here. You should also try carefully to evaluate a very important factor which there is no point in my discussing: the architect's personal impression on you.

Skilled labor can be hired on a largely rational basis. Objective tests can be given, and length and variety of experience ascertained. Even so the results of personal interviews are used in such a way that hiring is partly intuitive. In the case of an architect, despite the above criteria for judgment, there are really *no* highly reliable objective tests, and the significance of an architect's experience and reputation are not easily evaluated. Choice of architect remains largely irrational and intuitive. Objective criteria should be put in their place: important but inconclusive. You need not reject an architect because a contractor says "He sure cost me a bundle." Nor need you accept an architect because one of your friends says "He's wonderful." All too often an architectural commission hinges on one such statement.

Much of the general material in this book should become clearer when a specific building project is described. Therefore, inserted at appropriate places, you will find installments in the story of the design and building of a real house. Not only should clarity thus be served, but also you can vicariously experience something like the actual experiences of persons involved in the building process.

To avoid revealing personal information about real people, all the persons connected with this illustrative project have been fictionalized. Reversing the usual process of designing a house to suit a family, I have "designed" a family to suit a house. The relationship between the real house and the fictitious family, however, is just as consistent and credible as was the relationship between the house and its real family.

The illustrative project is a house, but I want to emphasize again that events are basically the same for all types of buildings, of whatever cost; whether the owner is an individual, a group, or a corporation; and whether the architect is an individual, a partnership, or a large firm.

Dr. and Mrs. John Hauswirth lived in a small town just beyond the commuting radius of a large city. The doctor practiced general medicine. His patients were from the families of farmers, small businessmen, and workers in light industry.

After their second child was born the Hauswirths bought sixteen acres of farmland outside the town limits. It was mostly pasture, but the back third was a thick grove of trees; a small stream, parallel to the road, bisected the property. The land on both sides pitched irregularly down to the stream, and without presenting any spectacular views, the property was attractive in its variety of feature.

Although not especially lucrative the doctor's practice provided enough income for the Hauswirths to pay off the mortgage on their house in town, and deny themselves nothing they really wanted for their health, comfort, or amusement. As they disliked being in debt it was not until several years after purchasing the country property that they had saved enough to build without mortgaging.

Then they happened to visit new acquaintances and greatly admired their house. So the Hauswirths got the architect's name and made an appointment to see him about designing a house for them. Before the appointment, however, they ran across an article in the metropolitan newspaper about an application of hyperbolic-paraboloids in house design. There were plans and photographs of a small-scale model. The house, weird to their first glances, fascinated the Hauswirths enough that, through continued scrutiny, the weirdness vanished. Harriet Hauswirth, who had always liked mathematics in school, remembered a little about hyperbolic-paraboloids, too. The Hauswirths decided to visit Marshall Shaper, the architect of the hyperbolic-paraboloid house, as well as George Plum, their friends' architect.

Plum proved to have a personal style. Most of the houses he had designed displayed a similar mixture of stone and wood, rooves of similar pitch and overhang, and a sort of equivalence of mass, all of which contributed to a family resemblance. He was Imitative in a hitherto unmentioned way: he copied himself. The Hauswirths liked his work very much. After they had described their sixteen acres, Plum began sketching possible house designs for them. They might have retained him there and then but were due at Shaper's in half an hour and were embarrassed to cancel the appointment so late.

Shaper was too young to have been in practice very long. His work consisted mostly of small industrial and commercial buildings, and some residential alterations, none of it especially interesting to the Hauswirths who had a new house in mind.

"That house you had in the newspaper," began the doctor. "Would something like that be practical for us?" Shaper said he didn't know.

The Hauswirths described their site and ideas for the house. They wanted the usual living, dining, and kitchen facilities; two child's bedrooms, a bedroom for themselves, a sitting room—a "private place"—for Harriet, a study for the doctor, a guest room, a two-car garage, and "plenty" of bathrooms and closets. The only unusual need was for a large studio for Harriet's painting and sculpturing.

"Do you think we can manage all that for $50,000?" she asked.

"No," said Shaper, "but if your budget is $50,000 we may be able to save money by combining some of the elements you've mentioned. And if you'll be satisfied with inexpensive interior and exterior finishes, it may then be possible to stay within the budget. First, though, does the $50,000 include the architect's fee?"

Harriet hesitated.

"No," said John.

"Does it include carpet, curtains, and furniture? How about landscaping?"

"Well," said Harriet, "I guess we can get along with our present furniture until we can afford new things. My brother can get us carpet cheaply, so we'll leave that out of the budget. We won't landscape because we like the property the way it is—John hates to mow. We might plant a small lawn later. I'll do some gardening . . . after I make the curtains."

"Now," asked John, "what about hyper . . . whatayacallems?"

"It really is too soon to tell if they make sense in this case," replied Shaper.

"But I thought it said in the newspaper they were so cheap," protested Harriet.

"They're potentially cheap," said Shaper, "because they use less material than conventional alternatives, but the cheapness could only be realized by mass-production and high-volume sales, which are not likely to occur in the near future. Using them in your house would increase the cost, and would make sense only if you liked them for their own sake and they were esthetically appropriate to the rest of the design, and if their physical adaptation to the house were so simple and direct that the added cost would be minimal."

The Hauswirths went home. "Plum will do us a nice house," said John.

"Just like all his other houses," said Harriet.

"Well, we *like* his other houses," said John. "Shaper would come up with god-knows-what."

"But it would be *our* house. Plum just designs houses for Plum."

"But Plum's fee would be seven percent of construction cost, he said; Shaper wants $5,000, which is 10 percent."

"Everybody we've talked to says a good architect charges 10 percent for houses."

"Yeah, but charging 10 percent doesn't make him a good architect," objected John.

"Shaper's younger, and not so set in his ways," ventured Harriet.

"Shaper's younger and not so experienced," countered John.

"Let's get them out to look at the site separately, and then decide," suggested Harriet.

The following Saturday the Hauswirths led Shaper deep into the woods on rising ground far from the road. "This is where we have always pictured the house," said Harriet. As they walked back Shaper paused on a small plateau near the side lot line and on the road side of the stream.

"I think the house should go here," he said.

"Why here?" asked the doctor.

"You'll need only half as much driveway, which will save money and require a lot less work to clear off after snowstorms. And by building here you won't need to build a vehicle bridge over the stream. But I think the house should go here mostly for the view down into the stream and across into that clearing to the southwest. As far as privacy from the road is concerned, we're four hundred feet from it: That's enough, but you can still see the road, which, I think, is nice in the country."

When the Hauswirths took Plum on a tour of the site and showed him the spot in the woods where they thought the house should be, he said "certainly, anywhere you say."

Later John telephoned Shaper. "I know where you think the house should go, but are you willing to put it where we want it?"

"Yes," said Shaper.

To his wife, John summarized. "All right. Plum has a house formula, and we happen to like it, but he's indifferent to anything that doesn't violate the formula, so outside of its dictates he'll leave everything up to us. Shaper has no formula and no apparent preconceptions or prejudices. He'll question anything we say we want, and try to talk us out of it anytime he thinks he can come up with a better idea. That could be irritating sometimes. Nevertheless I think we will get a cheaper, better house for us from Shaper than from Plum."

"And I think he's right about the location too," said Harriet.

Chapter 6

PUT IT IN WRITING

ONCE you have tentatively chosen your architect, you and he will discuss the project, his services, and his fee. As soon as you agree on the details of these matters, the architect can start working. At this point, if you have in fact reached agreement, then you and he have entered into a contract. It need not be written down to be "legal," but common sense dictates that it be in writing to insure against lapse of memory and to minimize the possiblity of misunderstanding. A contract is a mutually protective device. It will benefit you as much as the architect.

There are people who have an aversion to signing things. They suspect clever lawyers have laid traps in the fine print. In the early stages of a building project this aversion may be heightened if the client still looks upon the venture as somewhat tentative.

The architect will probably propose that you and he execute a *Standard Form of Agreement Between Owner and Architect.* This widely used form is published by the A.I.A., and there are several, slightly different versions to allow for different methods of determining the fee. There is no "fine print," and the wording is simple and straightforward. A thorough reading may be rather dull, but is not a formidable task. A sample form is printed at the end of Chapter 7. Almost everything in it will be discussed as we go along, so that when you get to it, it should be comprehensible and contain no surprises. If you have qualms about what you are letting yourself in for by signing such an agreement, talk it over with your lawyer. The standard form includes a termination clause for use if you should decide to cancel the project or fire the architect.

This contract between you and the architect, for convenience, I shall call the *Agreement,* with capital A. The later contract between you and the contractor I shall call the *Contract,* with capital C.

The Agreement is the beginning of a series of written and graphic records whose importance I wish to stress. The series includes the building program, construction cost estimates, all drawings and specifications, and all correspondence relating to the project. It should *also* include memorandums covering telephone calls, conferences, and even some casual conversations. There are thousands of details involved in the genesis of a building, and if decisions are not put in writing, some of them are almost bound to be forgotten, or worse, remembered differently by you and the architect. It is all too easy, in the beginning, faced with broad, unforgettable considerations, to be lax in the tedious taking and preserving of notes. Who, for example, can forget that a proposed building is to be ten stories high? Well, once the president of a large corporation, after a third martini, told his architect to add two stories to a building then being designed. When the architect later duly confirmed the order in a memorandum, the client soberly wrote back to cancel it. Memorandums are like insurance premiums: a small price to pay for protection against potentially disastrous forgetfulness.

Most of the burden of recording decisions falls on the architect. He uually furnishes the forms and writes up the building program. He makes the drawings and specifications and initiates the bulk of the correspondence. He also should note decisions made at conferences, conversations, and over the telephone. From time to time he should send you a summary of important transactions occurring since the last summary. You don't *have* to do anything more than keep what he sends you, just as you keep canceled checks as a matter of record. Yet, as he will be acting in accordance with those letters and memorandums, you should review them to make sure he has not left out or misunderstood something. It is also a good idea occasionally to review the written and graphic material in order to have in mind what orders to the architect are in effect. The architect, as the project develops, often needs your decision, and if your mental picture of the job is up to date, you are in a position to deal rapidly and intelligently with problems as they arise.

If you can summon the energy, I advise you not to leave record-making entirely up to the architect. He is not infallible. Like anyone else, he may have his attention diverted after talking to you and before writing down his notes, and so forget something. There is extra safety in making your own notes. These can be used to verify his summaries later. You may learn, too late, that the architect of your choice, a jewel in all other respects, is remiss about keeping records. Prodding may not change him. Prudence then directs that you take pains to record transactions yourself to avoid future arguments.

Architects and their clients, on rare occasions, get into disagreements that have to be resolved by lawyers or courts. This unhappy situation is less likely if all transactions have been recorded and notes exchanged.

Here is an example of things irksome to write down but easy to forget. At a conference with the architect you approve a color scheme he shows you. The next day you telephone him and request that one color be changed. He agrees. Nothing else happens. Ten months later the wrong color appears on the building. In retrospect, the architect should have confirmed the telephone order in writing, and you should have complained when he didn't. The fault, it seems to me, is basically his, but you were a bit careless too.

If neither of you makes notes, if you both gamble on unassisted memory, there is a chance that you will end up perfectly satisfied with the job. It is most likely to happen on a small job, rapidly executed, without changes in any initial decisions. You can't count on it, however, and it is a gamble I advise you not to take.

Chapter 7

FEES

THE first thing most clients want to know about the architect's fee is "how much?" and a fairly accurate answer is not difficult if normal service is expected. In addition to the size of the fee, however, it is important to consider *how* it is determined; and finally you will want to have an idea of the size and timing of payments.

THE SIZE OF THE FEE

According to architects, clients are prone to attach too much importance to the size of the fee. Architects point out that the difference between, say, a 5 percent and a 6 percent fee is only 1 percent of construction cost, which is very slight as far as the client is concerned, but is the difference between profit and loss to the architect. In reply the client may say that the same argument is equally valid for every person furnishing labor or materials to the job, and if each of *them* added one-fifth to his charges the project cost would increase, not one percent, but 20 percent, and this is certainly not slight.

Warming to the discussion, the architect replies that the planning of a project must be granted equal importance with its execution. If the fee is 5 percent, which is one-twentieth of construction cost, then every dollar's worth of architectural service decides the wisdom with which a total of twenty construction dollars are spent. Omit a dollar's worth of planning and you jeopardize many more dollars' worth of construction. A badly designed building may cost very slightly less, but it will be *worth* a great deal less.

The size of the fee is neither a matter of whim nor based on "what the traffic will bear." Reputable architects everywhere will ask for roughly the same fee once the type of building is known and its construction cost predicted. Fees are listed in fee schedules. Some are prepared by individual architects and others are standard for a state or region. A typical schedule is shown on pages 63-64. First establish whether the proposed building is classified as type *A,B,C,D,* or *E.* Next find the conjunction of the building type with the construction cost and read off the fee, which is expressed as a percentage of construction cost. Schools, for example, are found classified as type *B.* The fee for a $500,000 school is found in the table by reading across from $500,000 to column *B.* The value given is 6.9, which means "6.9 percent of construction cost." If actual construction cost turned out to be exactly equal to this predicted cost, the architect would receive 0.069 x $500,000 or $34,500. In this schedule the fee covers complete professional services, which include architectural work plus normal air-conditioning, plumbing, electrical, and structural engineering work.

The percentage is seen to decline as the size of the project increases. The reason for this decline is that some of the architectural work is independent of project size. Detail drawings of classroom window installation, for instance, will be drawn just once, regardless of the total number of classrooms to which those details apply; thus multiplying classrooms does not increase the architectural work in the same ratio.

Architects have also discovered that their work for complex or elaborate buildings takes more man-hours than for simple buildings even when construction cost is the same. Thus the classifications *A,B,C,D,* and *E* are groups of building types arranged in the order of increasing complexity with correspondingly higher fees.

Houses are in a class by themselves. They are the most complicated building type, so the fee for them is highest. No fee is shown for houses costing over $100,000 because they are both rare and of unpredictable complexity.

Whatever its cost, after preliminary discussion with you, your architect may decide that your project has special features. These may either complicate or simplify his work. A house that must be hurricane-proof, for example, will probably require more work than an ordinary house costing the same to build. If so, the architect will probably request a fee slightly higher than the schedule shows.

SCHEDULE
RECOMMENDED BASIC COMPENSATION

Construction Cost*	BASIC COMPENSATION—% OF CONSTRUCTION COSTS					
	Type A	Type B	Type C	Type D	Type E	Type F
Up to 5,000						15.0
10,000						13.0
25,000						12.0
50,000	7.0	8.0	9.0	10.0	15.0	11.0
100,000	6.5	7.5	8.5	9.5	12.0*	10.0*
200,000	6.3	7.3	8.3	9.3		
300,000	6.1	7.1	8.1	9.1		
400,000	6.0	7.0	8.0	9.0		
500,000	5.9	6.9	7.9	8.9		
600,000	5.8	6.8	7.8	8.8	*Over $50,000	
800,000	5.6	6.6	7.6	8.6		
1,000,000	5.4	6.4	7.4	8.4		
1,500,000	5.2	6.2	7.2	8.2		
2,000,000	5.0	6.0	7.0	8.0		
2,500,000	4.8	5.8	6.8	7.8		
3,000,000	4.7	5.7	6.7	7.7		
4,000,000	4.6	5.6	6.6	7.6		
5,000,000	4.5	5.5	6.5	7.5		

*When Construction cost falls between amounts shown, the fee shall be determined by interpolation.

For construction contracts involving remodeling, alteration of or addition to existing buildings add an additional factor, depending upon the complexity of the project, to the basic compensation rates shown above to determine the basic compensation for that portion of such contracts.

For construction contracts involving reuse of construction documents compensation is normally less than the basic compensation for original use, plus an hourly rate or fixed fee for any required changes. Variations shall be determined to suit the particular circumstances.

SEPARATE CONTRACTS:

The schedule of basic compensation applies when all construction is let under a single building construction contract. Increased compensation is required if separate building construction contracts are let, thereby increasing the architect's services, expenses and responsibilities. In situations where separate bids are taken and the successful bidders are assigned as subcontractors to the general contractor, the increased compensation to the architect may be less than when contracts are awarded.

COMPENSATION FOR ARCHITECTURAL SERVICES BASED ON PERCENTAGE OF CONSTRUCTION COSTS

Reprinted from Michigan Society of Architects Document No. 65-8 "ARCHITECTURAL SERVICES"

TYPES OF CONSTRUCTION PROJECTS

TYPE A:

Garages
Parking Ramps
Loft Buildings
Simple Industrial
Simple Stores
Utility Buildings
Warehouses

Other structures of simple utilitarian character which are without complication of design or detail and require a minimum of simple finish, mechanical finish, mechanical and electrical work.

TYPE B:

Apartment Buildings
Armories
Auditoriums
Banks
City Halls
College Buildings (See also Type C)
Department Stores
Dormitories
Detention or Custodial Buildings
Fire Stations
Complicated Industrial
Food Service Buildings
Hotels
Public Housing
Schools, Public and Private
Laundries
Libraries
Office or Administration Bldgs.
Recreational Buildings
Shopping Centers
Theaters
Process Buildings

Other structures of conventional character requiring normal care in design, detail and equipment.

TYPE C:

Convalescent Homes
Health Clinics
Hospitals
Laboratories
Medical, Dental or Veterinary Offices
Power Plants

Buildings for Research, Teaching of Medicine, Veterinary Medicine, Chemistry or other Sciences.

Other structures of exceptional character requiring the greatest skill in design and containing comparatively large amounts of complex scientific, mechanical and electrical equipment.

TYPE D:

Churches
Chapels

Religious Educational Facilities (other than day schools)

TYPE E:

Private residences

TYPE F:

Site Development and Landscaping

Furnishings consisting of fixed and movable equipment for buildings of Type A, B, C, D and E above.

Fee schedules are based on experience. Architectural service requires a roughly predictable number—hundreds or thousands—of hours of work by designers, draftsmen, and so forth. They receive wages and require a place to work; office rent and other overhead costs must be paid. Salaries, wages, and overhead account for 80 to 90 percent of the fee. The rest is profit. There is little latitude for variation. The important thing to remember is that you will get just about what you pay for. An architectural firm that asks a fee significantly lower than usual is almost certainly planning to furnish less than normal service. A firm that quotes higher is probably either very busy or basing its fee on the value of a famous name. If you have carefully selected your architect, it is likely that whatever fee he asks will be as close as anyone can come to the "right" fee.

Aside from the fee the architect will have some expenses for which he is customarily reimbursed. These include the cost of blueprinting, travel (and sometimes living), and a few other minor expenses. The sum of them all is usually less than 5 percent of the fee. The cost of topographical surveys and soil testing is also paid by the client, but directly, not as a reimbursement to the architect.

METHODS OF DETERMINING THE FEE

So far we have tacitly assumed that the fee was determined by the common, traditional percentage method. There are two other methods, called the *lump-sum,* and the *cost-plus.* Understanding the three different methods is a requirement for choosing among them, but the actual choice also depends on the architect's preference, which in turn is influenced by his evaluation of the project and the nature of his own firm.

1. Percentage Method

The Agreement between you and the architect will outline the services he is to perform and will also state the fee you are to pay in return. The Agreement will first state the predicted (or budgeted) construction cost, unless the uniqueness of the project makes this impossible. Then, if the percentage method is used, the Agreement will state that the fee is some percentage of the construction cost. Thereafter the architect commences work. As he proceeds, changes affecting construction cost usually occur. These changes produce corresponding changes in the amount of architectural work. The percentage fee method works to raise or lower payments to the architect to match increases or decreases in construction cost. The advantage of the percentage method lies in this self-regulating quality.

A disadvantage of the percentage method is that it subjects the fee to variations in the construction market. If contractors are busy they bid higher, the construction cost rises, and the architect receives an unearned bonus. If building activity is slack contractors bid lower, and the architect's pay is reduced even though his work is not. Perhaps a more serious disadvantage of the percentage method is that it penalizes the architect for discovering ways of building more cheaply. If, by exercise of his ingenuity, he enables contractors to submit exceptionally low bids, the architect should be rewarded, but the percentage method will penalize him instead.

The percentage method is best applied when construction cost is a subordinate consideration. This is the case when the facilities of the proposed building—number and size of rooms, and so forth—are of primary concern, and cost, although important, is secondary.

2. Lump-Sum Method

To determine the lump-sum fee a schedule can be used in the same way as for the percentage method, but one more step is required. The percentage fee for a $500,000 school was found to be 6.9 percent of construction cost. The lump-sum fee for the same job would be 6.9 percent of $500,000, or $34,500. The lump-sum fee is the percentage fee multiplied by the construction cost. The agreement between the architect and client will state that the fee shall be a certain number of dollars—in this case $34,500—rather than a certain percentage of the cost of construction.

The advantages and disadvantages of the lump-sum method are just the opposite of the percentage method. The self-regulating feature of the percentage method is sacrificed, but in return the lump-sum method frees the architect's remuneration from unpredictable variations in the construction market. It also avoids penalizing the architect for discovering ways of building more cheaply. Low bids do not reduce his pay, nor do high bids increase it.

In the good old days the client would come to the architect, describe the house he wanted, and say "I want to spend about $100,000." The architect would mumble a little and then diffidently point out that the house as described would cost nearer $150,000. The client would answer "That much? Well! I guess there's no help for it." The design would proceed, the client would request a cupola here, a gazebo there, and the bids would come in at around $200,000. Afterward the client's feigned annoyance at the *architect's* extravagance was a way of indirectly boasting about the cost of the house. In view of the elastic building budgets of the past the percentage method was usually best.

Nowadays the client describes the house he wants and says "My $20,000 plus a $40,000 mortgage is top. If the low bid comes in over $60,000, I can't build." The story is the same with other types of buildings: The voters, or the directors, establish an inflexible budget. The architect must usually exercise considerable ingenuity to meet it. Of course if the low bid matches the budget, the amount of the fee will be the same whether it is determined by the lump-sum or by the percentage method. But if the client wants to do whatever possible to have the low bid come in at *less* than the budget, the lump-sum method is superior.

A problem arises with both methods if changes are made in the building after the architect begins work. Suppose that after working drawings and specifications are completed for a ten-story office building, it is decided to reduce it to eight stories to save money. The architect will have completed about three-quarters of his work and is clearly entitled to three-quarters of his original fee. With the lump-sum method the amount is easily calculated, but with the percentage method payment to the architect must be based on what the construction cost of the ten-story building would have been, not on the low bid for the revised, eight-story building. Payment for the remaining quarter of the architect's service can be adjusted downward to agree with the reduced construction cost.

There is still another problem. The architect will have to do far more than merely erase the two unwanted stories from the drawings. If money is to be saved, foundations must be redesigned to take advantage of the lightened load from above. The air-conditioning system can be reduced in capacity, which means redesigning ducts and equipment. One of the elevators may be eliminated. In fact, all the architectural and engineering work should be reviewed and much of it revised. The architect is entitled to extra payment for this extra work. Either the agreement must include some supplementary provision to cover possible extra work, or a basis for payment must be negotiated when and if the need arises.

3. Cost-Plus Method

There are several variations of the cost-plus method ("time and overhead," "payroll basis," and others), but they all have this in common:

Payment to the architect depends on the actual amount of work his firm performs rather than on the cost of constructing the building his firm designs. The amount of work performed is learned from an inspection of employees' time cards. Their hours of work on any project, multiplied by their respective hourly wages, add up to the "productive payroll cost." The architect bills for productive payroll cost plus an agreed additional amount to cover overhead and profit.

The variations in the method are mostly variant ways of conveniently calculating overhead and profit. Sometimes, for example, the salaries of principals of the firm are considered as part of productive payroll and sometimes they are considered as part of overhead. In either case the architect assumes that the ratio of overhead to productive payroll is constant. A typical firm may find it allocates half its income to productive payroll, three-eighths to overhead, and one-eighth to profit. Its income thus needs to be twice its productive payroll, and the firm can be expected to do cost-plus work on this basis. In the Agreement the rate may be phrased "payroll plus 100 percent." Alternatively it might be agreed that overhead and profit would be separately calculated and paid for directly rather than as a fraction of payroll. This alternative is impractical unless the entire firm, or a separate office, devotes itself exclusively to one project, which it may do in the case of a very large project.

The cost-plus method is most appropriate when the required amount of architectural work is unpredictable, as often occurs with alterations or additions to existing buildings. The work required for unique buildings may also be impossible to assess in advance: The first building on the moon will probably be designed on a cost-plus basis.

One disadvantage of the cost-plus method is that employees of the architectural firm realize they can work slowly or even loaf a little and still get paid. Employees who expect to be laid off at the end of the job are most likely to yield to this temptation. The opportunity to loaf, however, is equally an opportunity for them to do their best, most careful work. With the right architect the cost-plus method, in return for a sometimes slightly higher fee, will encourage and facilitate design of the highest quality.

4. Combinations of Methods

Preparation of the building program, or program plus preliminary design, is the most important part of the development of any project. One might reasonably have this portion of the work done cost-plus to insure optimum results. The balance of the architectural work, which is largely routine, can then be performed on a lump-sum or adjusted percentage basis.

In the example of the ten-story building cut to eight stories we noticed that neither the lump-sum nor the percentage method in itself provided for paying the architect for his extra work. If one of these methods is used for the basic fee, the Agreement may additionally provide that extra work will be paid for on some definite cost-plus basis.

"BASIC" AND "ADDITIONAL" ARCHITECTURAL SERVICE

Basic service includes (1) consultation on the building program, (2) schematic and preliminary design, (3) making rough cost estimates, (4) preparing the Contract Documents, (5) assisting in obtaining bids, and (6) general administration of the construction Contract. Additional architectural work, which usually entails extra payment, will be mentioned occasionally in succeeding chapters. You can review these additional services now, if you wish, by consulting the *Standard Form of Agreement Between Owner and Architect,* Article 4, Architect's Additional Services. The Basic Services are described in Article 3 of the same form.

PROGRESS PAYMENTS ON THE FEE

If the architect is working on a cost-plus basis, you will receive periodic bills for the exact cost of the work performed, plus overhead and profit for the period just completed. The bills will usually be monthly, but may be weekly on large projects. When the basis of payment is a percentage or lump-sum the timing of the bills is the same, but their size will depend on the architect's estimate of progress instead of on the time cards.

The following example of progress payments also illustrates the operation of the cost-plus method. Again taking a $500,000 school, we can assume that the size of the fee will be about $34,500, whatever method is used. With $10 per hour as a hypothetical average charge for cost-plus work (based on average wages of $5 per hour) the architectural firm can predict that it will devote 34,500 divided by 10, or 3,450 hours to the project. Preliminary design will account for the first quarter of the work, about 860 hours, and will probably take three months. Working drawings and specifications will account for the next half of the work, about 1,720 hours, but might take no more than an additional three months because more employees can work simultaneously during this stage. During the next month the job is "out for bids" and there is little for the architect to do. Then construction begins, and the final quarter of the architect's fee will be distributed nearly uniformly over the construction period, except for a rise at the end because of the time required for final inspections. In any situation proceedings will vary, of course, but the main outlines of the pattern will be the same. The billing is tabulated below:

Month	*Stage of work*	*Time-card hours*	*Hours times $10 equals monthly billing*
1	Preliminary Design	288	2880
2	Preliminary Design	287	2870
3	Preliminary Design	287	2870
4	Drawings and Specifications	576	5760
5	Drawings and Specifications	576	5760
6	Drawings and Specifications	576	5760
7	Out for Bids	—	—
8	Construction	165	1650
9	Construction	165	1650
10	Construction	165	1650
11	Construction	165	1650
12	Construction	200	2000
	Totals	3450 hours	$34,500

THE AMERICAN INSTITUTE OF ARCHITECTS

AIA Document B331

The Standard Form of Agreement Between The Owner and The Architect

on a basis of

Professional Fee Plus Expenses

AGREEMENT

made this 21ST day of MARCH in the year of Nineteen Hundred and

BETWEEN

JOHN T. HAUSWIRTH AND HARRIET HAUSWIRTH, the Owner, and

MARSHALL SHAPER the Architect.

It is the intention of the Owner to

ERECT A RESIDENCE COSTING ABOUT $50,000 AT 202 ACACIA DRIVE, HECTOR, MICHIGAN,

hereinafter referred to as the Project.

The Owner and the Architect agree as set forth below.

I. THE ARCHITECT shall provide professional services for the Project in accordance with the Terms and Conditions of this Agreement.

II. THE OWNER shall compensate the Architect, in accordance with the Terms and Conditions of this Agreement, as follows:

a. *FOR THE ARCHITECT'S BASIC SERVICES,* as described in Paragraph 1.1, a Professional Fee of FIVE THOUSAND dollars ($ 5000.00). If the scope of the Project is changed materially, the Professional Fee shall be changed in the same proportion. ~~[illegible]~~.

b. *FOR THE ARCHITECT'S* ~~[illegible]~~ *ADDITIONAL SERVICES,* as described in Paragraphs ~~[illegible]~~1.3, a sum computed as follows:

Principals' time at the fixed rate of FIFTEEN dollars ($ 15.00) per hour. For the purposes of this Agreement, the Principals are:

MARSHALL SHAPER

Employees' time computed at a multiple of TWO & ONE-HALF (2½) times the employees' Direct Personnel Expense as defined in Article 4.

Services of professional consultants engaged for the normal structural, mechanical and electrical engineering services at a multiple of ONE POINT TWO (1.2) times the amount billed to the Architect for such services.

c. *FOR THE ARCHITECT'S REIMBURSABLE EXPENSES,* amounts expended as defined in Article 5.

d. *THE TIMES AND FURTHER CONDITIONS OF PAYMENT* shall be as described in Article 6.

ARTICLE 1
ARCHITECT'S SERVICES

1.1 BASIC SERVICES

The Architect's Basic Services consist of the five phases described below and include normal structural, mechanical and electrical engineering services.

SCHEMATIC DESIGN PHASE

1.1.1 The Architect shall consult with the Owner to ascertain the requirements of the Project and shall confirm such requirements to the Owner.

1.1.2 The Architect shall prepare Schematic Design Studies consisting of drawings and other documents illustrating the scale and relationship of Project components for approval by the Owner.

1.1.3 The Architect shall submit to the Owner a Statement of Probable Construction Cost based on current area, volume or other unit costs.

DESIGN DEVELOPMENT PHASE

1.1.4 The Architect shall prepare from the approved Schematic Design Studies, for approval by the Owner, the Design Development Documents consisting of drawings and other documents to fix and describe the size and character of the entire Project as to materials, structure, mechanical and electrical systems, and such other essentials as may be appropriate.

1.1.5 The Architect shall submit to the Owner a further Statement of Probable Construction Cost.

CONSTRUCTION DOCUMENTS PHASE

1.1.6 The Architect shall prepare from the approved Design Development Documents, for approval by the Owner, Working Drawings and Specifications setting forth in detail the requirements for the construction of the entire Project including the necessary bidding information, and shall assist in the preparation of bidding forms, the Conditions of the Contract, and the form of Agreement between the Owner and the Contractor.

1.1.7 The Architect shall advise the Owner of any adjustments to previous Statements of Probable Construction Cost indicated by changes in requirements or general market conditions.

1.1.8 The Architect shall assist the Owner in filing the required documents for the approval of governmental authorities having jurisdiction over the Project.

BIDDING OR NEGOTIATION PHASE

1.1.9 The Architect, following the Owner's approval of the Construction Documents and of the latest Statement of Probable Construction Cost, shall assist the Owner in obtaining bids or negotiated proposals, and in awarding and preparing construction contracts.

CONSTRUCTION PHASE — ADMINISTRATION OF THE CONSTRUCTION CONTRACT

1.1.10 The Construction Phase will commence with the award of the Construction Contract and will terminate when final payment is made by the Owner to the Contractor.

1.1.11 The Architect shall provide Administration of the Construction Contract as set forth in Articles 1 through 14 inclusive of the General Conditions of the Contract for Construction, AIA Document A201, Tenth Edition, dated September 1966, and the extent of his duties and responsibilities and the limitations of his authority as assigned thereunder shall not be modified without his written consent.

1.1.12 The Architect, as the representative of the Owner during the Construction Phase, shall advise and consult with the Owner, and all of the Owner's instructions to the Contractor shall be issued through the Architect. The Architect shall have authority to act on behalf of the Owner to the extent provided in the General Conditions unless otherwise modified in writing.

1.1.13 The Architect shall at all times have access to the Work wherever it is in preparation or progress.

1.1.14 The Architect shall make periodic visits to the site to familiarize himself generally with the progress and quality of the Work and to determine in general if the Work is proceeding in accordance with the Contract Documents. On the basis of his on-site observations as an Architect, he shall endeavor to guard the Owner against defects and deficiencies in the Work of the Contractor. The Architect shall not be required to make exhaustive or continuous on-site inspections to check the quality or quantity of the Work. The Architect shall not be responsible for construction means, methods, techniques, sequences or procedures, or for safety precautions and programs in connection with the Work, and he shall not be responsible for the Contractor's failure to carry out the Work in accordance with the Contract Documents.

1.1.15 Based on such observations at the site and on the Contractor's Application for Payment, the Architect shall determine the amount owing to the Contractor and shall issue Certificates for Payment in such amounts. The issuance of a Certificate for Payment shall constitute a representation by the Architect to the Owner, based on his observations at the site as provided in Subparagraph 1.1.14 and the data comprising the Application for Payment, that the work has progressed to the point indicated; that to the best of his knowledge, information and belief, the quality of the Work is in accordance with the Contract Documents (subject to an evaluation of the Work as a functioning whole upon Substantial Completion, to the results of any subsequent tests required by the Contract Documents, to minor deviations from the Contract Documents correctable prior to completion, and to any specific qualifications stated in his Certificate); and that the Contractor is entitled to payment in the amount certified. By issuing a Certificate for Payment, the Architect shall not be deemed to represent that he has made any examiantion to ascertain how and for what purpose the Contractor has used the moneys paid on account of the Contract Sum.

1.1.16 The Architect shall be, in the first instance, the interpreter of the requirements of the Contract Documents and the impartial judge of the performance thereunder by both the Owner and Contractor. The Architect shall make decisions on all claims of the Owner or Contractor relating to the execution and progress of the Work and on all other matters or questions related thereto. The Architect's decisions in matters relating to artistic effect shall be final if consistent with the intent of the Contract Documents.

1.1.17 The Architect shall have authority to reject Work which does not conform to the Contract Documents. The Architect shall also have authority to require the Contractor to stop the Work whenever in his reasonable opinion it may be necessary for the proper performance of the Contract. The Architect shall not be liable to the Owner for the consequences of any decision made by him in good faith either to exercise or not to exercise his authority to stop the Work.

1.1.18 The Architect shall review and approve shop drawings, samples, and other submissions of the Contractor only for conformance with the design concept of the Project and for compliance with the information given in the Contract Documents.

1.1.19 The Architect shall prepare Change Orders.

1.1.20 The Architect shall conduct inspections to determine the Dates of Substantial Completion and Final Completion, shall receive written guarantees and related documents assembled by the Contractor, and shall issue a final Certificate for Payment.

1.1.21 The Architect shall not be responsible for the acts or omissions of the Contractor, or any Subcontractors, or any of the Contractor's or Subcontractors' agents or employees, or any other persons performing any of the Work.

1.2 PROJECT REPRESENTATION BEYOND BASIC SERVICES

1.2.1 If more extensive representation at the site than is described under Subparagraphs 1.1.10 through 1.1.21 inclusive is required, and if the Owner and Architect agree, the Architect shall provide one or more Full-time Project Representatives to assist the Architect.

1.2.2 Such Full-time Project Representatives shall be selected, employed and directed by the Architect, and the Architect shall be compensated therefor as mutually agreed between the Owner and the Architect as set forth in an exhibit appended to this Agreement.

1.2.3 The duties, responsibilities and limitations of such Full-time Project Representatives shall be as set forth in an exhibit appended to this Agreement.

1.2.4 Through the on-site observations by Full-time Project Representatives of the Work in progress, the Architect shall endeavor to provide further protection for the Owner against defects in the Work, but the furnishing of such project representation shall not make the Architect responsible for the Contractor's failure to perform the Work in accordance with the Contract Documents.

1.3 ADDITIONAL SERVICES

The following services are not covered in Paragraphs 1.1 or 1.2. If any of these Additional Services are authorized by the Owner, they shall be paid for by Owner as hereinbefore provided.

1.3.1 Providing special analyses of the Owner's needs, and programming the requirements of the Project.

1.3.2 Providing financial feasibility or other special studies.

1.3.3 Providing planning surveys, site evaluations, or comparative studies of prospective sites.

1.3.4 Making measured drawings of existing construction when required for planning additions or alterations thereto.

1.3.5 Revising previously approved Drawings, Specifications or other documents to accomplish changes not initiated by the Architect.

1.3.6 Preparing documents for alternate bids requested by the Owner.

1.3.7 Providing Detailed Estimates of Construction Costs.

1.3.8 Providing consultation concerning replacement of any Work damaged by fire or other cause during construction, and furnishing professional services of the type set forth in Paragraph 1.1 as may be required in connection with the replacement of such Work.

1.3.9 Providing professional services made necessary by the default of the Contractor in the performance of the Construction Contract.

1.3.10 Providing Contract Administration and observation of construction after the Contract Time has been exceeded by more than twenty per cent through no fault of the Architect.

1.3.11 Furnishing the Owner a set of reproducible record prints of drawings showing significant changes made during the construction process, based on marked up prints, drawings and other data furnished by the Contractor to the Architect.

1.3.12 Providing services after final payment to the Contractor.

1.3.13 Providing interior design and other services required for or in connection with the selection of furniture and furnishings.

1.3.14 Providing services as an expert witness in connection with any public hearing, arbitration proceeding, or the proceedings of a court of record.

1.3.15 Providing services for planning tenant or rental spaces.

ARTICLE 2
THE OWNER'S RESPONSIBILITIES

2.1 The Owner shall provide full information regarding his requirements for the Project.

2.2 The Owner shall designate, when necessary, a representative authorized to act in his behalf with respect to the Project. The Owner or his representative shall examine documents submitted by the Architect and shall render decisions pertaining thereto promptly, to avoid unreasonable delay in the progress of the Architect's work.

2.3 The Owner shall furnish a certified land survey of the site giving, as applicable, grades and lines of streets, alleys, pavements, and adjoining property; rights-of-way, restrictions, easements, encroachments, zoning, deed restrictions, boundaries and contours of the site; locations, dimensions and complete data pertaining to existing buildings, other improvements and trees; and full information concerning available service and utility lines both public and private.

2.4 The Owner shall furnish the services of a soils engineer, when such services are deemed necessary by the Architect, including reports, test borings, test pits, soil bearing values and other necessary operations for determining subsoil conditions.

2.5 The Owner shall furnish structural, mechanical, chemical and other laboratory tests, inspections and reports as required by law or the Contract Documents.

2.6 The Owner shall furnish such legal, accounting and insurance counselling services as may be necessary for the Project and such auditing services as he may require to ascertain how or for what purposes the Contractor has used the moneys paid to him under the Construction Contract.

2.7 The services, information, surveys and reports required by Paragraphs 2.3 through 2.6 inclusive shall be furnished at the Owner's expense, and the Architect shall be entitled to rely upon the accuracy thereof.

2.8 If the Owner observes or otherwise becomes aware of any fault or defect in the Project or non-conformance with the Contract Documents, he shall give prompt written notice thereof to the Architect.

2.9 The Owner shall furnish information required of him as expeditiously as necessary for the orderly progress of the Work.

ARTICLE 3
CONSTRUCTION COST

3.1 Construction Cost shall be determined as follows, with precedence in the order listed:

3.1.1 For completed construction, the total cost of all such Work;

3.1.2 For work not constructed, the lowest bona fide bid received from a qualified bidder for any or all of such work; or

3.1.3 For work for which bids are not received, (1) the latest Detailed Cost Estimate, or (2) the Architect's latest Statement of Probable Construction Cost.

3.2 Construction Cost does not include the fees of the Architect and consultants, the cost of the land, rights-of-way, or other costs which are the responsibility of the Owner as provided in Paragraphs 2.3 through 2.6 inclusive.

3.3 Labor furnished by the Owner for the Project shall be included in the Construction Cost at current market rates. Materials and equipment furnished by the Owner shall be included at current market prices, except that used materials and equipment shall be included as if purchased new for the Project.

3.4 Statements of Probable Construction Cost and Detailed Cost Estimates prepared by the Architect represent his best judgment as a design professional familiar with the construction industry. It is recognized, however, that neither the Architect nor the Owner has any control over the cost of labor, materials or equipment, over the contractors' methods of determining bid prices, or over competitive bidding or market conditions. Accordingly, the Architect cannot and does not guarantee that bids will not vary from any Statement of Probable Construction Cost or other cost estimate prepared by him.

3.5 When a fixed limit of Construction Cost is established as a condition of this Agreement, it shall include a bidding contingency of ten per cent unless another amount is agreed upon in writing. When such a fixed limit is established, the Architect shall be permitted to determine what materials, equipment, component systems and types of construction are to be included in the Contract Documents, and to make reasonable adjustments in the scope of the Project to bring it within the fixed limit. The Architect may also include in the Contract Documents alternate bids to adjust the Construction Cost to the fixed limit.

3.5.1 If the lowest bona fide bid, the Detailed Cost Estimate or the Statement of Probable Construction Cost exceeds such fixed limit of Construction Cost (including the bidding contingency) established as a condition of tihs Agreement, the Owner shall (1) give written approval of an increase in such fixed limit, (2) authorize rebidding the Project within a reasonable time, or (3) cooperate in revising the Project scope and quality as required to reduce the probable cost. In the case of (3) the Architect, without additional charge, shall modify the Drawings and Specifications as necessary to bring the Construction Cost within the fixed limit. The providing of this service shall be the limit of the Architect's responsibility in this regard, and having done so, the Architect shall be entitled to his fees in accordance with this Agreement.

ARTICLE 4
DIRECT PERSONNEL EXPENSE

4.1 Direct Personnel Expense of employees engaged on the Project by the Architect includes architects, engineers, designers, job captains, draftsmen, specification writers and typists, in consultation, research, designing, producing drawings, specifications and other documents pertaining to the Project, and services during construction at the site.

4.2 Direct Personnel Expense includes cost of salaries and of mandatory and customary benefits such as statutory employee benefits, insurance, sick leave, holidays and vacations, pensions and similar benefits.

ARTICLE 5
REIMBURSABLE EXPENSES

5.1 Reimbursable Expenses are in addition to the Professional Fee under Paragraph IIa herein, and to the compensation for Basic and Additional Services under Paragraph IIb herein, and include actual expenditures made by the Architect, his employees, or his consultants in the interest of the Project for the incidental expenses listed in the following Subparagraphs:

5.1.1 Expense of transportation and living when traveling in connection with the Project and for long distance calls and telegrams.

5.1.2 Expense of reproductions, postage and handling of Drawings and Specifications, excluding copies for Architect's office use and duplicate sets at each phase for the Owner's review and approval; and fees paid for securing approval of authorities having jurisdiction over the Project.

5.1.3 If authorized in advance by the Owner, the expense of overtime work requiring higher than regular rates; perspectives or models for the Owner's use; and fees of special consultants for other than the normal structural, mechanical and electrical engineering services.

ARTICLE 6
PAYMENTS TO THE ARCHITECT

6.1 Payments on account of the Architect's Professional Fee shall be made as follows:

6.1.1 An initial payment of ten per cent of the Professional Fee, payable upon execution of this Agreement, is the minimum payment under this Agreement;

6.1.2 Subsequent payments of the Professional Fee shall be made monthly in proportion to services performed to increase the total payments on account of the Professional Fee to the following percentages at the completion of each phase of the Work:

Schematic Design Phase................ 15%
Design Development Phase............. 35%
Construction Documents Phase......... 75%
Bidding and Negotiation Phase.......... 80%
Construction Phase....................100%

6.2 Payments for Principals' time, employees' time, and services of professional consultants as provided in Paragraph IIb and for Reimbursable Expenses as defined in Article 5 shall be made monthly upon presentation of the Architect's statement of services rendered.

6.3 No deductions shall be made from the Architect's compensation on account of penalty, liquidated damages, or other sums withheld from payments to contractors.

6.4 If the Project is suspended for more than three months or abandoned in whole or in part, the Architect shall be paid his compensation for services performed prior to receipt of written notice from the Owner of such suspension or abandonment, together with Reimbursable Expenses then due and all terminal expenses resulting from such suspension or abandonment.

ARTICLE 7
ARCHITECT'S ACCOUNTING RECORDS

Records of the Architect's Direct Personnel, Consultant and Reimbursable Expenses pertaining to the Project and records of accounts between the Owner and Contractor shall be kept on a generally recognized accounting basis and shall be available to the Owner or his authorized representative at mutually convenient times.

ARTICLE 8
TERMINATION OF AGREEMENT

This Agreement may be terminated by either party upon seven days' written notice should the other party fail substantially to perform in accordance with its terms through no fault of the other. In the event of termination due to the fault of others than the Architect, the Architect shall be paid his compensation for services performed to termination date, including Reimbursable Expenses then due and all terminal expenses.

ARTICLE 9
OWNERSHIP OF DOCUMENTS

Drawings and Specifications as instruments of service are and shall remain the property of the Architect whether the Project for which they are made is executed or not. They are not to be used by the Owner on other projects or extensions to this Project except by agreement in writing and with appropriate compensation to the Architect.

ARTICLE 10
SUCCESSORS AND ASSIGNS

The Owner and the Architect each binds himself, his partners, successors, assigns and legal representatives to the other party to this Agreement and to the partners, successors, assigns and legal representatives of such other party in respect of all covenants of this Agreement. Neither the Owner nor the Architect shall assign, sublet or transfer his interest in this Agreement without the written consent of the other.

ARTICLE 11
ARBITRATION

11.1 All claims, disputes and other matters in question arising out of, or relating to, this Agreement, or the breach thereof, shall be decided by arbitration in accordance with the Construction Industry Arbitration Rules of the American Arbitration Association then obtaining. This agreement so to arbitrate shall be specifically enforceable under the prevailing arbitration law.

11.2 Notice of the demand for arbitration shall be filed in writing with the other party to the contract and with the American Arbitration Association. The demand shall be made within a reasonable time after the claim, dispute or other matter in question has arisen. In no event shall the demand for arbitration be made after institution of legal or equitable proceedings based on such claim, dispute or other matter in question would be barred by the applicable statute of limitations.

11.3 The award rendered by the arbitrators shall be final, and judgment may be entered upon it in any court having jurisdiction thereof.

ARTICLE 12
EXTENT OF AGREEMENT

This Agreement represents the entire and integrated Agreement between the Owner and the Architect and supersedes all prior negotiations, representations, or agreements either written or oral. This Agreement may be amended only by written instrument signed by both Owner and Architect.

ARTICLE 13
APPLICABLE LAW

Unless otherwise specified, this Agreement shall be governed by the law of the principal place of business of the Architect.

This Agreement executed the day and year first written above.

OWNER John T. Hauswirth

ARCHITECT Marshall Shaper

Architect's Registration No. 9836

Chapter 8

BUILDING PROGRAM AND SITE CONDITIONS

BEFORE the architect starts to design a new building he needs information. Complete data on conditions at the building site are necessary, as is knowing how much you can spend for construction. He will also discuss with you the detailed requirements of the building itself. The sum of these requirements is called the building program. It is the seed from which the building grows, and it controls all subsequent work by the architect. Unlike site conditions, which can be precisely determined, the program is based on aims and desires, some of which are difficult to explain, or even to perceive clearly in your own mind. This complication caused me to say earlier that telling the architect what you want is harder than it sounds. The way you do it does not merely reflect your approach to architecture; the program literally *is* your approach to architecture.

THE BUILDING PROGRAM

One way of telling the architect your requirements is to say, for example, "we want four bedrooms, two bathrooms," and so forth. You can specify the approximate size of each room, and their arrangement with respect to each other. You can add details such as "tiled bathrooms," and so on. You can even specify the general visual appearance of the results. In short, you can *describe a building;* not a "real" building, of course, but a hypothetical building you want "realized."

If you thus describe a building, it will probably be composed of elements of other buildings you have experienced. In a magazine you saw a photograph of a bathroom that appealed to you. A friend's house contains your ideal of a living room. Out driving you once saw a house whose exterior appearance is just what you want. Your present kitchen has revealed its inadequacies; you feel they can be remedied by certain modifications. And everyone wants more closets. Thus, over a period of time, you have built up in your mind an image of the parts of an ideal house. When the time comes to write the program, you describe this image to the architect. It will probably be less than complete, but basically you see the future building as an amalgam of elements of known, existing buildings. This is nothing more nor less than the Imitative approach to architecture.

Alternatively, instead of describing a building, you can *describe its future contents, occupants, and their activities.* This is the Abstract approach. Using this information, the architect himself will work out what rooms will be necessary, how large they should be, and their desirable arrangement. This, in fact, is what architects are trained to do. It is part of the process called "designing a building." If you describe the building you want instead of its occupants and their activities, you are doing the architect's work yourself.

The Abstract aim is economical physical and psychological utility. To achieve it, the architect needs to be told how the building will be utilized. In telling him, you assume the role that best suits you: that of expert in matters such as how much the building can cost (it's *your* money); the age, sex, and numbers of future occupants (they are *your* family, friends, associates, employees, or tenants); what furniture, equipment, and supplies they will have; and the details of the activities in which they will engage. You may not yet have given enough thought to these matters to enable you to rattle them off to the architect, but he will help. His questions and suggestions will both promote and channel your thinking to this end.

As was pointed out in discussing approaches to architecture, probably neither a purely Imitative nor a purely Abstract approach is practical. However Imitative your approach, you will expect the architect to give some attention to the building's occupants and their activities. However Abstract your approach, you will also describe certain desired physical arrangements based on your own experience with other buildings. The problem is to arrive at the optimum compromise, and the solution is easy. Merely tell the architect what you want in your own terms, not worrying about whether you are being Imitative or Abstract. Next, cooperate fully if he thinks any of your stated requirements can be improved. Permit him to probe your reasoning, answer his questions, and carefully consider the alternatives he suggests.

Some of your stated requirements may appear to him to be mutually exclusive. You cannot have a brick house for the price of wood. Small-paned windows preclude easy washing. If two bathrooms (which serve bedrooms) and the kitchen on the same floor are arranged so that each backs up to both the others (for minimum plumbing cost), then one of the three rooms will be windowless. When the architect points out such things, you may be unpleasantly surprised. They are not his fault, however, and if you realize as much, you will probably recognize that one of his suggested alternatives is satisfactory. Millions of people like wood siding. Windowless bathrooms have proven quite tolerable, and so forth.

The architect may also suggest revisions to the program simply to make it more Abstract, and therefore flexible. If you request a recreation room 14 feet by 16 feet, it may occur to the architect that a room of almost the same total area but measuring 12 feet by 18 feet would permit ping-pong playing. So he asks your reasons for requesting a room 14 feet by 16 feet: the question diverts your attention from size to activities, that is, from Imitation to Abstraction.

In general, the architect will take a more Abstract view of the building's requirements than you will. This leads him to ask questions that sometimes seem impertinent, and to make suggestions that may appear as unwarranted interference. He is not trying to tell you how to live your life or run your business. But to the extent that the program specifies room size or arrangement, to that extent it embodies solutions to architectural problems. Often the architect believes he can discover a better solution if you will only tell him the *basis* for your solution. Solving architectural problems, after all, is his job. Final approval is up to you.

After discussions with you the architect will write out a finished program and send you a copy for approval. It may all be on one page, but will probably be longer. I once worked on a program for a six-million-dollar building that ran to 105 pages. When you receive a copy, review it carefully. As you read it over, something new may occur to you. Also the architect may have accidentally omitted or misunderstood something you told him. You may have changed your mind about some of the building's requirements. Unless afterthoughts and corrections can be cleared up by telephone or letter, you and the architect should get together for a second program conference.

The written program will not be absolutely complete. It will not state that the proposed building must be attractive, soundly constructed, and weatherproof: These qualities are understood. Some desirable provisions will not be mentioned because they were never actually discussed: locating the garage near the kitchen to ease the labor of carrying in groceries may be desirable, but no one thought to say so. It is not, in fact, practical to specify all conceivable minor conveniences of a building in the written program. Furthermore, it is impossible to include all of them physically in the building itself. Nevertheless it is a good idea to mention those conveniences that come to mind: The mere fact that they occur to you indicates they probably have extra importance in your case.

The architect will revise the program to incorporate the additions or changes you request, and send you a new copy. You may decide it needs still more changes but you hate to delay progress by requesting them. Request them anyway. The program determines the form the building will take. Many other factors—the cost of plaster, the strength of steel—are influential but outside your control: You control the program. The program, and construction money, are the essential contributions you make to the building. Give program preparation patience and the best effort of which you are capable.

SITE CONDITIONS

It is unfortunate that building sites are usually purchased before the architect is hired. Of course, if real estate is bought for speculative purposes and the decision to build on it comes later, then it is inevitable for site to be chosen before architect. If possible, however, you should select the architect and establish the building program before spending money for land. Using the program, but without actually designing the building, the architect can determine some of the desirable as well as undesirable features of its future site. Lot size consistent with building size is an obvious consideration, but there are many others of which you will probably have general knowledge but of which the architect has expert knowledge.

You may discover an odd parcel of land that is offered for a song because it has some drawback such as constricted shape or low elevation. Sometimes an architect can perceive an ingenious and unexpected way to wed your particular building to that particular site: He may thus save you thousands of dollars.

Whether or not you hire the architect before you buy the land, he should have all pertinent site data before starting to design the building. Collecting the data involves expenses you will have to approve. The data include:

1. Soil Information

Underground conditions may have to be investigated to insure that the earth will support the building. Borings and other soil tests by specialists may cost several hundred dollars; thorough investigation over a large area will cost several thousand dollars. If the site is not marshy or covered with uncompacted fill, soil-testing for one- or two-story buildings will probably be unnecessary. The timing and desirability of testing should be determined by the architect. He will explain his conclusions, and have your decision executed.

2. Topographical Survey

On a level lot the property description given in the deed may substitute for a regular survey. The description must be augmented by information from utility companies on location of mains, sewers, and power lines. If there are any complications, such as trees or sloping ground, however, the architect will probably recommend that a topographical survey be made by a licensed land surveyor. Survey and soil testing costs, although there is no connection between them, tend to be of the same order of magnitude. Both are additional to the architect's fee.

For the architect to adapt the building to the site, he must have accurate, complete topographical data. Otherwise the site has to be adapted to the building in unpredictable ways after construction begins. Expensive extra grading and filling, tree removal, driveway lengthening, and so forth may be required. If he thinks a survey is desirable you will almost certainly save money in the long run by paying a surveyor in the beginning.

3. Miscellaneous Site Conditions

The architect will ascertain or acquire the following at negligible cost, but you should be aware that the information is factual, inescapable, and influential in designing the building. The architect will often refer to it in the course of explaining his drawings and justifying his recommendations.

(A) View and Neighbors

The architect will visit the site, probably several times, to study it first hand before commencing design. He may take photographs to supplement the survey. The proposed building should take advantage of pleasant views, but be sensitive to potential loss of privacy resulting from neighboring streets and buildings (actual or predictable). Streets are a source of traffic noise from which some parts of the building should perhaps be insulated. Visual harmony with nearby buildings and scenery should be considered by the architect.

(B) Climate and Orientation

The directions from which the sun shines and the winds blow—with daily and seasonal variations—should be taken into account when designing. The layout and capacity of air-conditioning systems depend on climatic data, such as temperature and humidity ranges.

(C) Codes, Ordinances, and Restrictions

To some extent the design of buildings almost everywhere in the country is controlled by law. Most of the laws are embodied in the local building code and the zoning ordinance. The code will be crammed with provisions, such as "All buildings must have two separate exits from each floor," "Stress in mild steel shall not exceed 20,000 lb./sq.in. in flexure," "Water closets located more than 3′ from a vent stack shall be back-vented," and so forth. Building codes come in book form and typically contain about four hundred pages.

Zoning ordinances usually contain a map of the city, or other area, with the various "zones" outlined and labeled. The ordinance states what types of buildings are permissible in each zone, and what activities can be carried on in them. For example, probably only houses, churches, and elementary schools may be erected in a "residential" zone. No manufacturing activity is allowed in a "business" zone. No business activity is allowed in a "residential" zone, and so forth.

The Federal Housing Administration publishes *Minimum Property Standards,* which lists requirements houses must meet to qualify for F.H.A. insured loans. This book resembles a building code. Even if you do not need an F.H.A. mortgage to build, if your house fails to conform to their standards, you cannot later sell it to anyone who does need an F.H.A. mortgage.

Most new houses nowadays are built in residential subdivisions: A tract of several acres is platted, and lots, or lots complete with ready-built houses, are then sold. The subdivider in such cases will probably prepare "deed restrictions" which are registered in the appropriate municipal office and can be thought of as part of the sales contract for each lot. Such restrictions resemble both building codes and zoning ordinances, but they pertain to fewer topics and cover each more stringently than the municipal ordinances. They may, for instance, specify that each house in the subdivision shall have an incinerator. The ostensible purpose of deed restrictions is to prevent loss of value to any one buyer through degradation of other property in the subdivision. The premise is that if your neighbor, for example, builds his house closer to the street than his neighbors, then his neighbors' houses lose value. You and your architect should study the deed restrictions, preferably before you buy the lot.

The architect either has or will obtain the building code. You are responsible for getting him copies of the zoning ordinance and deed restrictions. The architect is then responsible for the conformity, to all these regulations, of the building he designs.

REMODELING

Remodeling means alterations or additions to existing buildings. Everything in this book that applies to new buildings applies equally to remodeling work, but remodeling also involves additional problems.

A typical residential remodeling might include some interior rearrangements, such as the relocation or removal of certain partitions, plus some exterior changes, such as the addition of a new bedroom or the enlargement of the living room, and so forth. In other buildings common remodeling jobs include rearrangement of office partitioning, addition of school classrooms, adding new wings, and so forth. In remodeling the amount of architectural work per dollar of construction cost is usually higher than for new buildings because the new work must be adapted to the complexities of an existing building. Thus architectural fees, considered as a percentage of the total cost, run higher for remodeling.

During programming for remodeling, it is usually necessary for the architect to take careful measurements, and then make accurate drawings of the existing building, or part of it. The fee for this work may be figured separately or included in the higher basic fee.

The desire to remodel develops from your experience with the actual building. You decide you want additional facilities or the correction of inconveniences. As you are living with the problems you want to correct, the tendency is to try to solve them yourself to the extent of figuring out which walls to move, where to add the new room, and so forth. All these are architectural decisions, and yours may be good ones, but a good architect may be able to improve on many of them. Therefore, as with new buildings, try to think mainly in terms of what the remodeling should accomplish and let the architect worry about how: Tell him your ideas but encourage him to improve them.

In choosing an architect for remodeling you should give first consideration to the architect who designed the original bulding. He may no longer be available, of course, but even if he is, there are other considerations.

Remodeling work presents a rather special challenge to an architect. The "site" is not just a piece of land: It is an existing building—something more complex than topography. This complication calls for a corresponding ingenuity if the final result is to be economically achieved, and if the new work is to harmonize with the old. An architect who enjoys this special challenge can surprise you with his ingenuity. If there is some serious deficiency in your building, it is well worth consulting an architect even if you believe the deficiency is impossible to correct: He may find a way.

MASTER-PLANNING

If a young married couple build a house and plan on expanding it with the advent of children, the expansion will be cheaper and better looking if it can be incorporated in the original design even though omitted from the original construction. Generally speaking, if the future growth of a building, or future need for additional buildings on the same site, can be effectively anticipated, then the project in its full future scope should be considered in the original programming and design. Doing so is called master-planning.

A simple illustration of master-planning might be the development of a new university. The board of trustees decides to assume, on the basis of study, that the ultimate size of the university will be *X* students and *Y* faculty members, accommodated in the appropriate number of classrooms, laboratories, and housing; supplemented by suitably sized library, athletic facilities, offices, and so forth. Initial construction, however, need serve only a fraction of the predicted ultimate size. What is needed is a master plan that provides for logical, orderly growth, and what is equally important but often slighted, a plan that provides that, at each stage of future growth, the complex of then existing buildings and facilities add up to a workable, harmonious whole. Planning for this type of expansion is difficult, and it is perhaps even more difficult to write the program for it. Successful programming in such cases requires a combination of imagination, hard-boiled realism, mature judgment, and intellectual effort. The rarity of this combination is attested by the thousands of unrealized master plans yellowing in obscure pigeonholes.

Sometimes, however, master-planning is not very difficult. You can, with little extra effort, write the program and prepare the preliminary design for a church complete with Sunday School; then build the church now and the Sunday School a few years hence, without significant loss of economy, and never have a "bad-looking" project. Nor is it impractical, in the design of a house, to anticipate extra bedrooms, or future conversion of part of the basement into a recreation room.

It is always advisable, when preparing a building program, to look beyond today's needs and try to predict future developments. You must then assign to your predictions whatever degree of reliability they deserve and instruct the architect to take the predictions and their reliability into account. He should then recommend master-planning to whatever extent his judgment indicates. This course will tend to minimize the difficulties, decrease the cost, and improve the results of future remodeling.

An architect should naturally be paid extra for additional work. In the case of the university considered above, the architect might prepare a master plan for a twenty-million-dollar complex of buildings and site improvements (utilities, landscaping, parking). Initially, perhaps, only part of the project would be built, and actual first-stage construction cost might be only five million dollars. The architect is then clearly entitled to a full fee for the five million dollars worth of project actually built, and additionally entitled to a partial fee for the remaining fifteen million dollars worth of project that was planned but not built. You may be able to agree on a lump-sum for this partial fee, but it will usually be wiser to compute his fee by the cost-plus method. It is also possible to pay for master-planning on a percentage basis. First you must agree what fraction of a full fee is represented by the work of master-planning. It will probably be about 15 percent. Then you can agree to pay him 15 percent of what his full fee would be for the fifteen million dollars worth of project that he master-planned.

WHERE ARE WE

In the process of creating a new building we have arrived at a wasp-waisted stage. Broad ideas about architecture have been sifted and reduced to a building program. The infinite details of the building's future environment have been culled and embodied in a survey, printed restrictions, and the architect's observations of the neighborhood. Now the process of concentration is to be reversed. Design ideas in both graphic and verbal form will begin to proliferate, and then the building will take on physical form. To the continuing labor of making decisions you can begin to add the pleasure and excitement of seeing the architect's drawings, and then watching construction.

"As long as we're cutting down to save money, let's combine the study with the guest room," suggested John, when the Hauswirths met with Shaper to work on the building program.

"And I've decided to do without a separate sitting room," added Harriet. "I'll have the studio and I can put my desk and a comfortable chair in the bedroom."

"What about bathrooms?" asked Shaper, making a note.

"One for us and one for the children," said Harriet. "And it would be nice to have a guest lavatory, but we can get along without if we have to."

"How often do you have guests?" Shaper inquired.

"We have one or two couples for dinner every month or so. We have evening parties with ten or twenty people sometimes. We usually feed them buffet style. Sometimes they feel like dancing too, by the way."

"In the living room?" asked Shaper.

"Now they do, but a basement recreation room would be better, and the children could use it too," said Harriet.

"Leaving the living room for conversation and . . . ?"

"I have a baby grand piano," announced John. "That goes in the living room, along with the television, radio, and record player. We also need bookshelves, and we want a fireplace."

"All right," said Shaper, "what about eating arrangements?"

"We all cook," said Harriet, "even the children. Of course, I do most of it, but John sometimes makes dinner. And when we have guests they all seem to be in and out of the kitchen—and in and out of the way, but I like it. I think we could eliminate the dining room and eat in the kitchen, even with guests. The family does now."

"I think it would be better to eat in one end of the living room," said John.

"But it's so easy to set the table, and serve, and clear off, if the table is in the kitchen," objected Harriet.

"The table could be arranged as an extension of kitchen counter into the living room," interjected Shaper. "It should be as convenient as the arrangement you have in mind, Mrs. Hauswirth . . ."

"Call me Harriet."

". . . and also satisfy you . . . John," concluded Shaper.

After some further discussion the Hauswirths agreed.

Shaper then asked for details of the studio.

"It takes up our whole two-car garage now," said John.

"And I still need more space and a higher ceiling," added Harriet.

"Where do you keep the car?"

"We keep them both in the driveway." said John.

"Do you mind leaving them outdoors?"

"Only when it rains or snows."

"Would a carport suit you?"

"They never really seem to work, do they? Snow and rain blow in the side."

"If the sides had some protection?" queried Shaper.

"I suppose that would be all right," said John.

"Now, as for the studio," interposed Harriet, "I just need a big room where I can arrange things to suit myself. I paint and sculpture, and I have a loom. I also have a bench saw, and I need space for a workbench, a couple of tables, cabinets, shelves, and so forth. I want lots of light, natural and artificial. And garage doors in opposite walls."

"Why is that?" queried Shaper, surprised.

"You'll laugh, but every year I build a float for the Hector Memorial Day parade. They bring me the chassis and run it into the studio. Other people help me build the float, and then it goes out. But it's forty feet long, so only one end can be in at a time. With doors in opposite walls we can push it part way through and back to work on either end indoors."

"OK," said Shaper, "I guess you really do need the garage doors, and obviously the studio can't be in the basement. Speaking of the basement, aside from a recreation area and mechanical equipment, what will you use it for?"

"Well, not much for storage," answered Harriet. "Things we don't use we throw away."

"The deep freeze and the laundry should be in the basement," said John.

"I'd rather have the washer and dryer upstairs near the bathrooms or in the kitchen," said Harriet. "Either place is near where dirty linen comes from and goes back to."

"Marshall, what did you mean by 'mechanical equipment'?" asked the doctor.

"Oh . . . water heater, air conditioner, water softener—if you need it —incinerator: things like that."

"We will need a water softener because the well water will undoubtedly be hard. And we want an incinerator. But do you think we need air conditioning out in the country?"

"Yes, it can get just as hot there as where you live now. Besides summer-cooling is getting relatively cheaper and more common all the time. More people expect it, and not having it will hurt the resale value of the house."

"How much does it cost?" asked John.

"It will add about twelve hundred dollars, I would guess."

"I've always had a yen for central air conditioning," mused John. "Harriet?"

"You decide," she said.

The discussion then shifted to the children. Like their parents, Larry, fifteen, and Cheryl, eighteen, read books. They did school work in their rooms, were visited by friends, gave parties for teenagers a few times a year, and went out on dates. Each had a record player, and there would be a second television for their use in the recreation room. Larry had inherited his mother's manual dexterity and used the studio as his workshop, but to build and experiment with electronic apparatus rather than art.

"Neither of them will be living at home much longer," Harriet pointed out, "whereas John and I expect to live in this house until he retires, which will be at least twenty years. In fact we might stay here until we get too old to keep house for ourselves."

"We aren't like a lot of people we know," put in John, "who can't wait to retire to Florida. We like snow in winter."

Shaper asked about overnight guests. "Do you ever have to put up crowds of people, for instance?"

"John has his sisters and his cousins and his aunts," said Harriet, "but none lives nearby. If one or two stop to see us they can sleep in the guest room. If we have a lot of Thanksgiving or Christmas guests, they can go to a motel."

"In a few years your children will be coming to visit and bringing *their* children," pointed out Shaper.

"Well, yes. So their rooms should be large enough for double beds, and the grandchildren can take the guest room, or Larry's children can take Cheryl's room, or vice versa."

The conversation shifted to a discussion of materials. The Hauswirths acquiesced to Shaper's recommendation that the exterior be painted plywood, cheaper than masonry; that interior partitions be faced with drywall, cheaper than plaster. They also agreed that "liquid tile," a plastic coating, would be a satisfactory inexpensive substitute for ceramic tile in the bathrooms. They agreed to eliminate hardwood flooring from areas to be carpeted.

Before they left, the Hauswirths arranged to meet Shaper at the site in a few days to perform the topographical survey.

Shaper and the Hauswirths were middle-class, college-educated, white, Midwestern Americans. Their ages differed by less than a dozen years. In addition, both John and Marshall practiced professions. These socioeconomic and cultural similarities enabled Shaper to make valid assumptions as to numerous facets of the Hauswirths' lives never expressly stated by them. They didn't need to tell him, for example, that their bedroom would be used for sleeping, dressing, and making love: Shaper (and the reader) could assume as much. If there are cultural differences between architect and client, such assumptions might be false.

An American firm built a cement factory in a Near-Eastern desert. Several hundred Bedouin were hired to man the factory. Perhaps because tribal cohesion was lacking, the camp the Bedouin created for themselves and their families, outside the factory fence, soon degenerated into semianarchic, unhealthy squalor.

The American firm, acting from both economic and altruistic motives, hired an architect and built a modern, permanent village for the Bedouin. Everyone was proud of the functional, attractive buildings; and the spacious, well-planned community areas. The Bedouin moved in to enjoy central heating and running water for the first time in their lives. A few months later they all moved out.

The puzzled Americans, after investigating, determined that what was necessary, bizarre as it sounds, was to announce that the water main was sick and turn off the water. The Arabs moved back.

BUILDING PROGRAM: RESIDENCE

5 May 1965
Job No. 65-01

Dr. and Mrs. John T. Hauswirth
202 Acacia Drive,
Hector, Michigan

1. Family Living Area: essentially a single zone.

(a) Living Area: reading conversation, entertainment of adult guests. Space for television, radio, record player, baby grand piano. Seating, fireplace, bookshelves.

(b) Dining Area: family and guests. Immediately adjacent to kitchen but visually screened.

(c) Kitchen Area: food storage and preparation facilities. Electric range, oven, and refrigerator. Screened from living area but easily accessible.

(d) Laundry: in kitchen or near bathrooms. Washer, dryer, space for ironing. Sink and counter.

2. Adult Bedroom, Bathroom Zone:

(a) Parents' Bedroom: two clothes closets. Space for two sets of drawers, dressing table, double bed, desk, upholstered chair.

(b) Guest-Bedroom, Study: clothes closet. Space for set of drawers, double bed, bookshelves, upholstered chair.

(c) Bathroom: lavatory, water closet, bathtub with shower, medicine chest, mirror.

3. Children's Bedroom, Bathroom Zone:

(a) Cheryl's Room: clothes closet. Space for set of drawers, double bed, bookshelves, desk, upholstered chair.

(b) Larry's Room: same facilities as Cheryl's.

(c) Children's Bathroom: same facilities as parents'.

4. Studio: acoustic isolation from rest of house. 600 sq.ft. High ceiling. Garage doors at grade in two opposite walls.

5. Garage or Carport: two-car.

BUILDING PROGRAM: RESIDENCE (CONT.)

5 MAY 1965
JOB NO. 65-01

DR. AND MRS. JOHN T. HAUSWIRTH

6. RECREATION ROOM: CAN BE IN BASEMENT. ACOUSTIC ISOLATION FROM FAMILY LIVING AND ADULT BEDROOM ZONES. SPACE FOR TELEVISION, TEENAGE PARTIES, GAMES.

7. MISCELLANEOUS:

   (A) BROOM CLOSET

   (B) LINEN STORAGE

   (C) DEAD STORAGE: MINIMAL

   (D) MECHANICAL EQUIPMENT: AIR CONDITIONER, WATER HEATER, WATER SOFTENER, INCINERATOR, DEEP FREEZE.

In their investigation the Americans had learned that one of the few excuses for Bedouin women to leave their abodes was to go to the community well for water. When water was on tap in each apartment, the women found themselves denied an essential part of their social lives. As a result they brought so much pressure to bear on their husbands that the families moved back to the unwatered tents of the old camp. When the Americans turned off the water in the new village, they finally made it an acceptable place to live.

The case of the Arabs and Americans concerns great cultural differences, but smaller differences, closer to home, can also have unfortunate results.

An architect might be raised in a family that used their family room for most "living" activities, and kept their living room largely unused but expensively furnished for "show." An architect with such upbringing may make some unconscious assumptions leading to a house design that is unsuitable for a family like the Hauswirths, who "live" in their living room.

When the Hauswirths bought their property a boundary survey was made. Now it was necessary to establish earth contours and plot the location of trees and other features. Shaper, although not a surveyor, could "shoot grades," find trees, and draw a topographical plan. He suggested that he do the necessary surveying for the project, and that the Hauswirths assist him, a plan of action that would increase his knowledge of both the site and his clients.

On a sunny Monday morning Shaper, with rented transit-level, rod, and tape, met the Hauswirths at the site. Harriet brought a picnic lunch. John brought an insulated bucket of ice cubes and a bottle of bourbon.

Shaper set up the instrument. The Hauswirths, using the north boundary fence as a reference, taped off a grid as Shaper indicated, and held the rod at each point of intersection for Shaper to read the elevation and write it down. After lunch Shaper "swung angles" with the transit from two different positions to locate the trees and stream with respect to the fence and road.

As there was no sewer in the neighborhood, the house would require a septic tank and drainage-tile field. The absence of a water main meant driving a well and installing a pump and pressure tank. No gas main, plus the high cost of bottled gas, meant installing a buried oil tank. "I want a *big* one," said John, "enough capacity for a whole heating season. If you run out in early spring, when it's still cold or slushy, it's hard to get the fuel oil people to deliver out here, the neighbors say; and if you buy oil in summer you sometimes get a bargain price."

On his way home Shaper stopped at the Township Office, where he acquired a copy of the Building Code and Zoning Ordinance.

Back at his office Shaper used his field notes to draw the topographical survey. It showed only the northeast corner of the property, but included as much as necessary to site the house and driveway.

Shaper mailed two copies of the building program to the Hauswirths. A few days later Harriet telephoned to say that they approved it but wanted to add a sink in Larry's room. She said he was increasingly interested in photography and could use his bedroom as a darkroom if it had a sink. She also thought a sink in one of the children's bedrooms would be handy when infant grandchildren came visiting in the future.

Shaper was now ready to begin designing the house. The question of the practicality of a hyperbolic-paraboloid roof would soon be decided.

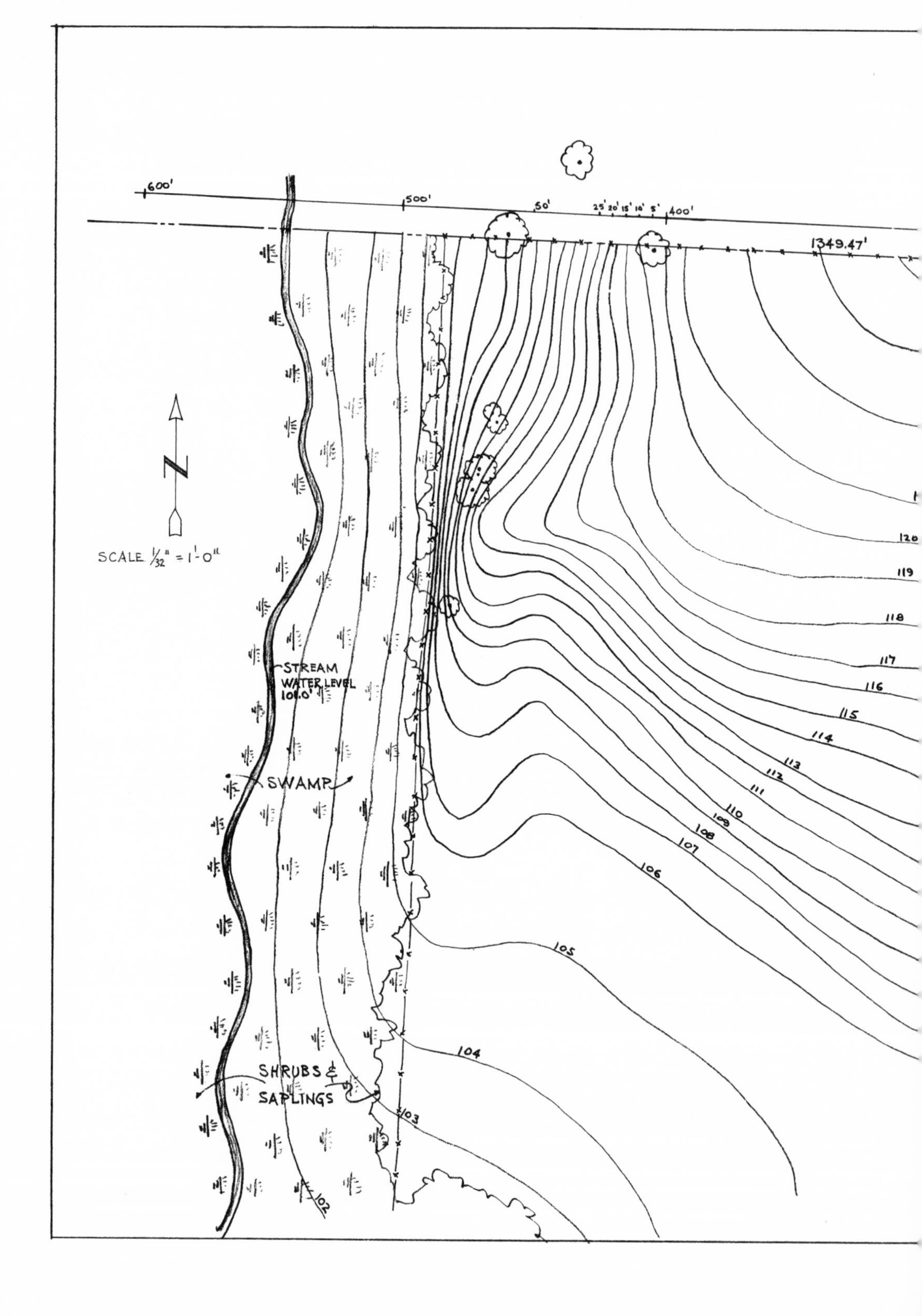
600'
500'
50'
25' 20' 15' 10' 5'
400'
1349.47'
SCALE 1/32" = 1'-0"
STREAM
WATER LEVEL
100.0'
SWAMP
SHRUBS &
SAPLINGS
120
119
118
117
116
115
114
113
112
111
110
109
108
107
106
105
104
103
102

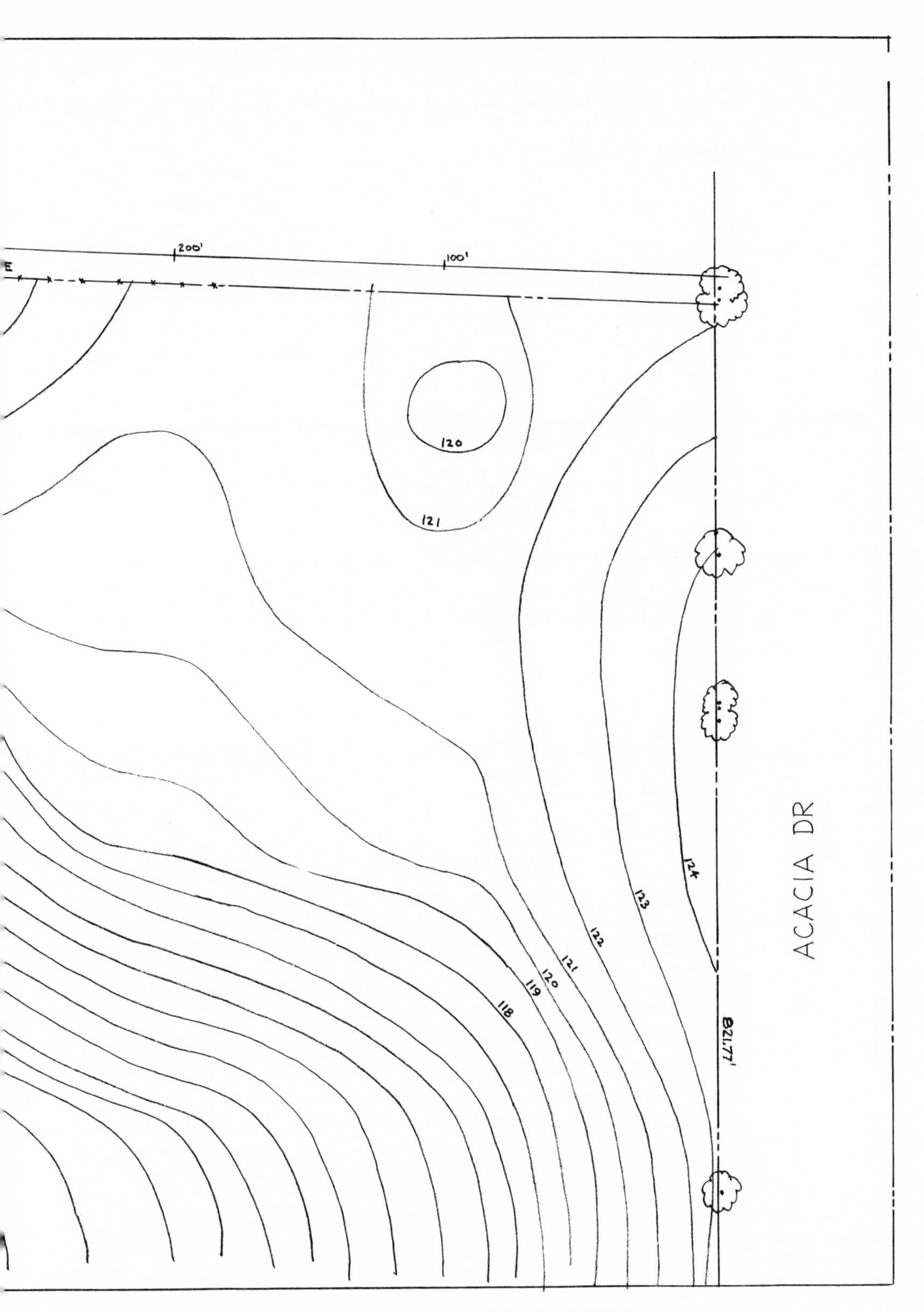

PARTIAL TOPOGRAPHICAL SURVEY FOR J. A. HAUSWIRTH RESIDENCE

Chapter 9

BUILDING BUDGET VS. CONSTRUCTION COST

For which of you, intending to build a tower, sitteth not down first, and counteth the cost, whether he have sufficient to finish it? Lest haply, after he hath laid the foundation, and is not able to finish it, all that behold him begin to mock him, saying, this man began to build, and was not able to finish.

—LUKE 14:28–30

IT may surprise you to learn that sometimes the architect's client claps no ceiling on construction cost. The building budget is left open. The program will state what facilities are required and the object will be to obtain these facilities *economically,* whatever they may cost.

Planning a new building offers many opportunities for good investments. In most parts of the northern half of the United States, east of the Rockies, an investment in wall insulation 3 inches thick by reducing heat transfer, provides an annual return of around 30 percent in fuel costs besides amortizing itself. The return is guaranteed provided fuel and power costs do not greatly decline and the building is not abandoned. We are therefore encouraged to consider using 4-inch instead of 3-inch insulation. On analysis we learn that the extra inch will cost one hundred dollars to install and will save twelve dollars per year in fuel bills. This return is comparable to that of a land contract, but is more secure and therefore more attractive. If you don't have the extra one hundred dollars, however, you cannot make the investment no matter how attractive it is.

Funds are usually limited, so buildings are usually built on budgets. If there is a budget (which may be expressed either as a desired cost or as a ceiling cost), then meeting it is a building requirement like any other, and the budget should be made part of the building program.

It is common to discover that the budget is inconsistent with the rest of the progam. It proves to be impossible to build the desired facilities without exceeding the budget. Naturally you would like to know, preferably before the architect has earned any of his fee, whether your budget is high enough to construct the building you want.

FIRST COST ESTIMATE

To satisfy yourself on this score, you may come to the architect saying, "We want a four-bedroom house, with two bathrooms, living room, dining room, kitchen, basement, and two-car garage. How much will it cost?" You might as well ask "How long is a piece of string?" Too many things remain undetermined. How big is each room going to have to be? Is the house to be brick, wood, or something else? ($1,000 to $5,000 difference in cost). Will the air-conditioning system include summer-cooling? ($500 to $1,500 difference). Will there be built-in furniture, cabinets, or shelving? (up to $15,000 difference). A hundred other such questions could be asked, and it is too soon to answer many of them. The architect can only guess a minimum probable cost for facilities such as you describe. A minimum cost entails a rather Spartan building and you will very likely want something better than that, but how much better?

Even before visiting the architect, you probably found some way of satisfying yourself that your budget was not unreasonable. Most likely you inspected similar buildings and learned their cost. If so, until the program is completed, you have a better idea than the architect not only of what you want but of how much it will cost.

The first cost estimate, then, is the one you make yourself, but the architect can provide the degree of confirmation you need by stating that buildings like yours have been built within your budget. There are at least some limits to the length of the piece of string.

SECOND COST ESTIMATE

As the architect's work proceeds there is a gradual increase in the accuracy of the estimates he can prepare. When the program is finished, he can probably apply what is known as the *square-foot method* of estimating construction cost. (The cubic-foot method, aside from the obvious difference implicit in the name, is basically the same and will not be separately discussed.) A lot of misunderstanding exists as to the way it works, how it applies, and what it means.

The square-foot method uses the assumption that on the whole a future building will cost about the same as a similar existing building—one whose cost is known. The basic idea is simple enough, but the application is tricky.

To use the square-foot method you need to know or guess as much as possible of the following information: (1) Total enclosed floor area. This is usually calculable once the program is completed. (2) Principal materials of construction, such as walls and partitions, and whether the structural system will be masonry, concrete, wood, steel, or some combination of these. Also needed is a good idea of the character—luxurious, frugal, or in between—of interior floor, wall, and ceiling finishes. (3) General requirements of the air conditioning, and other mechanical and electrical work. (4) Anything else the architect can think of that will have a marked effect on construction cost. A bad soil condition requiring expensive foundations is an example. Absence of sanitary sewer or city water are others.

With the foregoing facts and assumptions in mind the architect will search his files and literature for existing buildings that resemble your future building as closely as possible in those characteristics already mentioned, and which are nearby and were recently constructed. If he is extremely lucky, he will find an existing building that is like yours in almost all respects. If so, he can tell you with some confidence that your building will cost about the same as the one he has found. Despite the general similarity between the two buildings, however, there will probably be some difference in size. So to improve the estimate, divide the total cost of the existing building by its total area, which gives the cost per square foot. This figure is then multiplied by the total area of your building. The result is the estimated total cost of construction, calculated by the square-foot method.

More often than not the estimator will not find an existing building that is quite similar to your future building. Instead he will have to deal with several buildings, each similar in only some respects. He will then calculate the cost per square foot of each, survey the range of results, and try judiciously to strike an accurate medium to be used as the predicted cost per square foot of your building. As before, he will multiply this figure by the total area of your building to get the estimated total cost.

The result can easily err by twenty five percent. Underlying other inaccuracies in this method of estimating is the obviously false assumption that one is buying "square feet." If one is buying wheat, the cost per bushel, multiplied by the total number of bushels purchased, gives an accurate total cost. Buildings, unlike wheat, are not homogeneous, so that while a "square foot" of building that happened to contain the furnace burner might cost two hundred dollars, a "square foot" of floor in the middle of a room might cost only two dollars. If your building has, say more bathrooms or more partitions (resulting from smaller rooms) for its total size than the buildings whose costs are used as an index, then your building will cost relatively more per square foot. Other things being equal, larger buildings usually cost less per square foot than smaller buildings.

The problem of estimating accurately by the square-foot method is always difficult and should not be attempted by the inexperienced. At this stage of progress a square-foot cost estimate is the best available, however, and its result should be compared with the building budget.

If, as so often happens, the budget is lower than the estimate, it would seem that either the program must be revised or the budget raised. Sometimes the budget can't be raised, and revising the program to reduce the requirements seems too painful to be borne. An alternative is to leave things as they are and forge ahead with the preliminary design. When the design is completed, a more accurate third cost estimate can be made, and it is just possible that the earlier estimate will turn out to have erred on the high side, although the chances for this happy outcome are probably slim. Even if the estimated cost is still too high, however, it may be easier to decide how money can be saved if you have an actual design to work with instead of just the program. On the other hand revision to the design may cost something extra in architectural fee, whereas revision to the program would not. Talk it over with the architect before you decide.

THIRD COST ESTIMATE

Let us jump ahead for a moment and consider the actual cost of a building which is the amount of money a contractor is going to charge you to build it. How does he know what to charge? Before the contractor submits a bid, he will make his own estimate of the cost of construction by taking the final working drawings, which show everything, and actually measuring or counting the quantity of everything, including not only things incorporated into the structure but also other items of cost involved in building. These include such things as crane rental and earth moving. Using the quantities measurable from the drawings, of the quality called for by the specifications, he applies "unit costs" based on past experience. For instance, he finds a total of 800 square feet of face brick on the drawings, and the specifications call for a type of brick that the contractor learns can be purchased from the manufacturer for $75 per thousand. Knowing how fast masons lay brick as well as how much masons are paid per hour, the contractor can estimate that each square foot of brickwork will cost, say, $1.25. Multiplying by 800 gives $1,000 as the total cost of the brickwork.

Returning now to the third cost estimate we find that as soon as the preliminary design is done, it is possible to make an estimate of the same kind that the contractor will later make, but at this stage it will be incomplete and less accurate than later. Still, it will be far more accurate than the square-foot method.

This third estimate is based on what can be called the *take-off method* because the actual quantities of materials can be "taken off"—measured from—the drawings. It is inaccurate because although the estimator can, for instance, measure the length of gutters and downspouts, it may not yet have been decided if they are to be aluminum or some other material. There will be a medicine chest, but the actual model, hence the price, is still undecided. The third estimate is incomplete because some additional building elements will be added later during preparation of working drawings.

If the estimate is still over the budget, now is probably the time for reconcilement. If you cannot or will not raise the budget you must agree to one or more of these four alternatives: (1) omit facilities, (2) reduce quality, (3) a little of each, or (4) provide for later adjustment by using the method of "alternates."

ALTERNATES

In addition to the above-mentioned error factors in the third estimate, you must realize that between now and the time contractors bid, the climate in the construction industry may change. Workmen's wages and materials prices may fall but will probably rise; the volume of construction activity may increase or decrease, with contractors consequently demanding higher or lower profits. The method of alternates allows adjustment of the construction cost at the time of accepting a bid, and it thus permits not only correction of all estimating errors, but also compensation for the current industry situation. The adjustment, however, depends on sacrifice of facilities.

The method works best in buildings that exhibit several quite similar facilities, some of which can be omitted without serious damage to the over-all design. In a school design, for instance, it is usually possible, both physically and esthetically, to eliminate two, four, six, or more classrooms. A multistory office building can often relinquish one or more stories without loss of anything important except the floor space itself. In such cases the architect can prepare the Contract Documents in such a way that bidders submit a "base" bid for, let us say twenty stories of the building; the base bid is then followed by a bid on Alternate No. 1, which is an additional amount for constructing the twenty-first story; followed in turn by Alternate No. 2, which is an additional amount for constructing the twenty-second story, and so forth. You can then select the base bid plus as many alternates as you can afford.

The method of alternates can actually be applied to almost any building. The base bid may be based on the use of face brick, and an alternate may then provide an additional amount for substituting the far more expensive glazed brick. The base bid may omit interior painting, which is then included in an alternate; if the additional cost of interior painting puts the total over the budget, you may decide to do the painting yourself. There are many other possible alternates.

Making provision for alternates in the Contract Documents sometimes requires a lot of extra work by the architect. It would be rather silly to have him include an alternate that would potentially save you $100 if including it entailed $50 extra in the architect's fee. Simple alternates that cost around 5 percent of the total construction cost are best.

CONTRACTORS' BIDS

During preparation of working drawings and specifications the architect will try, by careful selection of materials, and by ingenuity in the way they are put together, to minimize the cost of construction. After you have approved his work, contractors will be invited to bid.

Each bidder will make a thorough, accurate take-off as a basis for his construction cost estimate, and will incorporate his estimate into his bid. The difference between an estimate and a bid should be clearly understood. The contractor's estimate is the amount he predicts he will have to pay for overhead and to his workmen, his subcontractors, and materials suppliers in order to get the building built. His bid is the amount he wants from you in return for agreeing to build. An estimate is thus an opinion, whereas a bid is an offer to build.

EXTRA COSTS

During construction you will almost certainly want to make some changes in the design of the building. You may decide to move a doorway a few feet, extend a partition, repaint a wall, or add a bookshelf. No law says you have to make such changes, but experience indicates you must assume that a few will occur. Changes usually entail extra cost. If the budget permits you to make all the changes you really want, their aggregate extra cost may be in the neighborhood of 10 percent of the original contract amount. On a tight budget you will naturally exercise restraint, but it would be unwise to enter into a construction Contract so high that it left you with no money at all for changes during construction.

THE ARCHITECT'S DILEMMA

Whenever the architect's estimate of construction cost is higher than your budget, he has a problem. If he tells you truthfully that your purse is too thin or your sights too high, he knows from experience with some former clients that you may blame him for this state of affairs, and decide to look for another architect who will promise more building for less money. The result is a pressure, tending to make him underestimate construction costs. He may even sense that you actually want to be deceived, in which case estimating becomes a kind of game: The architect starts out giving you an "estimate" that is well within the budget and thereafter from time to time, using minor changes in the program or design as excuses, gradually ups the estimate. You grudgingly agree to each small increment and end up authorizing a $65,000 house that started out on a $50,000 budget. You resemble the person who prefers to remove adhesive tape slowly and painfully rather than rip it off in a single, agonizing jerk.

Design and program changes actually do cause real increases in construction cost. You must not assume that because the architect's estimate keeps increasing, he must be playing games.

All ethical architects will do their best to design the building you want for the price you can pay. Sometimes they find this task impossible. Therefore some architects, although they will try to meet a budget, will refuse to commit themselves to it. Some other architects will accept commitment to your budget only if you allow them what they believe is sufficient latitude in choice of materials, size of the building, or both. Only in those rare and happy cases where the architect perceives that your budget is quite adequate for the facilities desired does the problem of building budget vs. construction cost disappear.

Chapter 10

DESIGNING THE BUILDING

WITH your approval of the program the architect can start to design the building. *Design* is nearly synonymous with *invent,* and each can refer to both a process and its end result. That is, an inventor invents an invention; a designer designs a design. In architecture designing means inventing an arrangement of building elements that will satisfy the physical demands of the program and site and produce the desired psychological effects.

You can also think of designs and inventions as solutions to problems. Problem: Reduce the time required for long-distance communication—solution: Invent the telephone. Problem: House this family as specified in their building program—solution: Design their house.

Design is a solitary activity. You can neither help nor hurry the architect. When he finishes, he will show you drawings representing the new building, and you will have to decide what changes, if any, you want him to make. I am convinced that you can make such decisions better if you understand how the architect makes a design.

Parts of the design problem are like baking a cake: You open the cookbook to the right recipe and then follow step-by-step instructions. The size of a pipe or a beam can be determined this way; it can even be done by a computer. Other aspects of design cannot be performed by following simple directions. Creativity, inspiration, original thinking, or what have you is required. There are so many factors involved in the creative part of designing a building, however, that an architect can do it in less time than it would take to explain exactly how he does it. Nevertheless the design process can perhaps be made clear by a simple analogy.

Consider this "field" of nine dots: • • • • • • • • • and let it represent a building site. Assume that this pattern of dots stands for all the information available on that site: all the information of the type considered under *Site Conditions* in Chapter 8.

Now let us pose the following "design" problem: Compose four straight-line segments, without removing the pencil from the paper, so that all nine dots are connected. Let this statement represent the building program. Assume that it stands for all the requirement of the building agreed upon by you and the architect.

You have no recipe for solving this problem, unless you have solved it before, in which case it would be more accurate to say that there is no problem. If there is a problem, the would-be solver must first have the "program" and the "site" clearly in mind. Then he must make his mind prepare a possible solution, such as this:  . Next the possible solution must be tested, like this: 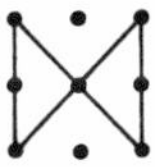 . The solution doesn't work. Now a second possible solution must be created and tested in its turn. In this problem, as in original architectural design, the procedure is the same: First the problem is memorized; second a possible solution is mentally generated; and third the possible solution is tested by reference to the terms of the problem. If the possible solution proves faulty, another possible solution must be generated and tested, perhaps again and again, until a satisfactory solution emerges.

In the design of a building there is naturally a great deal more to the program than a field of nine dots to be joined by four lines. There is so much more, in fact, that it is necessary in the beginning to simplify the problem by selecting only those program requirements that appear most important, and in the architect's experience, seem most likely to present difficulties in design. Minor requirements, such as a place to store the waffle iron, are ignored for the moment.

A typical simplification in designing a house might be to consider the living-dining-kitchen spaces as a single zone, the bedroom-bathroom spaces as a second zone, and the vestibule and garage as third and fourth zones. Representing each zone by a simple shape such as a rough oval, the architect might then generate a design that involved only a tentative arrangement of these zones, sketched on a background roughly representing the salient features of the site. The architect would then review the sketch to see if he could discover flaws in the arrangement. Finding flaws, he would try other arrangements. In each arrangement he would look for such characteristics as conveniently located points of entry to the house, living spaces oriented to the best view, sleeping zone oriented for visual and acoustic privacy, and many others. When the architect finally produces an arrangement that satisfies his own critical scrutiny, he can proceed to articulate the separate rooms within each zone and also work out the way adjacent zones will join each other.

Sometimes it may turn out that, although the arrangement of zones seems adequate in itself, the designer finds it impossible to accomplish the next step of planning individual rooms. Then he will have to junk the zone plan and start over.

The normal progress of a design is to move from the solution of the major to the minor aspects of the total problem. As the designer proceeds, he will sometimes find his progress blocked. This forces him to back up two or more steps and attempt to resume progress along new lines. The progress is embodied in sketches. The earliest ones resemble doodles or scrawls and are often intelligible only to the person who made them. Each time an impasse is reached and the designer has to back up and try another tack, one sketch is laid aside and another is begun. A couple of times, out of curiosity, I have counted the pile of rejected sketches for a single building. One of these, a small house, entailed sixty-three unsatisfactory partial designs before a satisfactory complete design was developed. On another occasion, involving an eight-million-dollar laboratory, after the client had criticized the first set of preliminary drawings, there ensued 116 abortive attempts to redesign the building to suit him, until on the 117th attempt the architect decided he had succeeded.

Even the nine-dot, four-line "design" problem admits of quite a few unsatisfactory solutions. Here are some:

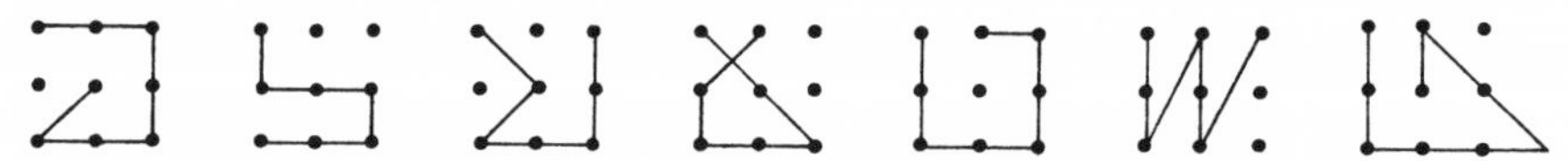

Looking these over we may observe a phenomenon that tends to plague the problem-solver: The unconscious assumption of an unnecessary restriction. Until just before his last attempt our would-be problem-solver seems to have assumed that the four lines must lie entirely within the field of dots. This restriction was not stated and is therefore not actually a requirement.

Designing a building is not as neat and simple as the nine-dot problem. Most of the factors cannot be precisely evaluated, and it is never known whether a perfect solution is obtainable, nor even if there is any such thing. A hundred different architects, as stated earlier, given the same design problem, will produce a hundred different designs and many of these will be good ones.

Often, while working on a design problem, the architect discovers something that leads him to suggest changes in the program. Perhaps the arrangement of rooms, as the design develops, appears to offer space for breakfasting on an extension of a kitchen counter, which would be less expensive than the separate breakfast nook called for in the program. There may turn out to be a little surplus space in the principal bathroom, which makes him think you might be glad to have the clothes washer and dryer there instead of wherever the program locates them. The architect will get in touch with you in such cases and explain his new ideas. If they appeal to you, by all means allow him to incorporate them. The program is not sacred. It should be the architect's guide, not his jailer; every chance to improve it should be seized.

In talking about architectural design so far we have considered only the arrangement of rooms on the site. The complete design must, of course, also determine the size, shape, and appearance of all the principal elements of the building. A sketch that shows just the arrangement of rooms and also shows or implies the paths of circulation is best called a *circulation diagram*. Usually it is the first step in design, but not always. An architect may start from an idea for the over-all shape or mass of the building, and into this shape or mass attempt to fit a satisfactory arrangement of rooms. This alternate approach might be called *designing from the outside in*, and was quite common before the "modern" revolution. The revolutionaries, as revolutionaries must, adopted the opposite slogan: *Design from the inside out!* The true aim should be to produce a building that is satisfactory in all respects, and whether the designer starts from the inside or the outside should be left to his own discretion.

Certain complex buildings, however, seem to insist on being designed from the inside out. In a hospital, patients, professional staff, service staff, and visitors must all have some separate facilities but also be allowed to come together efficiently in other joint facilities. Vehicular traffic and parking outside the building exhibit similar requirements. Circulation problems in such a building are severe and must undoubtedly be solved first if the building is to be workable.

SCHEMATIC DESIGN

When the circulation problem seems to be of primary importance, the architect will probably work out the circulation diagrams and seek your approval of them before he proceeds with the rest of the design. These diagrams, which the architect calls *schematics,* tell you little or nothing about the appearance of the building. Judge them for just what they are: diagrams that show how the architect is proposing to arrange the facilities of the building, without prejudice to forthcoming esthetic dispositions.

PRELIMINARY DESIGN

What is called the preliminary design of a building goes well beyond the schematic design. It includes an accurate representation of the shape, size, and arrangement of most of the visible elements of the building, such as roof, walls, partitions, doors, windows, landscaping, important furniture and equipment, and so forth. The set of drawings called preliminaries will thus permit you to evaluate not only the arrangement and provision of physical facilities, but also the visual quality of the design. The preliminaries will also either show or separately list the materials of construction, with additional notes in some cases as to quality or method of fabrication.

When the architect comes to you with the preliminary design he is saying in effect, "I think I have solved the design problem in a satisfactory way. My solution is contained in these drawings and notes, which I now submit for your study and evaluation. If you approve my work so far, I will go on to the next stage; if you want me to explain or discuss any aspects of the design I will gladly cooperate. If after discussion, you are dissatisfied with parts of the design, I'll go back to my office and try to revise it to your satisfaction. There will probably be no extra charge for revisions unless they require a great deal of extra work or unless they are tantamount to revisions of the program."

The solution to the nine-dot, four-line design problem, by the way, is as follows:

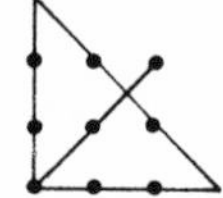

From approval of the program to completion of preliminary design might take no more than a week, if you are just remodeling your front porch, but a $50,000 house will take something like six weeks. Buildings in the million-dollar-and-up class will take several months for preliminary design. Design work depends partly on imagination, which is not subject to control by time schedules. We might say that the void is full of good ideas, but the designer can use only those that come to his mind. A good idea may come to his mind early in the game, but if he continues to cudgel his brains, he may get a better idea. Even after he is satisfied, it is usually advisable for him to shelve his work for a couple of weeks and then review it with a refreshed eye and mind. Some new criticisms will probably result. It is therefore unwise to try to hurry the architect through the preliminary design. If time is important, it is better to get him to agree to put more draftsmen on the production of working drawings when the time comes. That stage of the work lends itself to group accomplishment, whereas preliminary design should be essentially the work of a single mind.

When the architect brings you the preliminaries, you must first figure out what they mean, which some people take as a matter of course, but which others find very difficult. The following chapter is intended as aid and comfort for persons about to be confronted with architect's drawings.

After you have read the drawings and decided you know what they mean, you must evaluate the building the design of which they embody. The critical problem of architectural evaluation is the subject of the chapter after next.

The preliminary design does not include details of construction, nor complete, precise dimensioning. There is insufficient information at this stage for the contractor to be able to build. He will need what are called working drawings and specifications, which the architect will begin to prepare as soon as you and he are agreed on an acceptable preliminary design.

In the preliminary design all the big decisions are made. The building takes shape. The rest is detail. No good architect will underestimate the great importance of detail, but as far as you are concerned, the details should largely be left to the architect. For you, until construction is completed, the preliminaries are really the main event.

It seems unnecessary for the reader to follow the tortuous meanderings of the design of the Hauswirth residence up and down blind alleys and through indecipherable squiggles, which even the architect in some cases can no longer interpret. Here then, are just a few legible sketches representative of several distinct stages in the preliminary design: a half-dozen or so, culled from a total of about thirty.

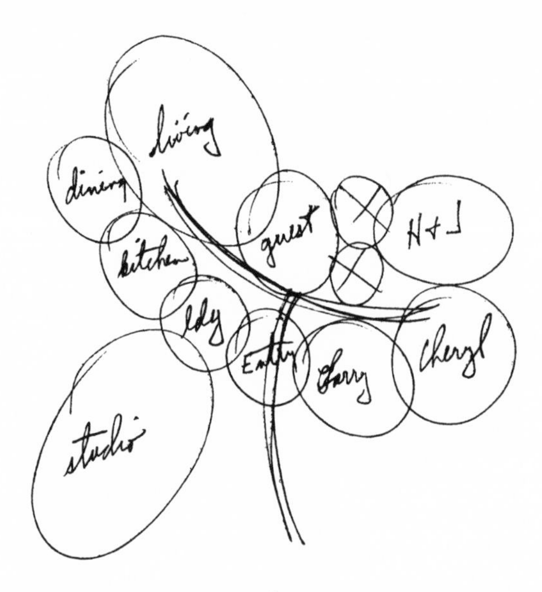

FIGURE 1

In the first sketch, where rooms are represented by circles or ovals, the heavy lines indicate main circulation: presumably hallways. The laundry area would separate the studio from the house to reduce noise transmission. The small circles containing *X*'s are bathrooms. The children's bathroom is meant to be accessible from the hall; the other bathroom from both the parents' bedroom and the study/guest room, but not from the hall, thus creating a private adult suite within the bedroom zone. The carport, or

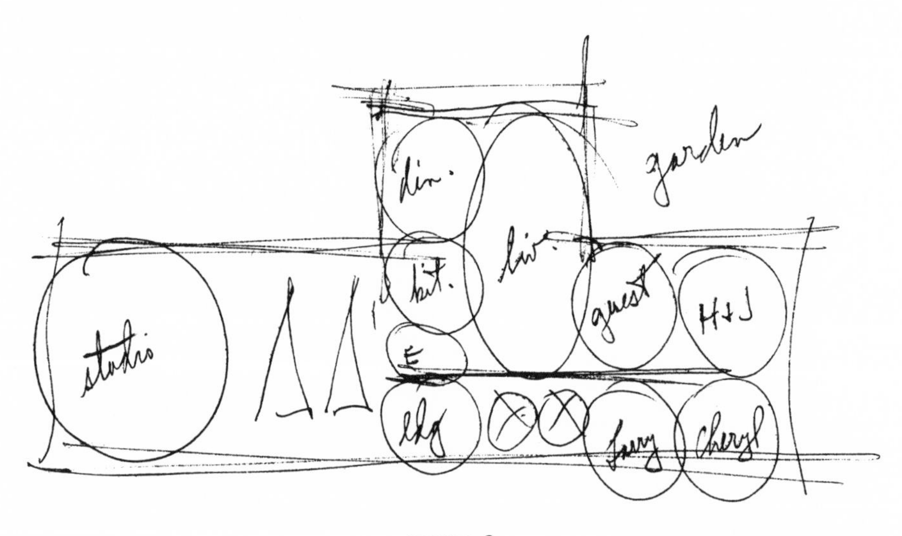

FIGURE 2

garage, is not shown, but would doubtless have to be near the studio on the entry side or the dining side, both of which locations would detract from the outlook from one or more rooms, a consideration that probably explains the abandonment of this general arrangement.

In Figure 2 the studio has been divorced from the house proper to insure noise-transmission reduction. Roofing the space between house and studio neatly creates a carport with protected sides. (The triangles that look like tepees represent automobiles.) The entry also gets protection from the carport roof, and the cars are right by the front door, reflecting the fact of modern life that in the suburbs people come and go by automobile, and an automobile, unlike a horse, need not be stabled downwind away from the house. In this sketch, however, the attempt to "square-off" the plan has led to putting the bathrooms in an inconvenient location. Also it is time to start thinking about a lower level, or basement, for the recreation area.

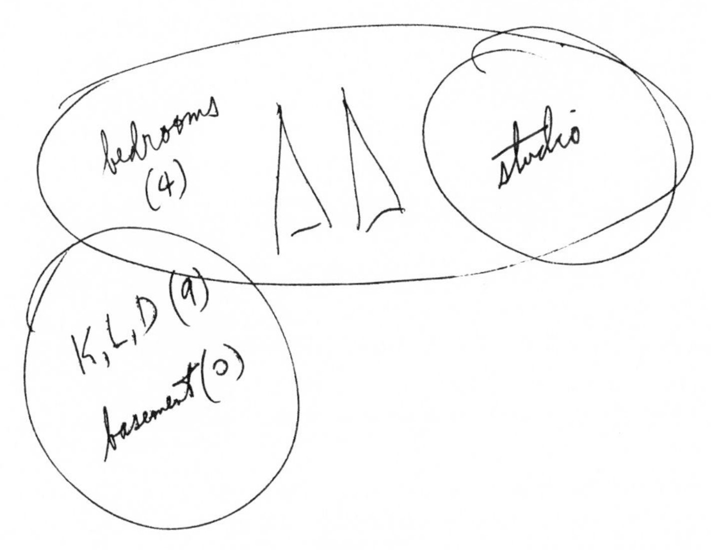

FIGURE 3

As the basement need not be large, the architect has tried in the third sketch to put the basement beneath only the living-dining-kitchen zone. The remainder of the facilities—bedrooms, baths, carport, and studio—occur at an intermediate level, apparently four feet above the basement floor. (The living-dining-kitchen zone appears to be nine feet above the basement.) This tri-level arrangement recognizes the slope of the site.

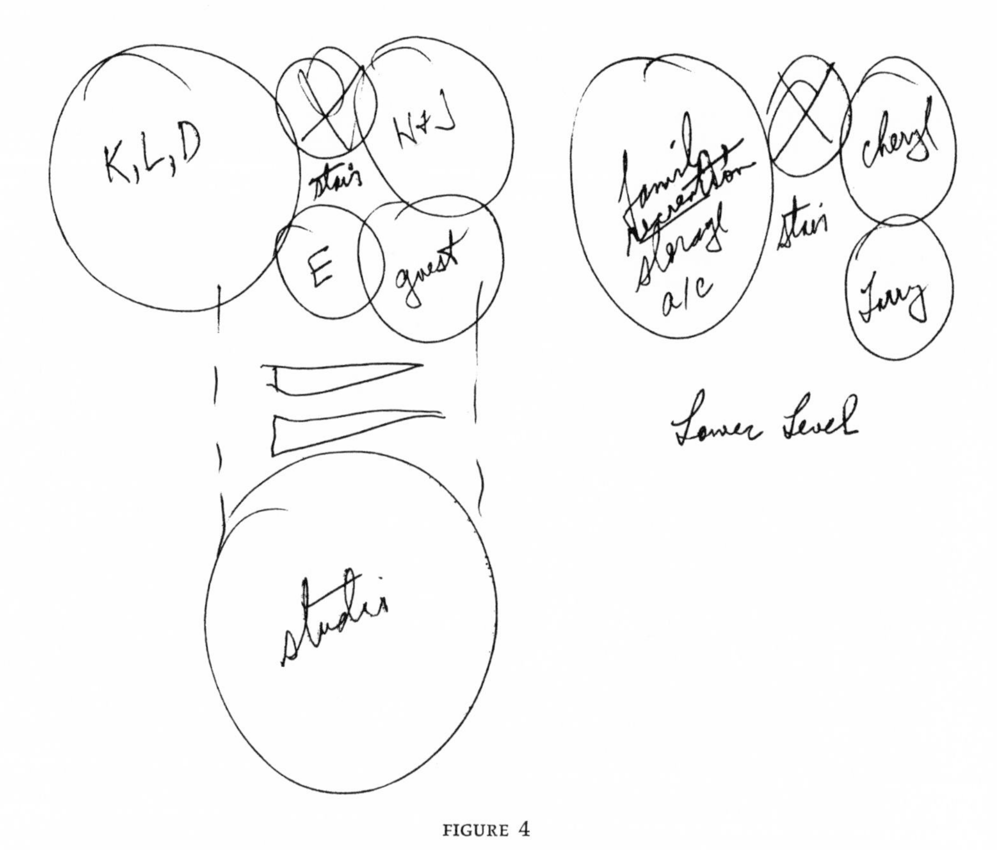

FIGURE 4

The fourth sketch refines the preceding one and shows a significant alteration: The childrens' bedroom-bath zone has been placed directly beneath the parents' bedroom-bath zone on a level with the recreation room, making the latter, in a sense, the children's living room, a notion that appealed to the architect. The overall arrangement is also far more economical than the one immediately preceding.

The sheet of small sketches on the opposite page confusingly reflects the working out of the design in more detail. An attempt is made to fit rectangular rooms together. The numbers represent tentative wall or partition lengths in feet. There is evidence of back-tracking and redesign to improve upon certain subdispositions of space. The upper left hand corner sketch (to read, rotate the book ninety degrees counter clockwise) is a cross-section showing a tri-level arrangement with basement children's zone on the lowest level, carport-studio-entry at an intermediate level, and living-adult zones at the highest level. This is the way the house was actually built.

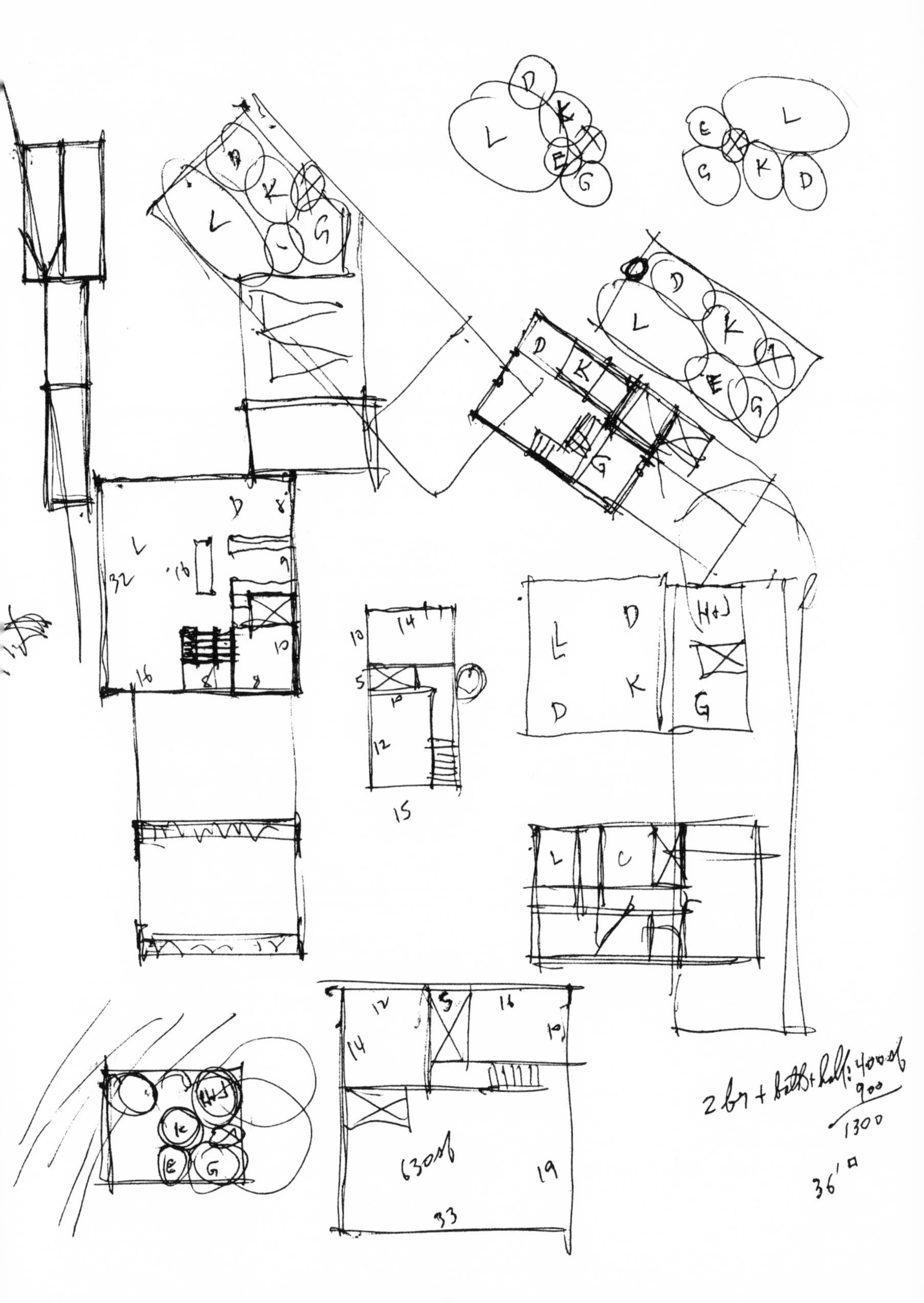

FIGURE 5

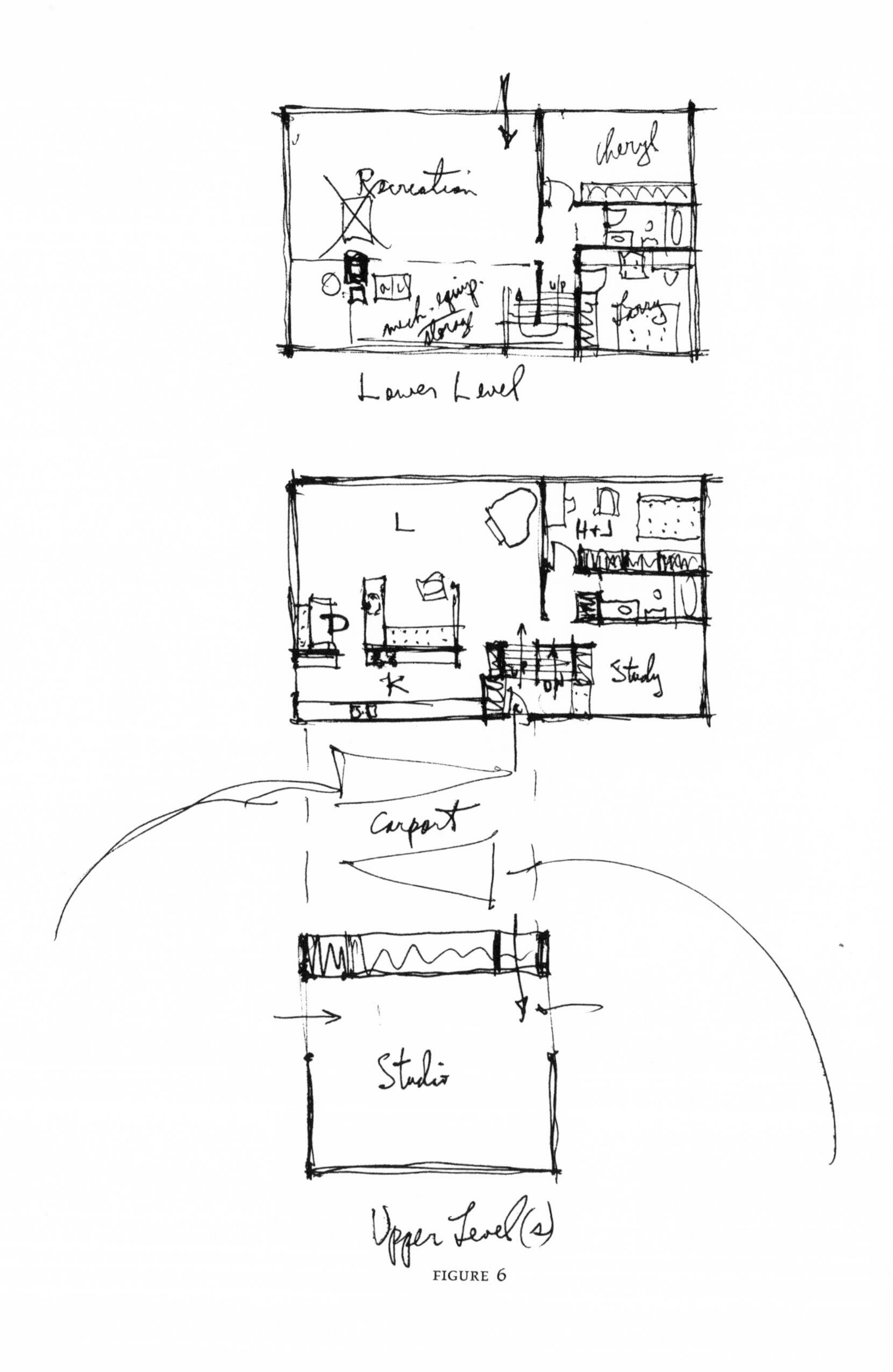
Recreation
cheryl
mech. equip. storage
Lower Level
L
K
Study
Carport
Studio
Upper Level(s)

FIGURE 6

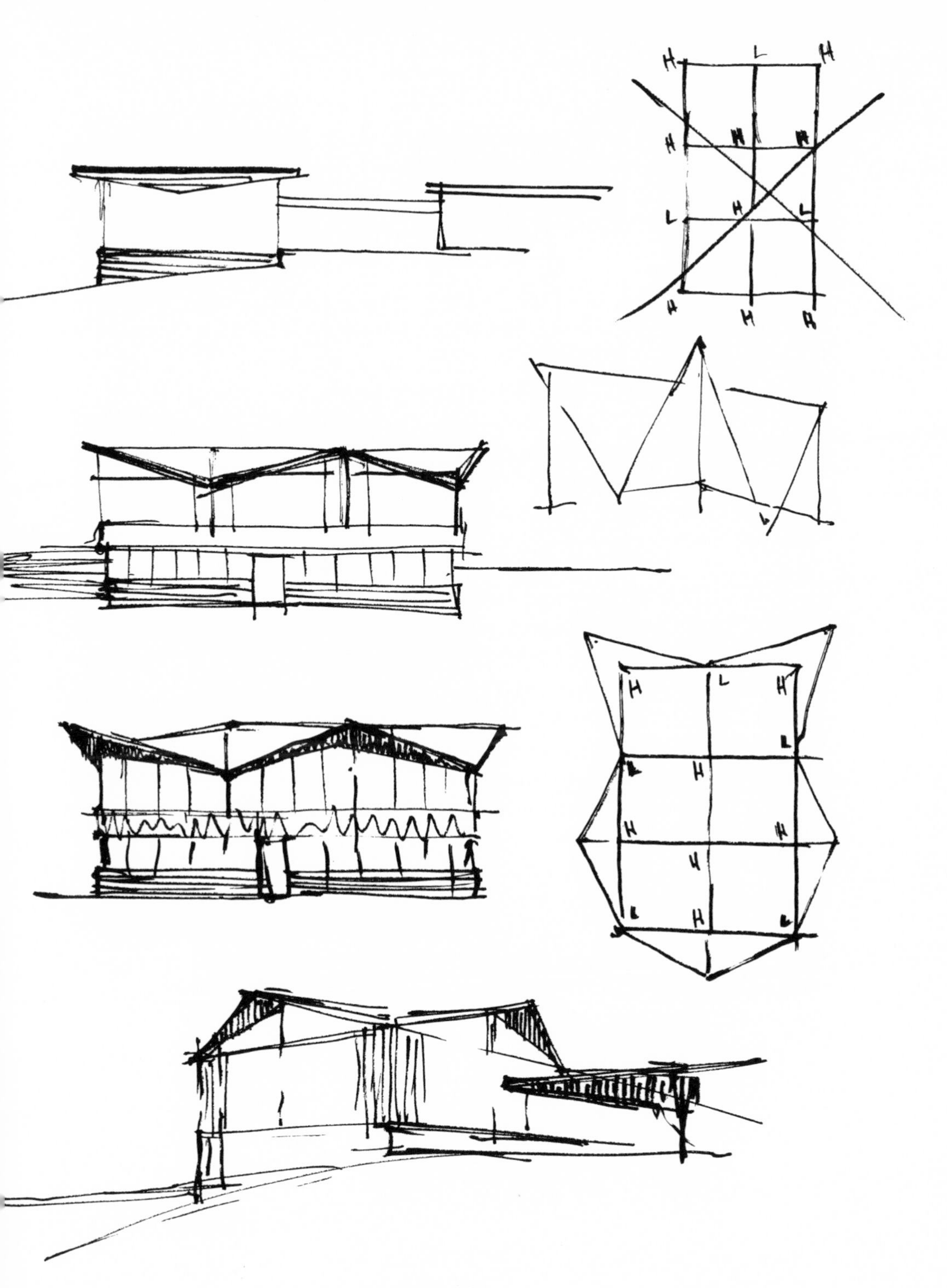

FIGURE 7

Figure 6 shows what was essentially the final plan. Rooms are drawn roughly to scale and some items of furniture are shown. Note the architect's idea for the driveway to run through the carport and circle the studio. One could drive in and out from either direction and never have to back up to turn around.

On page 117 are sketches of the evolving exterior design. Throughout his experimentation with various plan arrangements, the architect kept in mind, but did not sketch, the implications for exterior appearance of what he was doing. Now exterior sketches begin. The first, at the top of the sheet, indicates a level roof. Next come variations with warped roof surfaces: hy-pars (hyperbolic-paraboloids). The letters *l* and *h* on the two roof plans refer to high and low points of the warped segments.

Hy-pars resemble saddles or potato chips, and thus possess compound curvature, which is the source of their strength as it is in the case of eggs and automobile fenders. Happily the curvature of hy-pars is of a different kind from that of eggs and fenders, and hy-pars can be generated by straight lines. A hy-par roof segment can be built using straight timbers for temporary formwork, with thin boards bent over them in two layers at right angles to each other to form the permanent structural surface. Stiff, straight permanent members are required along each of the four edges of each hy-par segment, and once the layers of bent boards are attached to these edge members, the structure is complete and the formwork can be removed. The result is a rafterless curved roof the underside of which is a curved ceiling.

The architect finally concluded that the use of hy-pars was not impractical in the Hauswirth residence, and as they had indicated a liking for the form, he would design the house that way. Soon he completed the preliminary design. The drawings he made to show to the Hauswirths are used to illustrate the next chapter.

Chapter 11

DRAWINGS AND HOW TO READ THEM

FACED with architect's drawings, some people panic. Anyone who has firmly accepted the idea that he can't read drawings is very likely to try to avoid architects altogether. I sympathize: As one who can't carry a tune I try to avoid glee clubs and choirs. Graphophobes should take heart, however, because the ability to read drawings is not inherited: It can be learned.

Often the difficulty seems to lie in false expectations. Although many architectural drawings are nearly photographic and can be comprehended at a glance, others require careful study. Not realizing that patience is required, the viewer who can't comprehend such drawings instantly may conclude that he can't comprehend them at all. Nonpictorial and semi-pictorial drawings, like verbal language, have their own grammar, syntax, and vocabulary. Like verbal language they must be read, sometimes one line at a time. Anyone who troubles to do so should be rewarded with meaning gleaned from even the densest, eye-straining maze of fine lines.

Besides having patience, anyone who aspires to read drawings should also know in advance the kind of information he can expect to find and the manner of its presentation. The elements of architectural drawings may be well known to some but even the most experienced layman may discover one or two new morsels of information in the following.

Drawings for the most part consist of *plans, sections, elevations,* and *details.* Several of these may be assembled on the same sheet, with a border-line around it, and a title block in the lower right hand corner. Anyone can read a title block.

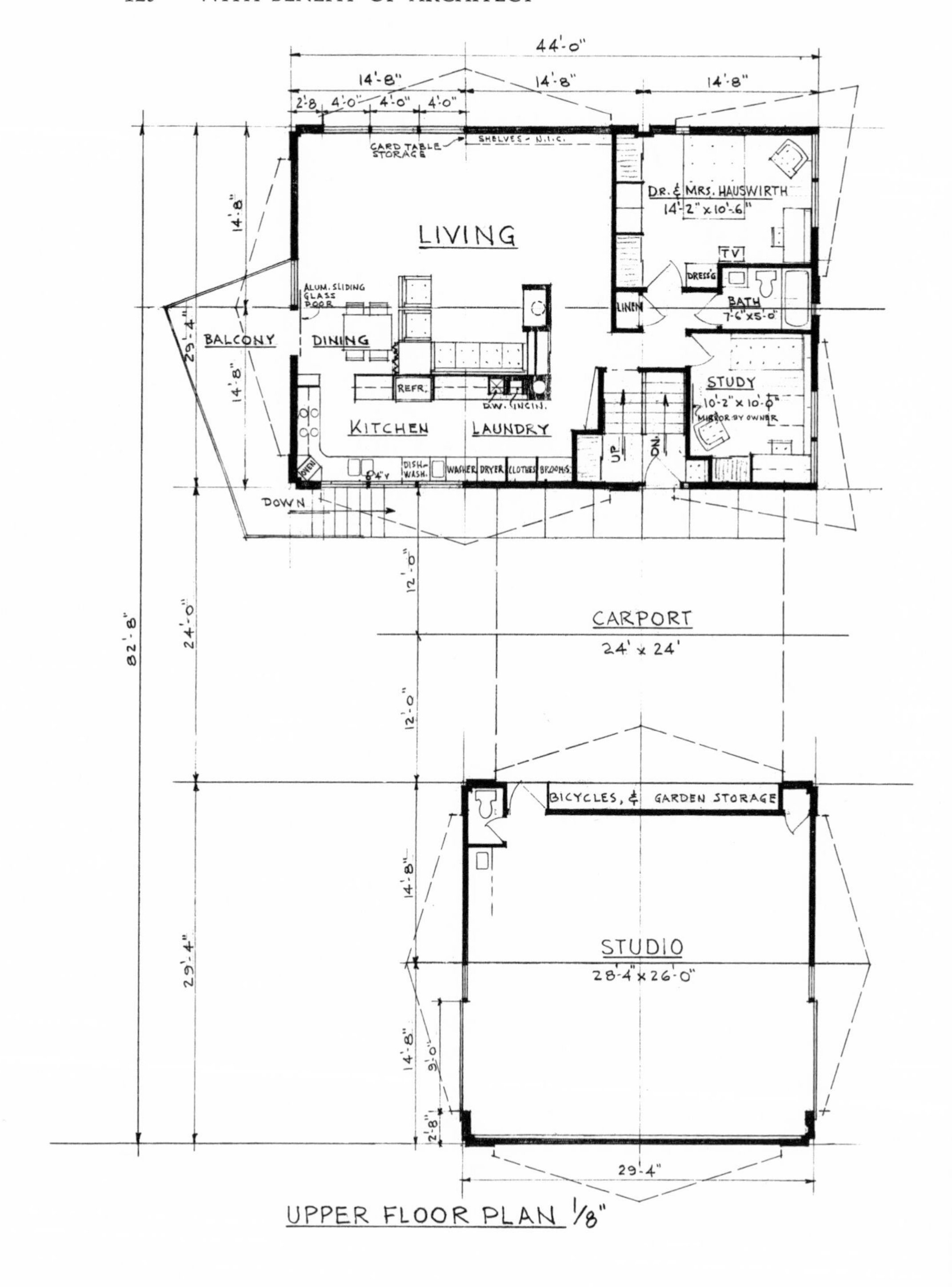

UPPER FLOOR PLAN 1/8"

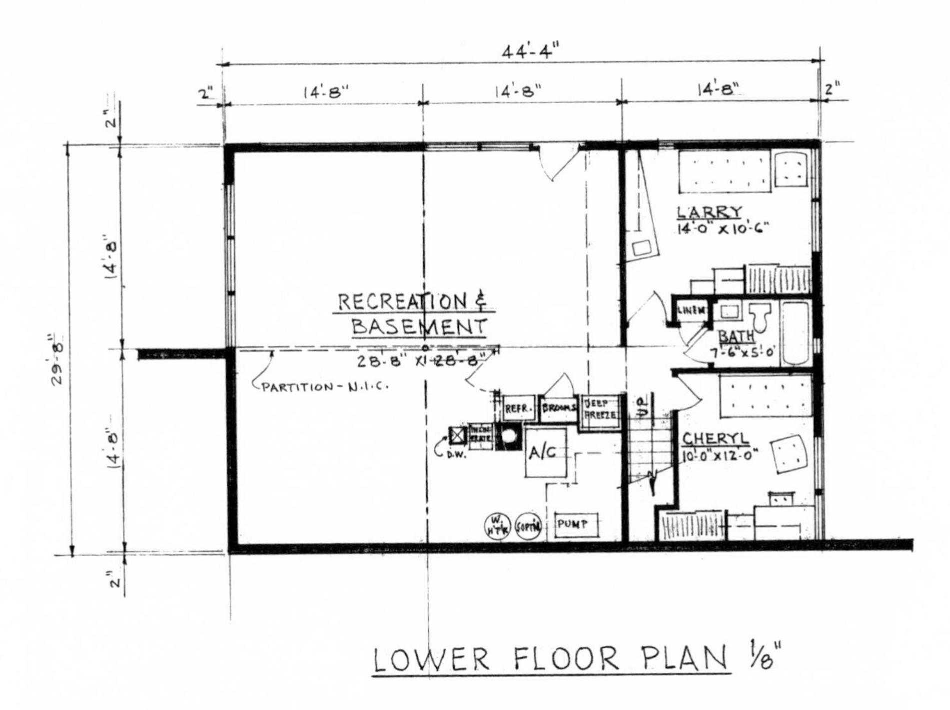

The floor plans of the Hauswirth residence, shown above and on the facing page, are not the first ones presented to the Hauswirths by their architect, but differ primarily in minor details. For example, Harriet Hauswirth liked the idea of separating the studio from the house for acoustic isolation and to improve the carport, but she decided that such separation made a toilet and lavatory necessary in the studio.

The addition of the balcony was Dr. Hauswirth's idea after he saw the first set of preliminary drawings.

FLOOR PLANS

Roughly speaking a plan is a map. It is what you would see (from above) if a giant razor had sliced horizontally through the building at a level just above the window sills, and then someone had removed all that part of the building above the slice. For precision it must be added that to "see" a plan you must imagine yourself infinitely high above the building; otherwise you would have an oblique glimpse of vertical surfaces such as areas of wall remaining below the slice. In a plan all vertical surfaces disappear as surfaces and their edges appear as lines. New horizontal surfaces created by the hypothetical razor when it cut through the walls are usually shown shaded or cross-hatched. Windows and doorways appear as gaps in otherwise solid walls. Floors are usually shown as blank areas surrounded by the shaded areas representing walls, but sometimes the draftsman will sketch in some lines to indicate tile or flagstone, or dots to indicate carpet, and so forth.

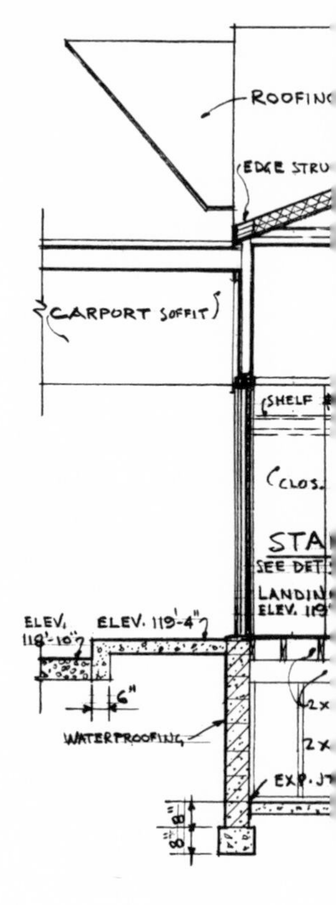

It often happens that no section drawings are included among the preliminary drawings. Such was the case with the Hauswirth residence. The section shown here is one that appears on the final working drawings. It is on Sheet No. 2 in the upper right hand corner: The complete working drawings are reproduced in Chapter 14.

SECTIONS

A section (short for cross-section) is like a plan except that the razor makes a vertical cut, and your line-of-sight is horizontal rather than vertical. Again, the cut-off part is removed, and you are looking head on at the cut surface.

To draw a plan the building is sliced in two by a razor moving horizontally: Thus what is called a *plan* can be thought of as a horizontal cross-section. To draw a section the building is sliced by a razor moving vertically: Thus what is called a section can be thought of as a vertical cross-section. In short, both plans and sections are varieties of cross-section.

CEILING PLANS

A plan shows the floor, but what about the ceiling? Ceilings are often pretty uninteresting, but the electrician has to be informed where to put the lights and there may be other things up there, such as air diffusers, a

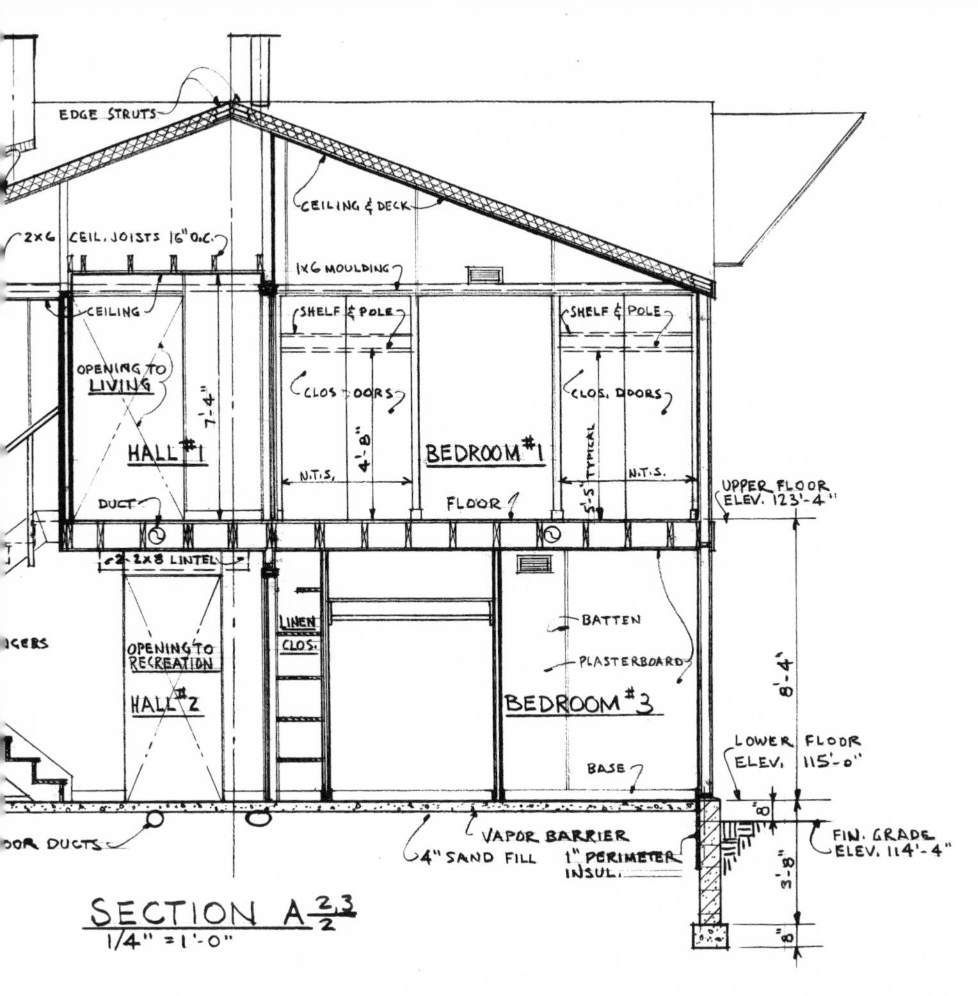

SECTION A $\frac{2,3}{2}$
1/4" = 1'-0"

trapdoor to the attic, and so forth. On the floor plan of a house the ceiling features are usually shown as though they had been cut loose and dropped to the floor. That is, they are drawn on the floor plan but understood to be physically located directly above, on or in the ceiling. In this case they are usually drawn with dashed lines to distinguish them.

Other buildings may have very complicated ceilings. They may contain lights and air diffusers, plus return-air grilles, loudspeakers, access panels, and height changes, as well as a patterned arrangement of acoustic tiles or panels mounted perhaps in an equally definite arrangement of metal strips. This situation calls for a reflected ceiling plan. To read one, imagine yourself as in the room. All projections have been removed from the walls, and the entire floor has been transformed into a mirror. If you look straight down at this mirror, you will see a reflection of the ceiling above, and this reflection is what the draftsman has drawn. You must also imagine that your own body is transparent or you would see yourself in the reflected ceiling plan.

Three sides of the Hauswirth residence were adequately shown in perspective drawings so only one elevation drawing was included among the preliminary drawings.

Stippled areas indicate roof. The vertically striated areas represent plywood siding. Glass areas have been left blank. The small circles in the two narrow windows in the center of the house proper are bathroom ventilating fan outlets.

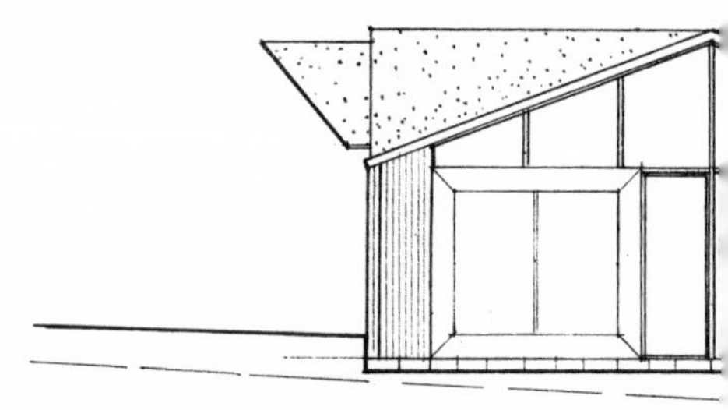

NORTHWEST E

SECTION LINES

We always know where the razor cuts to make a plan; the eighth floor plan is made by a cut just above the eighth floor window sills. Somehow we must also be informed exactly where the razor cuts to make a particular section. To provide this information for each section, the draftsman draws, on the appropriate *plan,* a line to represent the cut of the razor that made the section. If any section is made by cutting entirely through the building (we have been tacitly assuming this), a section line for the cut will appear on each floor plan.

The section line, as described, tells us where the razor cut, but by itself does not tell us at which one of the two cut parts thus produced we are supposed to be looking, and which one we are supposed to have thrown away. Let us assume that a razor aligned north and south cuts the building into an east half and a west half, and that the section drawn by the draftsman is actually a view of the west half with the east half removed. To view it, we assume therefore that we are standing to the east and looking westward. The draftsman indicates all this by drawing a north-south section line, as explained above, and then at each end of the section line drawing another line, short and *pointing west,* which means the section is what is seen by *looking westward* at the western piece.

The section of the Hauswirth residence shown above includes two floors.

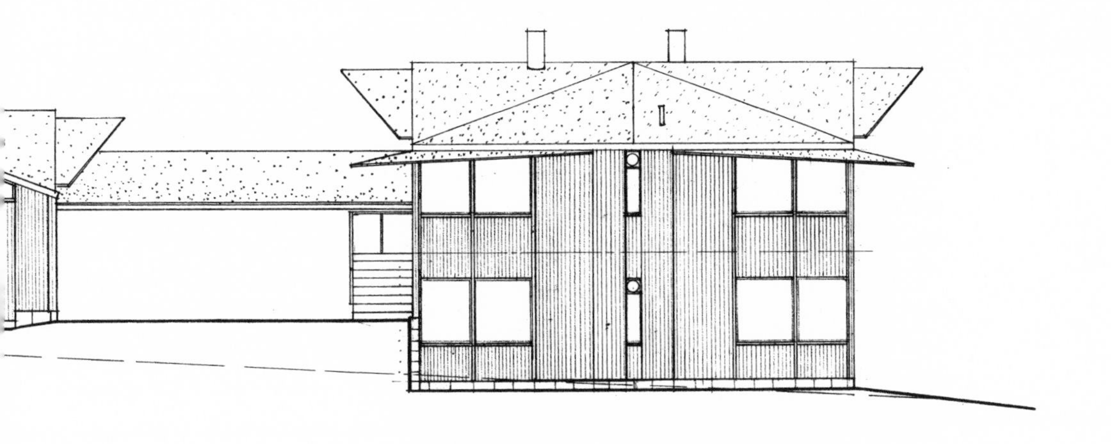

You will therefore find its section lines (in the working drawings, chapter 14) on both the lower floor plan (Sheet No. 2) and the upper floor plan (Sheet No. 3). The section designation—A-2,3/2—is explained as follows: The final *2,* under the line, designates the sheet on which the section itself is drawn; the other digits—*2,3*—designate the sheets containing plans of the floors cut by the section. The result is a cross-referencing of all sections to corresponding plans, which facilitates consulting them together despite their frequently being drawn on different sheets.

As views of buildings, plans and sections are remote from daily experience. A bomb may blow off the wall of a building, revealing what looks something like a section drawing, or an archeologist may excavate a ruin the roof of which is gone and the walls of which are destroyed down to the level of the windows, but few of us ever see the results. Remoteness from experience makes the understanding of plans and sections somewhat difficult, so the explanation of them has been rather long. Once they are grasped, however, the rest is relatively easy.

ELEVATIONS

Walking down the sidewalk, if you stop at a point directly opposite a building across the street, turn and face it directly, what you will see is approximately the same as an elevation drawing. To make it exactly the same, you must, as with plans and sections, imagine yourself at an infinite distance instead of just across the street. A certain objection to this may have occurred to you: If you get that far away you won't be able to see the building at all. Therefore, as an alternative to moving back to infinity, stand still and fancy instead that a very strong but nondestructive pressure has been inexorably applied to all the building elements, such as window sills, door knobs, pilasters, and so forth that project toward you from the surface of the principal wall. If the face of the building, without any other sort of distortion, is rendered perfectly flat, then you could drape a piece of tracing paper over the whole facade, trace every line, and come away with a perfect elevation drawing—full size, too.

Elevations carry labels such as *East Elevation*, which means "elevation drawing of the east wall seen from the east looking westward."

Elevations seen from outside the building are exterior elevations. Interior elevations are often drawn. In fact, when we cut a section through a building, one of the things it will show is the elevations of interior partitions or walls of each of the rooms that is cut.

ROOF PLANS, SITE PLANS, PLOT PLANS

A roof plan bears the same relation to a floor plan that an elevation does to a section. A roof plan is like a bird's eye view of the building, looking down at it from an infinite height. No razor slices are involved. You are seeing superficial features of the roof itself: chimney tops, plumbing vents, exhaust duct caps, and so forth.

After drawing the roof plan, the draftsman may enlarge the field of view to include a map of the surrounding land. The result is called, interchangeably, a site plan or a plot plan. Site plans show such things as walks and drives, trees and shrubs, property lines, telephone poles, underground piping, and so forth.

A plot plan, especially for a steeply sloping site, will also ordinarily display a number of irregularly curved lines, some or all of which meander all the way across the drawing, while others may curve back to meet themselves. These are called *contour lines*. Somewhere on each line there will be a number which represents an elevation (height) of the earth's surface above or below some arbitrarily chosen elevation called the *datum*. The

The preliminary drawings for the Hauswirth residence did not include a roof plan. The one shown here is taken from Chapter 14, the final working drawings, Sheet No. 3, upper left hand corner. A study of it may help you to visualize some characteristics of hy-pars.

The roof is composed of ten segments, each a hy-par. There are six over the house proper and four over the studio. The striations on the roof plan indicate the bent boards of the permanent structure. In the striated areas shown, a segment of upper layer boards has been removed to show the lower layer running at right angles as also indicated by the crossed arrows and the letters *u* and *l* for upper and lower layers.

A line drawn on any hy-par parallel to any of its edge struts (the stiff, straight, permanent members mentioned earlier) will be a straight line. Furthermore, any line drawn along any bent board will be a parabola. Finally, if we made a "topographical survey" of the roof, as though it were a plot of ground, and drew contour lines, we would find that the contour lines were hyperbolas. Hence the name *hyperbolic-paraboloid.*

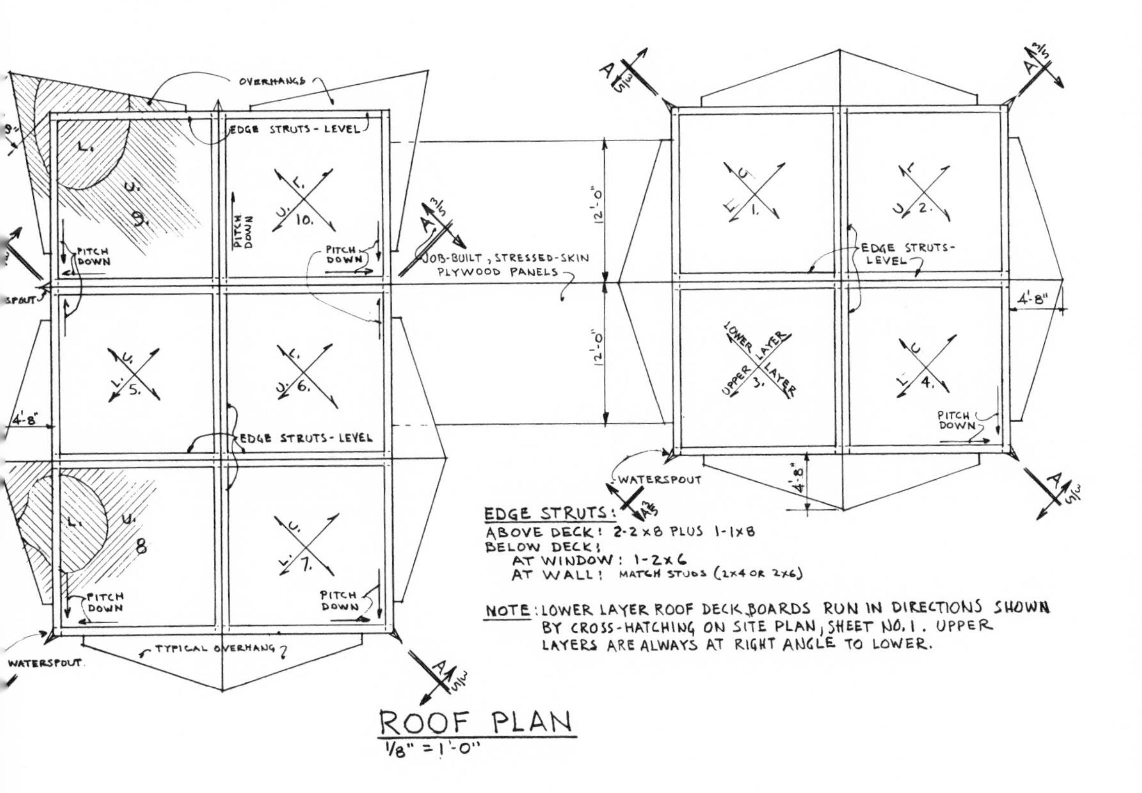

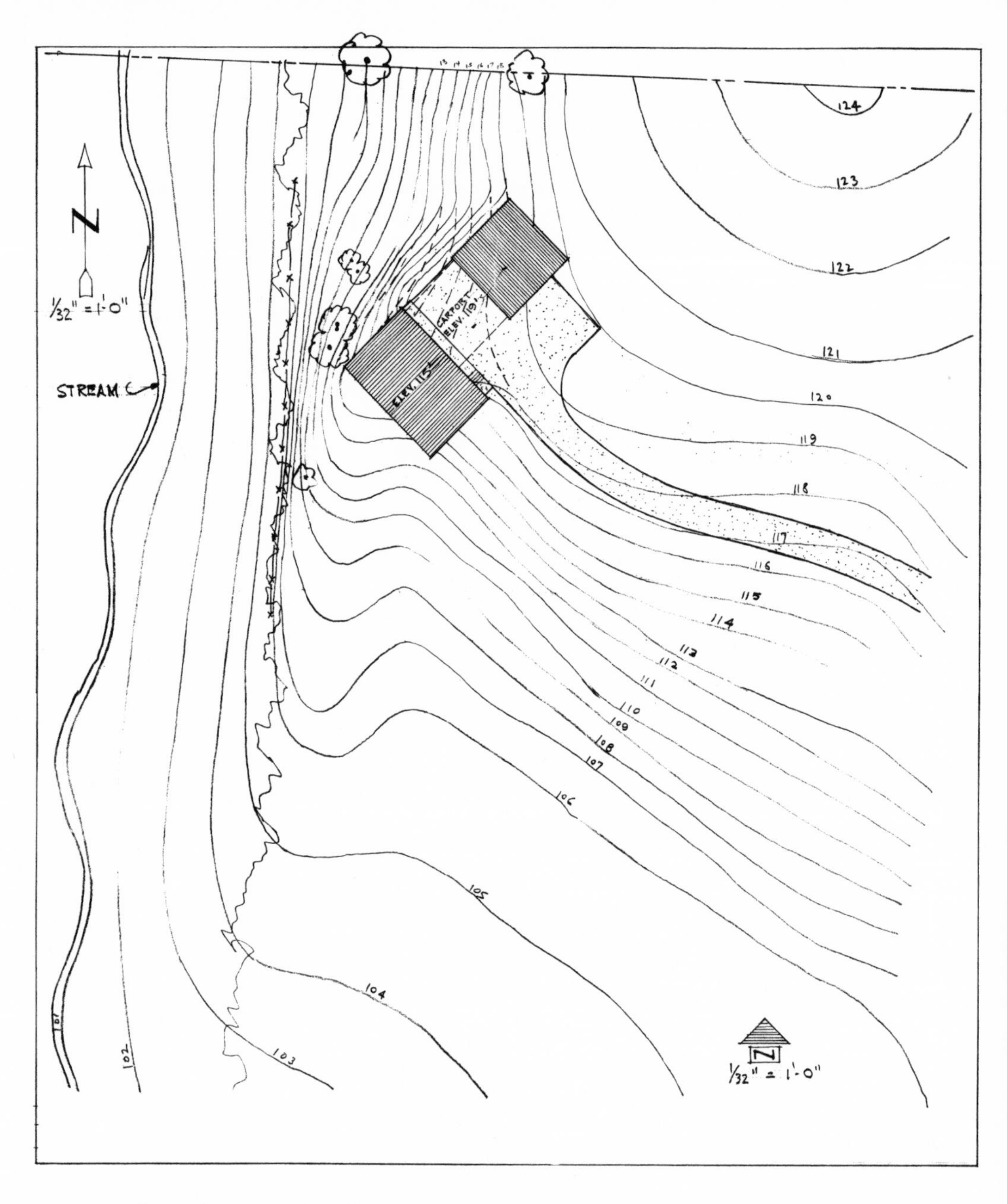

The preliminary plot plan of the Hauswirth residence shows the house and part of the driveway on a segment of the topographical survey. Note that it was decided not to encircle the studio with the driveway, as to do so would entail a substantial amount of earth fill to the northwest, which would be expensive and would also detract a bit from the pleasant outlook otherwise shared by all four bedrooms.

Note that reshaping of the earth has been indicated as explained in the text: The dashed lines show existing contours, and solid lines indicate finished contours.

datum may be sea level, but more often it is an imaginary point of no significance in itself. Take a contour line labeled *114'*. Here is its significance: All along that line the height of the earth's surface is 114 feet above something (anything). Now if you look at the adjacent contour lines, one of them may be labeled *112'* and the other *116'*; then the elevation of the earth along the 112-foot line is two feet lower than it is along the 114-foot line, and the elevation along the 116-foot line is two feet higher than it is on the 114-foot line. If these lines were actually marked off on the ground and you walked from the 114-foot line to the 116-foot line your path would take you two feet uphill. We don't care where the 000-foot line is: We are just interested in the rise and fall of land on the site itself.

If you have ever seen a hilly field that had been plowed by the contour-method you can easily perceive that each furrow of the plow would correspond to a contour line on a contour plan of the field. In an atlas you may have seen relief maps on which different elevations above sea level were represented by areas of different color. Often green is used for low-lying land, and white, suggesting snow, for mountain peaks, and so on. The borders of the differently colored areas are the same as contour lines.

Where contour lines are close together, they inform us that the earth slopes steeply. Where the lines are far apart the earth is relatively level. If the ground were dead level we would draw no contour lines at all.

A topographical surveyor makes measurements and takes readings at the site. These, followed by a little arithmetic, enable him to draw the contour lines on a map of your property. The architect uses the information on a contour map to relate the building to the vertical shape of the earth. He may decide that the shape of the ground should be altered, which he indicates to the contractor by drawing revised contour lines in the desired location, leaving the former contour lines to show as dashed lines. From such a drawing the excavator can actually compute how many cubic yards of earth he will have to move in the course of his work.

SCALE

A map is a "scale drawing" of the earth's surface. Somewhere on any proper map there will be a diagram called the *scale*. It will usually be a line marked off in definite increments. The divisions of the line will be numbered 0,1,2,3, and so on; and at the end of the line you will find a word such as *miles*. This means that the length of each division of the line represents one mile. Lay a ruler along the line and suppose you discover the length of each segment to be an inch. In that case the map is drawn to the scale of one inch equals one mile, which is just another way of saying that one inch on the map represents one mile on the earth. As there are 12 times 5,280, or 63,360, inches in a mile, we can further state that the earth is 63,360 times as large as the map, or that the scale is 1 to 63,360. If the cartographer had wanted to show more detail he might have doubled the scale of the map which would then be 2 to 63,360, or, what is the same thing, 1 to 31,680.

Architects' drawings are also scale drawings. Floor plans are most often drawn at the scale of one-eighth of an inch equals one foot, although floor plans of houses are usually drawn at the scale of one-fourth of an inch equals one foot. This means that one-quarter inch measured on the drawing represents one foot measured in the actual building. If you lay an ordinary ruler on such a drawing you might learn that the width of one of the bedrooms measures two and one-half inches. How wide is the actual bedroom to be? The answer is the number of fourths in two and a half, namely ten: The room is ten feet wide.

Other common scales for architects' drawings include ½-inch, ¾-inch, 1-inch, 1½-inches, and 3 inches equals one foot. To make or read a drawing at such scales with only an ordinary ruler requires too much tedious mental calculation of the "how many quarters in two and a half?" variety. Therefore architects use "scale rulers." Just as a scale drawing is a correctly proportioned miniature of the real thing, so a scale ruler is a correctly proportioned miniature of an ordinary ruler. The architect selects the ruler whose scale is the one he wants to use. Then the ruler readings will be the same as actual dimensions of the building.

Engineers use scales of the same general sort, but the ratios are typically one inch equals one hundred feet, one inch equals forty feet, and so forth.

Scale is a ratio of size, but the word is also applied to the miniature ruler itself. An architect's scale is graduated in a way that sometimes temporarily baffles the uninitiated, but anyone who knows how to use one can explain it to you.

DETAILS

A detail will be a plan, section, or elevation, but instead of showing most (or all) of the building at small scale, it will show a little bit of the build-

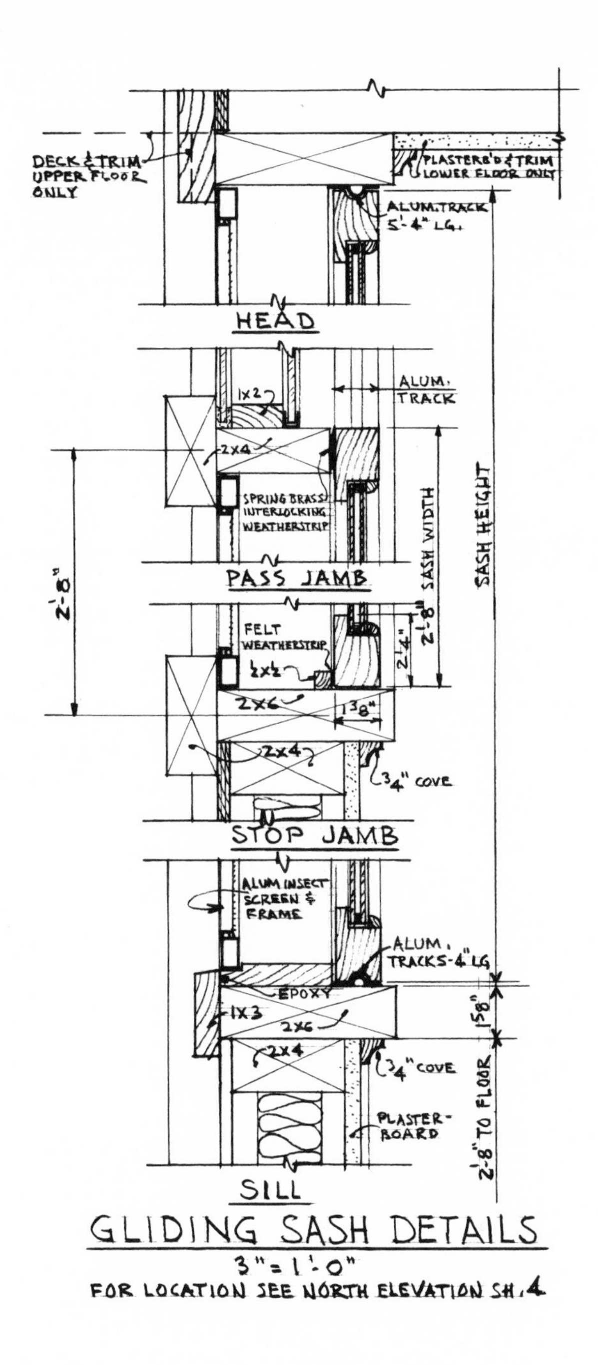

These window details are taken from the final working drawings of the Hauswirth residence, Sheet No. 1. They show the sill, jambs, and head of a type of window that occurs in each of the four bedrooms. In this detail, the note: "For location see North Elevation, Sheet 4," and the titles *Sill*, *Pass Jamb*, etc., make the use of a section designation unnecessary; nor are corresponding section lines required on the North Elevation, Sheet No. 4.

ing at large scale. The purpose of details is to convey precisely how the smallest elements of construction fit together. For instance, in the vicinity of a window sill any or all of the following elements may meet: studs, insulation, sheathing, lath, plaster, building paper, brick veneer, stone sill, wood sill, flashing, glass, glazing compound, glass stop, sash, frame, stool, and apron. A "sill detail" (which will be a vertical cross section), will show the shape, size, and means of joining together of all these elements.

Details rarely appear on preliminary design drawings. They may amount to 50 percent of the contents of working drawings.

SPECIFICATIONS

Drawings show how the parts of the building are related. Additional information is necessary and can be conveyed more conveniently in written than in graphic form. The written material is termed the *specifications.* Drawings will show shape, size, and location of footings, for example, and will note that the material is concrete. Specifications will describe this concrete as to composition, mixing, placing, finishing, and curing. Specifications are typed up and reproduced in quantity by mimeograph, or a similar process, for distribution to contractors. They are also bound in booklets separate from the drawings. Like drawings, specifications record certain decisions made by the architect, and approved by you. They constitute a book of directions for the builder.

Sometimes on small jobs the kind of information found in specifications is so brief that the architect will hand-letter it right on the drawings. This eliminates one pile of paper to be carried around on the job during construction.

Specifications accompanying preliminary design drawings are short, lack detail, and are called *outline specifications.* You should most certainly read them. The final specifications accompanying working drawings may, on a large job, be as bulky as a metropolitan telephone directory and about as interesting. For what to do with them consult the chapter on working drawings.

Hauswirth Residence

Job No. 65-01
21 March 1965

OUTLINE SPECIFICATIONS

1. Footings and Foundation Walls: concrete, with concrete block above to elevations shown. Bituminous waterproofing on concrete block walls above floor.

2. Floors on Grade: 4" concrete with wire mesh reinforcing over membrane waterproofing over 6" gravel fill.

3. Framing: wood walls and partitions above concrete block. Upper floor joists wood, with steel beam and column intermediate support.

   (a) Roof: Hyperbolic-paraboloid segments constructed of two layers 1x6 T&G boards with 3-2x8 (2x6 at ridge) wood edge struts epoxy-glued in place. Steel bar circumferential tie at living area and studio.

   (b) Carport: field-glued stressed-skin plywood panels.

   (c) Balcony: cantilevered wood joists.

4. Insulation:

   (a) Perimeter: 1" rigid.

   (b) Wall: 3" blanket.

   (c) Roof: 4" rigid.

5. Siding: 3/8" exterior plywood, no sheathing required. 2x4 vertical battens, 1x3 horizontal battens.

6. Sub-Flooring: 5/8" plywood (upper floor only).

7. Windows: fixed, insulating (double) glass.

   (a) Bedrooms and Study: one glide sash each.

   (b) Living Area: heat absorbing glass in southwest windows.

8. Doors: flush wood.

   (a) Dining Area to Balcony: aluminum sliding glass door.

9. Roofing: built-up, 20-yr bond type, with white marble chip surface. Metal flashing and waterspouts.

OUTLINE SPECIFICATIONS (CONT.)

10. FINISHES:

(A) EXTERIOR WOOD: WHITE-PAINTED PLYWOOD; GRAY-STAINED BATTENS AND CORNER PANELS.

(B) EXTERIOR CONCRETE BLOCK: GRAY-PAINTED.

(C) BALCONY RAIL AND DOORS: PAINTED ACCENT COLORS.

(D) INTERIOR: PAINTED DRYWALL WITH 1X¼ PAINTED WOOD BATTENS AT JOINTS. CEILINGS SHALL BE SOFFITS OF HYPERBOLIC-PARABOLOIDS, STAINED NATURAL.

(E) CONCRETE FLOORS: EPOXY PAINT.

(F) BATH, KITCHEN WALLS; BALCONY FLOOR: LIQUID TILE.

(G) WOOD FLOORS:

(1) KITCHEN, BATHS: RESILIENT TILE.

(2) OTHER: CARPET BY OWNER.

11. MISCELLANEOUS:

(A) KITCHEN CABINETS: JOB-BUILT WOOD; MELAMINE-FORMALDEHYDE COUNTERS.

(B) FIREPLACE: PREFABRICATED METAL.

(C) TRASH STORAGE: BELOW KITCHEN FLOOR, ACCESSIBLE THROUGH CHUTE AND FROM EXTERIOR.

(D) PACKAGE RECEIVER: KITCHEN EXTERIOR WALL.

12. SITE WORK:

(A) DRIVEWAY, CARPORT: ASPHALT WEAR SURFACE OVER GRAVEL.

(B) PLANTING: BY OWNER

13. MECHANICAL WORK:

(A) AIR CONDITIONER: CENTRAL, OIL-FIRED; BURIED TANK; EVAPORATIVE CONDENSER BENEATH BALCONY.

OUTLINE SPECIFICATIONS (CONT.)

13. MECHANICAL WORK (CONT.):

(B) INCINERATOR

(C) TEMPERATURE CONTROLS

(D) WELL: 10 GPM REQUIRED. PRESSURE TANK. WATER HEATER. WATER SOFTENER.

(E) DRAINAGE SYSTEM: 1000 GAL. SEPTIC TANK, TILE FIELD.

(F) PLUMBING: FIXTURES AND SYSTEM.

14. ELECTRICAL WORK:

(A) SERVICE: 220 VOLT, 200 AMP., UNDERGROUND.

(B) LIGHT FIXTURES

(C) ELECTRIC RANGE, VENT HOOD.

(D) ELECTRIC OVEN, VENT HOOD.

(E) EXHAUST FANS: BATHROOMS, BOY'S BEDROOM, STUDIO.

PERSPECTIVES

Of all types of drawings, a perspective most closely resembles the actual appearance of the building. A perspective drawing is what you would produce if you held up a piece of glass between you and a building, closed one eye, and with head held steady, traced in grease pencil on the glass the lineaments of the building seen through the glass.

The architect, of course, has the problem of producing perspective drawings of buildings not yet built. He can construct a perspective by using the plans and elevations and applying a moderately intricate process of projective geometry. The results are quite accurate. Alternately he may contemplate the plans and elevations, mentally visualize the finished building, and then sketch the vision. In this case he may be said to *eyeball* the drawing. The result will contain inaccuracies, but will be good enough for some purposes.

RENDERINGS

The realism of a perspective can be greatly increased by darkening some areas to indicate shades and shadows. This darkening is called rendering.

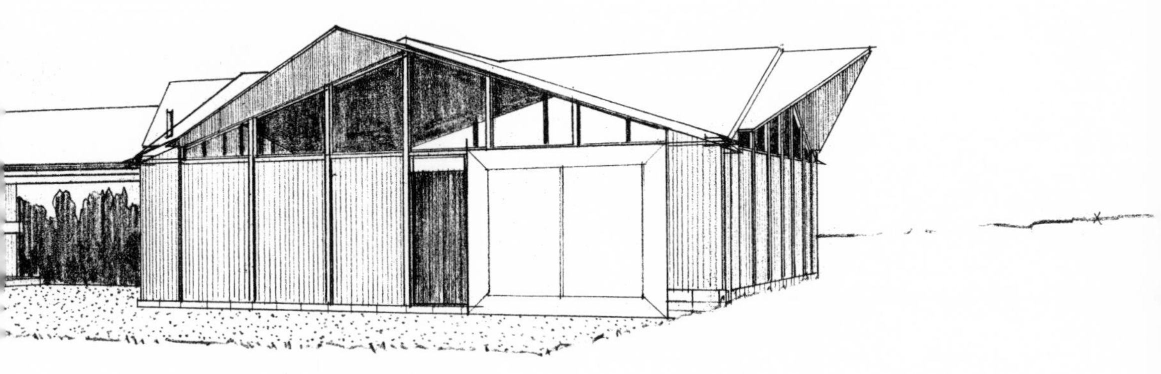

PERSPECTIVE VIEW FROM THE SOUTHEAST

The result is called a *rendered perspective,* or simply a *rendering.* If color is also used the result is called a *colored rendering.* Only preliminary drawings are either colored or rendered.

Sometimes elevations and even plot plans are rendered or colored or both, but again, only when they are preliminaries.

MODELS

Of all kinds of architectural representation a finished, complete model is the most realistic. As an aid in visualizing what he is doing, an architect sometimes makes rough models of parts of a building, but these are usually not meant to be displayed to the client.

RENDERINGS AND MODELS FOR DISPLAY

Preliminaries usually do not include models or finished perspective renderings suitable for public display. Houses aside, however, you may want to publicize the building before it is constructed. If so, tell the architect and arrange for him to provide suitable material, such as what newspapers

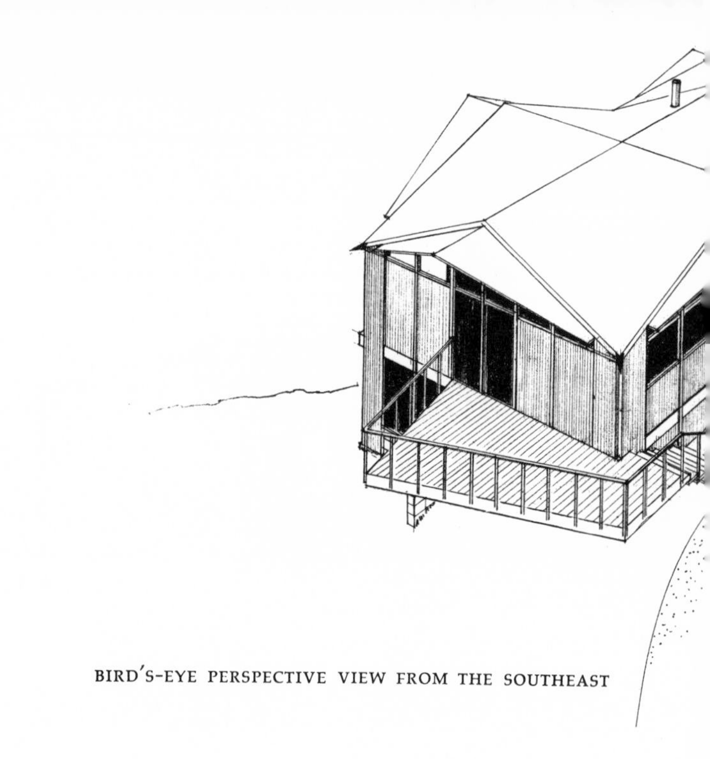

BIRD'S-EYE PERSPECTIVE VIEW FROM THE SOUTHEAST

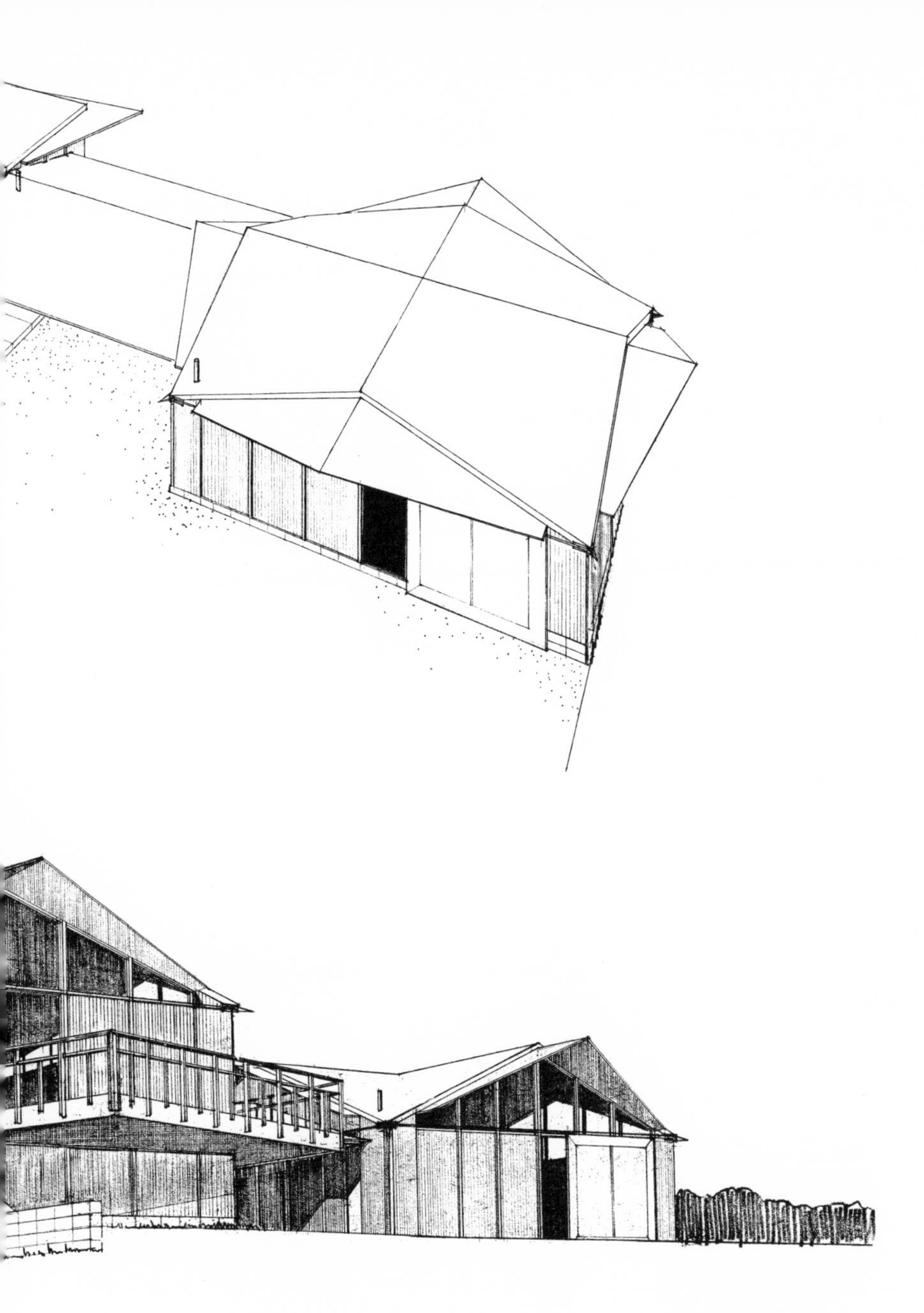

PERSPECTIVE VIEW FROM THE SOUTH

call an *artist's sketch.* A model can be displayed if a strategic location is available, or photographs of it can be publicized.

A suitable rendering will cost from $25 to $250 or more. A model will cost from $250 to $2,500 or more.

BLUEPRINTS, AND SO FORTH

In order to understand architects' drawings you must understand words like *plan* and *section.* There is another terminology, however, that refers to the physical form that drawings may take. Knowing the meaning of these terms is not very important, but as you will hear them bandied about, you should know enough to keep from being confused.

Drawing may refer to any graphic representation in any form. It means the original, or a copy, of anything drawn. Any plan, section, or detail is a drawing; and so is any single sheet of paper (or other material) containing several of these. *The drawings* usually means all the sheets of preliminary or working drawings for a single building project.

ORIGINALS

A sheet on which a draftsman has physically inscribed lines with pen or pencil is an original drawing. If you like rare words, you can call it a holograph.

Architects' drawings made with the use of triangles and T-square (or its equivalent) are classified as *ruled* drawings. To distinguish them, original freehand drawings are often called *sketches.* Sometimes preliminary drawings are drawn freehand, but a scale (ruler) is used for the more important dimensions. By extension such preliminaries are sometimes called *sketches,* but this use of the word is dying out along with the practice that entails it.

When drafting the working drawings, draftsmen often draw the parts, such as plans, elevations, sections, and details initially on separate sheets of cheap paper. These sheets are subject to frequent handling, erasure, and redrawing as the project develops. When these dirty scraps reach at least semifinal form, they are organized and traced neatly onto larger sheets of good grade translucent paper, cloth, or plastic film. The resulting sheets are called *tracings.* The dirty scraps have no name, but both they and the tracings are classified as original drawings.

REPRODUCTIONS

Architects, who are no less snobbish than the average man, have enjoyed many a snicker at ignorant usage of the word *blueprint.* When someone, likely as not a politician, talks about "drawing a blueprint for progress," gales of laughter seep out of the drafting room.

At the blueprinting company there is a large, wet, clanking machine with a "wringer" at one end and a table at the other. From time to time the architect's office sends tracings or other original drawings to the blueprinter. He feeds them one at a time into the wringer and after a brief disappearance they emerge where he can reach them and feed them in again. On the table at the other end of the machine, in due course, out comes a blueprint every time an original is fed in. Blueprinting is simply a specific process for cheaply reproducing any original drawing made on translucent paper or cloth. You can make blueprints of even typed letters or their carbon copies if they are on thin paper. A blueprint is also a negative image: The dark lines of the original come out white and the white, or clear background of the original comes out deep blue. Any time there is a need for expendable copies of architects' drawings, they can be blueprinted in the desired quantity and the originals returned to the files.

Blueprinting is an elderly process. Lately there has been a proliferation of alternate methods of making cheap copies of architects' drawings for the use of the many persons involved in construction. These processes include microfilming, photostating, photographing, whiteprinting, blacklineprinting, and others. The commonest of these at the moment, and the only one worth describing here, is whiteprinting.

A whiteprint is made in a large, humming machine, surrounded by an odor of ammonia. Like blueprints, whiteprints cost about a nickel per square foot, but unlike blueprints they are positive images: The dark lines of the original come out dark blue on the print, and the clear background of the original comes out white on the print. The average person appears to find whiteprints easier to read than blueprints, and thinking may make it so, although it has been demonstrated, for instance, that drivers more quickly grasp the message of roadsigns if they consist of light letters on a dark background than if they are the other way around. A real advantage of whiteprints, however, is that one can make notations on them with an ordinary pencil or pen. This is handy when two people are discussing the job over the telephone, and at other times as well.

Whiteprints are also called *blueline prints,* or simply *bluelines.* The word *print* always refers to a photographically reproduced copy of an original.

A *set of prints* or *the prints* means one copy of each original drawing for the job, usually stapled together with a brown wrapping paper backing. You have probably seen newspapers bound on a wooden stick in public libraries, and sometimes the same method is used in an architect's office. In such cases you may hear the prints quaintly referred to as *the stick.* Calling a set of prints *the plans* is slightly lowbrow.

DUPLICATE ORIGINALS

Blueprints and whiteprints can be made only from translucent originals. The prints themselves come out on relatively opaque paper. There are other processes for producing prints on translucent paper. A *sepia,* so called because it consists of light brown lines on a clear background, is both a photocopy and sufficiently translucent to be itself run through a blueprinter or whiteprinter to make blueprints or whiteprints or even other sepias.

There is another, more expensive process which makes copies by printing full size in black ink on tracing cloth. These and sepias are called duplicate originals: They are printable prints.

In a multistory building where many floors are almost the same, differing mainly in partition locations, a lot of drafting time can be saved by drawing the unchanging features of all floors just once and making duplicate originals to be used as the beginning drawing for each separate floor plan. It is possible to make changes on duplicate originals, but the relative difficulty of erasing their printed lines is a great disadvantage.

TRANSLATING THE DRAWINGS

Drawings in hand, start with No. 1 and use your head. Every line, note, and symbol has some definite meaning. If the meaning escapes you, ask questions. In writing the English language, we capitalize proper nouns. This is a convention. There are many conventions of a similar kind used in architectural drawings. Some of these are explained by a "symbol key" or "legend" included on the drawings. Others may require explanation by the architect.

Once I was showing the floor plan of a house to an acquaintance from South America. He professed total inability to comprehend the maze of chicken tracks before him. "Take this pencil," I said, "and pretend it is you. Put the point down here where it says 'garage.' Now you are in the garage. The walls are these thick lines that make a rectangle. But notice the gaps in the lines. The two wide gaps, close together, are the doors where the cars come in and go out."

"Aha!" he said.

"This smaller gap is the door for people to walk through. If you keep the pencil touching the paper you can move anywhere on the drawing that you could in the house, so long as you don't cross the thick lines."

"Like thees?"

"That's it. You are moving through the little gap. Now you are out of the garage. What is the label on the space where you are now?"

"Eet say 'keetchen.' "

"Right. Now you are in the kitchen. What does it say under 'kitchen'?"

"Ten eeks feefteen."

"That means ten feet wide by fifteen feet long." (What it said was "10'x15'.") "That is the size of the kitchen. It's about the same size as this room where we are sitting now."

"Eet ees then that I can go from garage to keetchen weethout goeeng outsides, no?"

"Eet, uh, it is so, yes."

Translating drawings means learning what the actual building will be like. The lines-on-paper universe generated by the architect is in itself of no direct interest or value to you. Your concern is with the real future building. One of your aims must be to avoid being misled by irrelevancies such as sloppy lettering on the one hand and overglamorous colored renderings on the other.

READING WITH IMAGINATION

Next to a model, a colored perspective rendering is the closest possible representation of the building. The real building, however, will exist in three dimensions, whereas the perspective must be drawn on flat paper in two dimensions. To convey depth the foreshortening of the drawing will be supplemented by shades and shadows. Very good, but this shows the building as it would appear on a sunny day: What will it look like in cloudy weather? Those verdant trees and shrubs, what will they look like in winter when the leaves have fallen? There are no trash cans in sight, but will it be possible to hide them after the building is occupied? Renderings

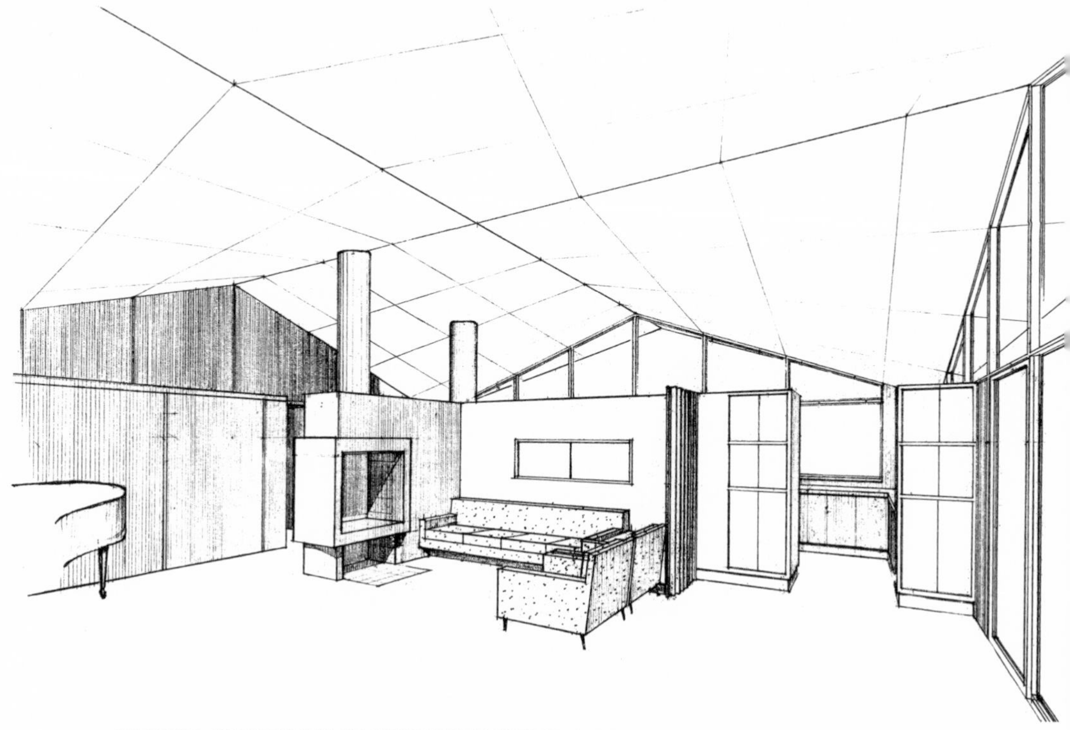

INTERIOR PERSPECTIVE OF HAUSWIRTH LIVING AREA

The fireplace shown here as stone or concrete was changed to a prefabricated metal type, noted in the outline specifications. The light lines that show on the ceiling are imaginary representations of the straight-line generators of the hyperbolic-paraboloids. The actual ceiling consists of bent boards running diagonally to the generators.

also have a special charm simply from being miniatures. This charm is similar to the appeal of models of boats and airplanes. The fact is that no matter how ugly an actual building is, it may be possible to make an attractive rendering of it. Conversely, no matter how attractive the building is, it is easy to make an unattractive rendering of it.

Avoid beguilement. Look closely at the drawings, but try to see the actual building. It is not too difficult if you exercise some imagination. Remember that songbooks are not music, scripts are not plays, and drawings are not architecture.

Certain deceptive qualities of both photographs and perspectives can be explained with the aid of the interior perspective of the Hauswirth living room. A camera held at the perspective viewpoint would show far less of the room unless it had an extreme wide-angle, or "fish-eye" lens, in which case the view would be greatly distorted. In one way, therefore, the perspective more closely approximates reality than a photograph, although the statement tends to be true only for interiors where one is prevented by walls from backing up far enough to get so much of the room on film.

In addition, the perspective drawing shown here can be taken in at a glance (if the book is held at arm's length), but a person standing in the actual room, at a point corresponding to the perspective viewpoint, could not take in as much at a glance as the perspective shows. A person would have to move his eyes and perhaps his head as well to see all that the perspective contains. To this extent the perspective gives an unreal impression.

The Hauswirth perspectives also reveal a visual quality, peculiar in my experience to hyperbolic-paraboloids. Their curvature does not show clearly in either drawings or photographs, although when one views a real hy-par its curvature is perfectly apparent. The difference seems to be that when experiencing achitecture, one can move eyes and head and can also move bodily past or through the structure. If so, then visual images in the mind must be composites of various individual views, and it would be impossible ever to apprehend completely the quality of architecture from two-dimensional representations.

Chapter 12

EVALUATING THE DESIGN

THE material in the preliminary design will include plans of every floor, a plot plan, exterior elevations, outline specifications, perhaps a section, and perhaps one or more perspective views. The architect will very likely show you this material in about the same order I have listed it, and he will provide a running commentary. He will also try to answer any questions you may raise as he goes along.

In a matter of minutes you will have viewed the whole design. These are exciting minutes, and your reaction is of the essence, because the fate of the building is being delivered into your hands.

The usual experience of people faced with preliminary designs is recognition that the building is indeed workable and good looking, but there are one or two things disliked or not understood. After discussing them with the architect, your doubts may be allayed, or he may agree that revisions to the design are in order.

After the first run-through, review the drawings at leisure in the days ahead. Hold further conferences with the architect if either of you thinks it advisable. After you have thoroughly comprehended the drawings, and your reaction to the design has become relatively stabilized, you will be in the best position to make final decisions as to what changes in the design, if any, you want the architect to make. Occasionally the preliminary design has to be revised several times before all parties are satisfied.

Sometimes disagreements develop between you and the architect. These are rarely serious, but when they are, a lot is at stake: namely thousands of dollars worth of future construction. There is danger that you or the architect has a wrong notion of how some part of the building will function. It more often happens, however, that you will be demanding changes that the architect fears will spoil the appearance of the building. The occurrence and magnitude of disagreements can be reduced, I believe, if you will adhere to the following five recommendations.

Each of these recommendations is accompanied by an attempt to amplify and justify it. The result is a sort of short course in architectural criticism. Do not be dismayed by either its length or apparent complexity. No one person will meet more than a fraction of the problems considered here and knowing how to deal with those problems will in itself tend to prevent their occurence.

AVOID HASTY ESTHETIC REACTIONS

This recommendation must be given first because as soon as you glimpse the design, you will tend to make an esthetic judgment in the form "I like its looks," or "I don't like its looks." Now, before the architect would present a design to you, he had to decide that it was good looking. If you agree, that makes two of you, and the outlook for successful architecture is favorable. If you dislike the design, however, you should realize that your dislike may change to approval as you study the drawings and become more familiar with all aspects of the building.

If the architect has done his work well all the parts of the building will be both interdependent and purposeful. Before accepting or rejecting any part of the design you should first learn its purpose and its relationship to the building as a whole, and this may take some time and study. The theory is that your esthetic approval stems from your recognition, partly unconscious, that what you are looking at will serve your purposes and hence is valuable to you. Esthetic dislike arises from a realization that something will not serve you or is potentially harmful.

An example divorced from architecture may support this theory. You have probably met a good-looking person who, with increasing familiarity, earned your dislike. He or she, by evincing dishonesty, disinterest, nasty habits, or what have you, proved unable to serve your purposes, which were friendship, support, or amusement. I suggest that when this happened, that person also ceased to be good-looking. Conversely, the homely person who turns out to have a heart of gold mysteriously ceases to seem homely. The point is not that "beauty is in the eye of the beholder," but rather that the eye sees what the mind believes. Anything you have learned to regard as good, true, or even just comfortable, tends thereby to acquire an attractive appearance.

You may have had a similar experience with architecture. On first glance some building, perhaps starkly unusual, struck you as ugly. Later, if you had occasion to learn that what looked unattractive was actually an efficiently planned, economical arrangement of space, the building began to look good to you. The process, of course, works two ways. The building you like at first may turn out to be poorly planned and pretentious, whereupon you come to loathe its appearance. Still again, familiarity may merely strengthen first impressions, not reverse them.

Even if you carefully apprehend the logic of a building design, however, your reaction may be warped by a personal "taste" that supersedes practical considerations. I will have more to say about taste after laying some additional groundwork.

COMPARE THE DESIGN TO THE PROGRAM

Using the program as a checklist, go through it item by item and verify that each requirement, including the budget, is met by the design. This is a mechanical process, requiring no great effort. Considering the labor you expended on the program, it is obviously prudent to insure that it has been carried out.

Don't be upset by small discrepancies between program and design. If they are oversights by the architect, he will correct them. His main concern has been to solve the big issues, and although he must be equally fastidious about providing places to store eggbeaters and old baby carriages, a few such requirements may have got lost in the shuffle. He may even have decided, on his own initiative, to make minor changes in the program with the expectation of convincing you that these changes were wise. If his reasons don't convince you, he will change the design to conform to the original program.

After seeing how the program works out in the actual design, you too may decide that the design might be better if the program had been different in some ways. This certainly doesn't mean that preparing the program was in any sense a waste of time; rather, we have reached the point where the program has served its purpose: It was an indispensable tool, but not an end in itself. The present problem is to evaluate the resulting design. If it can be improved, there is no need to let the program stand in the way.

VERIFY WORKABILITY OF THE PLAN

When guests arrive, to where do they drive? Where do they park? How do they unload? Where do they turn around? How do they drive away? Similarly, how does the design provide for doing the laundry? Preparing meals? Bringing in the groceries? Disposing of trash? Going to bed and arising? How does the design facilitate both the private activities of individual members of the family and guests plus the joint activities of these same occupants?

If the architect has followed the program, the building will contain all the facilities specified, but their arrangement should be reviewed carefully. Mentally trace out on the plan the activities of the building's future occupants and decide if these activities can be conveniently performed. Perfect circulation is impossible, but generally, the activities most frequently indulged in should be the ones requiring the shortest, least circuitous journeys. Also those trips likely to involve heavy loads, such as from garage to kitchen, should be short.

Insure that the furniture you plan to install will fit.

Climbing stairs requires more physical effort than most people realize: Be very critical of all stairs, even only one or two steps.

GRANT VETO POWER TO THE ARCHITECT

In the design of any building the laws of man and nature make some of the decisions. Wood is prone to warp in disregard for your wishes or opinions. The building code will ordain that the floor of your house be built strong enough to carry a live load of forty pounds per square foot whether or not you want it that strong. Architects, however, are not inexorable. They can be ordered to do what you wish and dismissed if they refuse.

As you review the design, therefore, you may tell the architect to move this door, raise the roof, lower that chimney, and so forth. Sometimes the architect will agree that what you want is reasonable, but in other cases he will believe that what you ask is unwise or unworkable. He may be able to give convincing reasons, but on the other hand his opinion may be intuitive and largely inexpressible.

The architect must grant that program decisions should be made by you. You are the world's greatest expert on what the building should accomplish, as an aggregate of physical facilities. At the same time you should grant that architectural design is the architect's profession, and that he is better at it than you are. Even so you don't want to wind up with a building you dislike, no matter how good it may be, "architecturally" speaking.

In cases of disagreement there is a form of compromise that almost always works: You veto whatever is unacceptable to you, and let the architect veto whatever is unacceptable to him, with the understanding that if he vetos something, he must produce an alternative acceptable to you. Unless you and he are seriously at loggerheads this method results in a building that is entirely acceptable to both of you. Knowing that you will always give him this much freedom, the architect's self-respect is maintained and his morale is improved, with beneficial results to the work he does. I do not mean to imply that in applying the method of joint veto you should avoid making suggestions on how you think the design could be improved: Your suggestions on revisions are invaluable, not only because they afford the architect a better understanding of your true needs, but also because you approach the design with a fresher eye than the architect now has. For instance, you may *insist* that the vestibule is too small, and *suggest* that it be enlarged by borrowing space from some adjacent room. The architect should agree to enlarge the vestibule but be free to do it the best way he can discover, although it helps him to learn that you are willing to sacrifice space in the adjacent room. When the basis of disagreement is esthetic rather than practical, the same injunctions apply, but then the difficulty of explaining the nature of your objections is much greater. The dangers to the success of the design are also greater if you insist on specific measures of esthetic revision.

Your position gives you the power to reject anything unacceptable to you. Be content with this. Don't force upon the architect anything unacceptable to *him*. In the long run you will have a better, more satisfying building if *both* you and the architect are pleased with it.

DON'T OVERRATE YOUR PERSONAL TASTES

The intent of this section is to show that "good taste," to deserve the name, should mean no other than the recognition of true value: "Bad taste" results from some deformation of natural instincts.

1. Definition of Taste

If we start by considering food and diet, where the meaning of taste is most obvious, it should be apparent that *good taste* means a liking for nourishing, healthy food. A person with good taste in food is one who, without needing to think about it, consumes a balanced diet. Experiments show that small babies do just that if given the chance. Turned loose amid open containers of milk, cereal, meat, fruit, ice cream, vegetables, whisky, and so forth, babies, without supervision, will instinctively eat what is good for them. Most of the rest of us cannot say the same. Our taste for chocolate cake or martinis is exaggerated, while we have an irrational dislike for a few nourishing foods such as spinach or liver. These exaggerated likes and dislikes are examples of "bad taste."

2. Origin of Bad Taste

Bad taste probably originates in something like the following way. After being punished a child unconsciously "reasons" thus: "I am unhappy. Therefore this chair is uncomfortable, our house is ugly, and my parents are hateful." The chair, house, and parents, of course, are actually loaded with benign past associations, so when the child's mood improves, his feeling for them reverts to normal. While still upset, however, he may be introduced to something entirely new to him: spinach, for instance. The resentment he is momentarily projecting into his surroundings will now also flow into the spinach, but there, encountering no contradictory earlier associations, the resentment will take permanent root. Thus when an emotional disturbance happens to coincide with a new experience, the emotion tends to color the experience, and the resulting "bad taste" lingers because the new experience had not previously acquired any other color.

Every experience was new once, but if afterward it was often repeated, the child almost had to adapt to it. Irrational aversion—bad taste—therefore tends to center on relatively rare experiences. Spinach and liver, being expensive or tedious to prepare, tend to be rare experiences, which explains why dislike of them is more common than dislike of milk and eggs. Life makes us swallow the everyday occurrences but usually permits us to spit out things like boiled squid and fried grasshoppers if we are so minded.

Bad taste includes irrational likes, which are as common as dislikes, and probably acquired in the same way, but from an opposite starting point. A child whose first taste of ice cream comes as a reward for good behavior finds the natural taste of the ice cream sweetened by the sense of approval that accompanies the experience. Thereafter the child's initial liking tends to be still further exaggerated each time his parents employ ice cream as a reward.

In esthetics the counterpart of spinach may be the hue purple. An appreciable number of people have a distaste for it. At the same time it is not so common that everyone must adapt to it. Nature feeds us mostly on light blue or gray skies, yellow-green foliage, and beige earth. She permits us to reject purple, and those whose first experience of it coincided with a period of resentment probably do dislike it.

3. Taste in Architecture

In general we can define bad taste as a predilection for what is unhealthy. Good taste is a natural liking for things that contribute to sustained physical and mental health. Good taste thus sounds very much like the Abstract approach to architecture, which, you may recall from Chapter 1, we defined as the pursuit of economical physical and psychological utility. The person exercising good taste and the person following the Abstract approach are on the trail of the same objective. The mechanism of taste is emotional and intuitive, however, whereas the mechanism of the Abstract approach is intellectual. Ideally the two should be combined.

Buildings sustain our physical health and contribute to our peace of mind in many obvious ways. They protect us from bad weather, insects, and other animal and human marauders. They also contribute to our well-being in subtle and not completely understood ways. Consider what is called *balance* in the visual arts. If balance has value, it must contribute to the sustained health of the onlooker. How can it? I think it is as simple as this: In art, balance means merely that the composition somehow tells the observer which way is up. This may sound absurd, but we constantly —although usually unconsciously—need to know which way is up so that we can keep our own balance with reference to the pull of gravity. Otherwise we fall down. We have an inertial guidance system in the inner ear, but we also seek visual clues because the inner ear sometimes becomes confused. Therefore we are disturbed by pictures that hang crooked on the wall, and by building designs that seem to lack "balance." The desire for esthetic balance is thus a matter of good taste.

Keeping our balance is an aspect of the general need for physical orientation. Another manifestation of this need is the desire to know how large things are in order to relate our own physical size and capacities to the size of our surroundings. In the case of a building the eye roams over it in search of keys to its size. The commonest clue is a door. Doors are usually just comfortably wider and higher than we are ourselves. Sensing this, we can, again usually unconsciously, treat a door as a kind of ruler laid up against the side of the building. The door size indicates to us such things as how far we must walk to get to the building, and whether we can see out of the windows while sitting down, and whether outsiders can see in, and so forth. A building that lacks clues to its size, or exhibits conflicting clues, is said to have bad "scale." If, for some unknown reason, a building had two doors, one exactly twice as wide and twice as high as the other, we would be at least momentarily disturbed, wondering if the big door was for people and the little door for dogs, or if the little door was for people and the big door for monsters—giants, guided missiles.

In buildings for people the desire for human scale, like a need for balance, is a matter of good taste, but there are other buildings in which something nonhuman takes precedence. In a Gothic cathedral a wooden panel is set in concentric stone arches and appears to be the door. Closer inspection shows that there is a smaller panel cut into the larger one. Recognition that this smaller panel is the actual door suddenly makes the whole building seem larger than it did at first. The designer is saying that the appropriate scale for the house of God is grander than the scale of mortal man.

The architect accepts the need for balance, and for some kind of rational scale in buildings, as principles of design. Color schemes can also be planned with reference to principle. You may recall the example of the successful restaurant wall color mentioned in Chapter 2. The orange that improved business was probably not the restaurant owner's favorite color, but I suspect that when he learned how well it served his purposes he acquired a taste for it. If so, his reaction illustrates the theory that liking stems from perception of value.

Another principle of color selection might be that the colors in mental hospitals should be "soothing," and the colors in commercial offices "nondistracting." As the eye finds it easy to ignore the everyday colors of most of nature—light blue, gray, light green, beige—these colors seem the most suitable for office walls. And I suppose that in nine out of ten cases they are the colors chosen.

4. The Architect's Taste

The architect is ethically obliged to serve the interests of his client. The architect must not indulge himself in the luxury of choosing blue simply because he likes blue. He should base esthetic choices on objective principles, but it is difficult or impossible in many cases to perceive valid principles for esthetic decisions. Therefore the architect must exercise his intuition as well as his brains. A professionally disciplined intuition, however, is one that is oriented outward to the design problem at hand, not inward to the prejudices—either good or bad—of the designer.

5. Your Taste

Your own tastes, like the architect's, are no doubt a mixture of good and bad, but you have probably not been trained to suppress them. Indeed, why should you? It is your building, built with your money, for your use and pleasure, and it is within your power to make the architect cater to your whim. The first recommendation in this chapter was that you avoid hasty esthetic reactions on the theory that careful study of the design would improve your ability to evaluate it. Now, however, we are talking about bad tastes so strong they don't yield to logic.

The best reason for not overplaying your personal tastes is "a decent respect for the opinions of mankind." This is not as altruistic as it sounds. Aside from your own likes and dislikes in architecture, your liking for your own building will probably be affected by your awareness of the attitude of others. If you sense that others dislike the building, one source of emotional satisfaction is denied you. "Others" means not only today's occupants and visitors. The building will be there for a quarter to half a century to entertain, please, bore, or exasperate hundreds or thousands of future observers.

There is also economic sense in holding your tastes in check. If the building is well designed, that is, in good taste, then in the long run most people will like it, and this means a better financial return when you sell it. And if you don't sell it, at least your heirs probably will.

Unlike private residences, commercial and institutional buildings are impersonal. The committee, board, or individual approving the design will tend to submerge personal taste as a matter of course, but it doesn't always happen that way. Sometimes the corporation president or the church pastor, perhaps unconsciously, inflicts his own tastes on a design, to the ultimate chagrin of the employees or parishioners. The results are equally unfortunate when a building committee tries to formulate and impose a set of esthetic standards for the architect to follow. The committee may think objectivity is thereby gained, but the fact is that each building sets its own esthetic standards. These standards, furthermore, originate in the design, not the program.

AFTER CRITICISM

Aside from paying for the building, it is the program, not the design, that is your essential contribution to the birth of a building. The design is the architect's essential contribution. As neither the architect's intuition nor his intellect is infallible, it is good for him and for architecture in general if you take a lively and critical interest in the design. No doubt you will, but the task should be approached as a pleasant privilege, not as an onerous duty.

If you decide that the design should be revised, you may be surprised either at how easy, or alternately, at how difficult it may be for the architect to make the change. Often what seems like a simple change is just that: a minor rearrangement of lines. Even major changes may be easy, although requiring correspondingly more drafting time. At the other extreme, however, some revisions that look easy produce seemingly endless complications resulting in redesign of large areas or even the whole building. There is no way to predict what complications a given revision will entail. A shower bath may be added merely by putting it in a space formerly occupied by a bedroom closet and relocating the closet by stealing space elsewhere in the bedroom. On the other hand the loss of bedroom space may result in insufficient room for the bed, and so on, so that creating space for the shower is like dropping a stone into a pool of water, causing ripples that spread over the entire surface and lap at the edges. Even the exterior appearance of the building may be affected.

If the changes you request in the design are a result of new ideas on your part—ideas not originally included in the program—then the architect is theoretically entitled to additional fee for the work involved. When such changes can be made by twenty minutes' erasing and an hour's redrafting, however, no architect is likely to bill you for extra work. If he has to rethink large portions of the design, on the other hand, involving days or weeks of work, he will naturally expect to be paid.

Don't make the economic error of paying an architect thousands of dollars to design a building and then accept something that is only, say, 80 percent satisfactory, when for a few hundred dollars more it could become 95 percent satisfactory. The same reasoning applies to the time involved. The building will be in use for many years, so don't begrudge a few extra days or weeks on improving the design.

After the architect has revised the first preliminary design it will probably meet your approval. If not, or if more improvements occur to you, take the time and spend the money to have these additional changes incorporated into the design, even if it has to be revised half a dozen or more times. Try at the same time to avoid mere vacillation. You can add something today, see the results in tomorrow's revised drawings, and decide you don't want it after all. If later you decide to put it back again, you are wasting time, and the paper on which the drawings are made will be getting dangerously thin from repeated erasures.

Harriet Hauswirth practiced the plastic arts and had devised various house plans for her family during her marriage. After Shaper was hired, however, she ceased even to consider the shape her house might take. The matter was now in professional hands: She did not want to warp her judgment by acquiring preconceptions. As for John Hauswirth, he was by nature disinclined to manipulate ideas of space. Nevertheless both Hauswirths brought strong preconceptions to their first viewing of the preliminary design.

Shaper first told them that the design included a hy-par roof. Harriet was pleased. John was diffident, fearing the cost. Then Shaper showed them the floor plans. The Hauswirths, keyed up by the mention of hy-pars, were shocked. They had assumed the house would be essentially a one-story building with basement recreation and storage. They were aghast to find the childrens' bedrooms "in the basement," and the studio "outdoors."

Shaper did not betray his awareness of his clients' perturbation. Levelly he explained the plans. "With a little cut and fill, plus short retaining walls, both the recreation room and childrens' bedrooms are slightly above grade. Then the earth slopes up to put the entry, carport, and studio at grade half-a-story higher. The living zone and adult bedroom zone are up another half-story, so they are essentially second-story rooms on the north and west sides.

"Separating the studio from the rest of the house assures its acoustic isolation, and the wall of the studio also protects the carport. At first I worried about the necessity to go outdoors to get to the studio, but now I look at it this way: it's only twenty-four feet away, and the route is sheltered from rain, snow, and the prevailing winds. Even without a coat on the coldest day of the year I doubt that you will experience any discomfort in traversing that distance.

"The two bathrooms are 'stacked,' which is economical. The living-dining-kitchen area is, in a sense, a single space, which I think reflects the way you will use the area, both when you're alone and when you have guests."

By this time the Hauswirths had recovered their aplomb and began to like the plan. Harriet observed that the part of the house she chiefly occupied was very compact: the circuit from car to entry to kitchen to laundry to living room to bathroom to her bedroom was short, whereas the physical separation of the studio nicely mirrored her own feelings about the psychological separation between her artistic and domestic life.

When Shaper displayed the perspective drawings, they proved to be less surprising to the Hauswirths than the plans had been.

"Well, Marhall, I like it, I like it," said John. "Still, I'm a little worried about the cost of those hy-pars."

"Oh, John," objected Harriet, "I think they're beautiful."

"I *said* I liked them," rejoined John, "but otherwise what value have they?"

"As to that," began Shaper, "we know they won't save any money: They'll cost a couple of thousand dollars extra. If they have any value it must be intangible, and I'll try to explain what I think that intangible value is.

"One thing that struck me about your family was the lack of segregation among the activities of cooking and eating and the activities of the living room. You all cook, and your guests are in and out of the kitchen. Although such things commonly occur in other households, I sense that their occurrence is felt to be irregular and slightly annoying. In your case, though, you seem to take pleasure in unifying these various activities. The hy-par roof, which is also the ceiling of the living-dining-kitchen area, expresses and emphasizes that unification. It works this way. First, there should be visual separation of the kitchen from the living area, but a visual barrier need rise only slightly above eye level, which it does as you can see from the interior perspective. But, now, the hy-par ceiling is much higher so that from the living area you can see the kitchen ceiling which gives a visual continuity to the whole living-dining-kitchen area. Furthermore, at each corner of the area the ceiling curves down giving a stronger sense of enclosure. The ceiling shape is unlike that of a dome but I think it has a comparable effect.

"The studio has the same kind of ceiling. It is high, as you requested, unifies the room in the same manner that it does in the living-dining-kitchen area, and harmonizes with the rest of the house.

"Within that same harmonious scheme the ceilings of the upstairs bedrooms are a variation on the main theme. There the hy-pars are inverted resulting in low ceilings, which are consistent with the intimate quality of small, private rooms. Furthermore the low ceilings of the bedroom and study will make the living area ceiling seem even higher by contrast, hence more spacious; and the high ceiling in the living area will make the low ceilings in the bedroom and study seem even lower by contrast, hence more intimate.

"But the true intangible value of these hy-par rooves cannot be expressed in words: It must be sensed. The explanation I have tried to give can only suggest viewpoints. It's what you see from those viewpoints that counts."

The doctor was not at all sure he fully understood what Shaper was trying to say, but the general effect of his words was convincing. There was further discussion of details. Harriet asked for the toilet and lavatory in the studio, as previously mentioned, and John suggested the balcony with a door from the kitchen-dining area for outdoor eating. Later, by telephone, Harriet asked that provision be made for a future partition to separate the recreation from the storage area in the lower level. She also requested an outdoor storage area for gardening equipment, bicycles, and so forth, which Shaper worked into the west wall of the studio, opening onto the carport. It then occurred to Harriet that a kitchen dumbwaiter would ease the movement of childrens' clothing and bed-linen from their bedrooms to the laundry and back, and would also facilitate the movement of drinks and food between the kitchen and recreation area. Shaper heartily agreed.

The drawings reproduced in the preceding chapter reflect all of the above modifications to the first set of preliminaries.

A sharp eye may detect a few inconsistencies. The balcony railing final design was incorporated on the view from the south but not on the other two exterior views. A window was omitted from the kitchen, but only one perspective was changed.

At Shaper's urging the Hauswirths compared the design, point by point, with the program and were satisfied that the two matched. About ten days after their first view of the preliminaries the Hauswirths approved them, and Shaper began the working drawings.

Chapter 13

LANDSCAPING AND INTERIOR DESIGN

THERE are four ways to supply the important final touches, indoors and outdoors, that change the new building from a shell into a complete design.

DO IT YOURSELF

Personal selection of elements of landscaping, furniture, and interior color scheme, may appear to you as a joyful pursuit, not to be relinquished to specialists in those fields. If so, good luck to you. Many like you have tried it, often successfully, or at least, to their own satisfaction.

The main advantage of acting as your own landscape and interior designer lies in the enjoyment you may get from the creative process and the sense of accomplishment it fosters. The disadvantages will become apparent as we consider alternatives.

NURSERYMEN AND DECORATORS

A nurseryman (or landscaper) is someone who contracts to do the physical work of landscaping: He sells and installs plant material and perhaps some kinds of outdoor furnishings. The decorator, who may call himself a designer, will contract to supply almost any indoor element, such as drapery and furniture, not included in the Contract Documents prepared by the architect. Decorators may work as independent dealers, in which case they buy from manufacturers for resale to you at a markup. Alternately they may work in a department store or for a furniture manufacturer at a salary.

Nurserymen and decorators inevitably possess a far wider knowledge than you of what things are commercially available, their characteristics, and cost. This knowledge is of value to you, and you should avail yourself of it to the maximum extent, even if your intention is to do the designing yourself.

Beyond acting as salesmen of landscape elements and furnishings, nurserymen and decorators readily offer their services as landscape architects and interior designers. Their preparation for these roles varies widely. Some, through training, natural talent, or both are quite competent. Others unscrupulously offer a mediocre or incompetent service as an inducement to buy their goods. In either case the nurseryman and decorator may claim that their design services are free. This is just another way of saying that you pay for it whether you use it or not. Design takes time. The design problem must be studied and a solution found. The designer has to make a living, so he must be paid somehow. If he or she works for a department store the salary is included as part of the store's overhead. If he is a nurseryman he is not likely to spend his time unprofitably if he can help it. In either case the cost of the design service is a hidden part of the price of the materials sold. The prudent buyer must always allow for the seller's probable bias. The nurseryman profits more if the landscaping design he produces requires a hundred shrubs than if it requires only seventy-five. The decorator's job is more secure, or he earns more, if the interior design he produces calls for leather upholstery than if it calls for wool. Each may be as honest as his commercial posture permits, but anyone who offers anything "free" is horsetrading.

LANDSCAPE ARCHITECTS & INTERIOR DESIGNERS

A person who offers landscaping or interior design service for a definite fee, and who is totally free of interest in the sale of materials, can claim professional standing. Professional landscape architects and interior designers, like architects and professional engineers, exhibit different degrees of ability, but all of them devote what talents they have to serve your interest, not the interests of a nursery, department store, or furniture dealer.

The activities of architects and professional engineers are deemed to affect public health and safety, so one is not allowed to practice these professions until he has been examined by the state. No such restriction is placed on the practice of landscape architecture and interior design. Practitioners in these professions do, however, usually receive college training equal to that required of architects and engineers.

You can retain the services of a professional landscape architect and interior designer on the same terms as you retain the services of an architect. Each will interview you to determine the program for his work; prepare preliminary drawings and proposals for your approval; make working drawings and specifications and the other Contract Documents; assist in securing bids from nurseries, landscape contractors, and furnishings suppliers; and finally, observe and certify the work of the contractor. For this work the landscape architect and interior designer charge fees in the same manner as architects do. The advantages of the services of professional landscape architects and interior designers are the same as the advantages of having buildings built through the services of an architect, which is to say that if you are sensitive to the value of professional design, the service more than pays for itself.

ARCHITECTS

For the types of building projects this book is about, if it is desirable to have a landscape architect or interior designer, it is best to have the architect arrange for and supervise their services. Different kinds of projects suggest different arrangements. The organization to design a power station might best be headed by a mechanical or electrical engineer, with other engineers and architects working under him. The team designing a public park should probably be headed by a landscape architect with a civil engineer and an architect (if structures are involved) on the team. When the dominant element of the project is a building or group of buildings, however, the design organization should be supervised by an architect and include such other professionals as the size and scope of the project indicate. The purpose of organizing in this way is to foster unity of design. Unity means that each element of the design not only complements the other elements but also is subordinate to the central theme of the whole design. If buildings dominate, then the central theme should originate with the architect, which places him in the best position to understand and interpret it. He should therefore be the one to coordinate the work of all members of the team.

Nothing in landscape or interior design is mysterious to the architect. In fact, some interior designers begin their careers as architects. The artistic and practical principles of the three professions are the same. All three shape space to produce economical physical and psychological utility. They tend to employ different elements, such as plants, walls, and furniture, but each freely borrows from the arsenals of the others.

On a small or medium-size building project the architect can ordinarily be allowed to decide if either a landscape architect or interior designer is needed. Even on a very small project the architect may perceive complications that call for professional assistance, but even on a relatively large project the architect may be quite capable of designing the interiors and landscaping himself, especially if he accepts assistance and advice from nurserymen and decorators as he would from other contractors.

The choice of landscape or interior design firm may be one you wish to reserve for yourself, but whether you make the selection, leave it up to the architect, or the two of you choose jointly (the best way), the architect's leadership of the team should be made clear to everyone involved. This is no more than the application of a sound principle of organization. As owner, you of course remain the ultimate authority, and all design proposals are subject to your approval.

The optimum time to start the landscaping and interior design for all types of buildings is at the beginning of the project. The building program should be expanded as needed to include landscaping and interiors. Programming the total project right at the start, even if execution of part of it is delayed, not only promotes unity of design but also results in better allocation of funds. The alternative is all too common: a nice house surrounded by raw earth and containing only grandmother's superfluous furniture.

Sometimes, usually about halfway through construction of the building, no previous arrangement for landscaping or interiors having been made, the owner of a building project hires a decorator or interior designer, and a nurseryman or landscape architect. He instructs them to do their work. He tells them to consult with the architect along the way. He asks the architect to cooperate. The outcome may be quite successful if all parties concerned are talented, lucky, and saintly.

Chapter 14

CONTRACT DOCUMENTS

AFTER you approve the preliminary design, the architect will prepare the working drawings, specifications, general conditions, and contract form. These papers taken all together are called the *Contract Documents.* In order to understand their peculiarities, we need to get a little ahead of the story and discuss briefly the purposes they serve.

After the contractor has been selected, you and he will sign a Contract. Its nature is as follows: In return for your agreement to pay him the amount of his bid, he will construct the building in accordance with the Contract Documents. These documents must therefore set forth clearly both the details of the building and the conditions under which it is to be built. These conditions include such things as insurance the contractor must carry, bonds he must furnish, and others which we will consider in more detail below.

Before contruction begins, bidders use the complete set of Contract Documents as a basis for cost estimating. The resulting estimates are the basis for their bids. Normally the low bidder becomes the contractor, and his bid becomes the Contract amount.

Good Contract Documents are clear, consistent, inclusive, and of course, based on sound decisions. It is not necessary that drawings be works of drafting art, although neatness may contribute to clarity; nor is it necessary that specifications be grammatically correct, provided they are not ambiguous.

We saw in Chapter 6 that the architect allocates 40 to 50 per cent of his fee to the preparation of the Contract Documents. Knowing the number of employees available to work on the job, and the architect's normal hourly charge, we can roughly calculate how long it will take to produce the Contract Documents. Some time, however, must be allowed for slippage. The mechanical designer may have to wait for the structural designer to finish part of his work. An architectural draftsman may be held up waiting for information from a product manufacturer. A specifications writer may be held up by anyone and everyone. Some questions may arise that require your decision, and you may have to mull over them for a few days.

Of the total time required to prepare the Contract Documents, the working drawings take nine-tenths or more, and the specifications take most of the remainder.

To save time, the architectural firm can work overtime, but to do so means adding premium wages to the fee unless the firm works overtime to meet a previously agreed upon deadline.

WORKING DRAWINGS

The working drawings repeat the preliminary drawings at larger scale. This enlargement permits addition of the copious notes and dimensions needed to show the exact size, shape, location, and identity of all elements of the building. Working drawings also usually include several sections of the building that were not among the preliminary drawings. A very noticeable addition to the working drawings is details. Prominent among them will be one or more wall sections. These show the footings, foundation wall, wall above grade, window head and sill, and junction of wall with roof. Other details show door and window jambs, heads, sills, mullions, thresholds, and so forth. Additional details depend on characteristics of the particular building.

In any building the plumbing, electrical, and air-conditioning systems must be shown. In a house the plans are usually drawn at a scale of ¼ inch to the foot, which may be large enough to permit these systems to be shown along with architectural features on the same drawings. In other buildings entirely separate sets of floor plans will be drawn, with the walls shown in light lines and the air-conditioning and other systems drawn in heavy lines.

If the building is supported by a steel or concrete framework, the structural system will ordinarily be the subject of another set of plans and details, which for clarity, omit all architectural, mechanical, and electrical features. The conventional wood structure of most houses may not be drawn separately, but if it is, floor and roof framing plans usually appear on the same sheets as the floor plans.

Working drawings for a medium-size house are commonly on sheets about 24 by 36 inches in size, with the total number of sheets in the range of from three to ten. On larger jobs the sheets may be twice as large, and there may be a hundred or more of them. The number of drawings on each sheet varies, but if you leaf through a set of drawings, starting with the first sheet, you will usually encounter the following drawings in roughly this order:

1. Plot Plan.
2. Floor Plans, starting with the lowest, and proceeding upward to, and including, the roof.
3. Exterior Wall Elevations.
4. Sections of the whole building or large parts of it.
5. Wall Sections.
6. Other exterior and interior Details (some of these are often scattered about on preceding sheets).

Next will appear the structural drawings, if separate; starting with a foundation plan, followed by framing plans for each floor and the roof, with sections and Details as needed.

The mechanical systems account for the next set of plans. If these systems are especially complicated, there may be separate sets of plans for plumbing and air conditioning. The electrical system accounts for the final set of plans.

If there is to be a substantial amount of sitework, the plot plan may be drawn at large scale and augmented by details, grading sections, and so forth. These may run to several sheets and will come first in the complete set of working drawings.

All six of the working drawings for the Hauswirth residence are reproduced on the following pages. The originals were eight or nine times as large but had to be reduced in size to fit on these pages.

SPECIFICATIONS

The specifications Title Page at the end of this chapter shows the division numbers and titles recommended by the Construction Specifications Institute, 1965. Not all buildings will utilize all sixteen Divisions. Also reproduced at the end of the chapter is a sample of one complete division: Carpentry, which is presented as typical. A review of it should reveal the kind of information to be found in specifications.

Specifications are written, rather than graphic, and are produced in book form. They are organized into chapters, called divisions, each of which deals with the materials and workmanship for a single element or related group of elements of building construction. Division 3, Concrete, for example, specifies type and quality of cement and aggregate, method of mixing, required strength, method of construction and removal of form work, quality of reinforcing steel, and hundreds of other, related details.

(In the front of the specifications book you will also usually find the Contract form, general conditions, and some miscellaneous items, but they are not termed part of the specifications.)

GENERAL CONDITIONS

The general conditions are often subdivided under three headings, which at first sight must seem unnecessarily obfuscatory. Add that the conditions are bound in the front of the specifications book, appear in fine print, and exhibit legalistic language, and you can understand why one of my colleagues calls them "the front garbage." Actually the subdivision of the conditions is reasonable, the language comprehensible, and you can wear your glasses if the print is too small for the naked eye.

To get an idea of the sort of thing to be found in the conditions, glance first at the "Index to the Articles" in the illustrated sample. Then read two or three of the articles themselves. That will be enough for the moment.

The general conditions are fairly well standardized: The ones shown below have been developed by the A.I.A. and embody a century of experience on the part of thousands of architects, contractors, and building owners. They are largely applicable to any job anywhere in the country. On any particular job, however, some of the standard general conditions must be modified. Differences in lien laws in the various states often require modification to *Article 32. Liens.* If no "time of completion" (of construction) is stated in the Contract, then *Article 18. Delays and Extensions of Time,* is meaningless and may be omitted. As architects and contractors are familiar with the standard form, the best practice is to stipulate the standard form and then set forth modifications to it under the heading "Supplementary General Conditions." If, instead, the architect rewrote the general conditions, the contractor would have to restudy all of them.

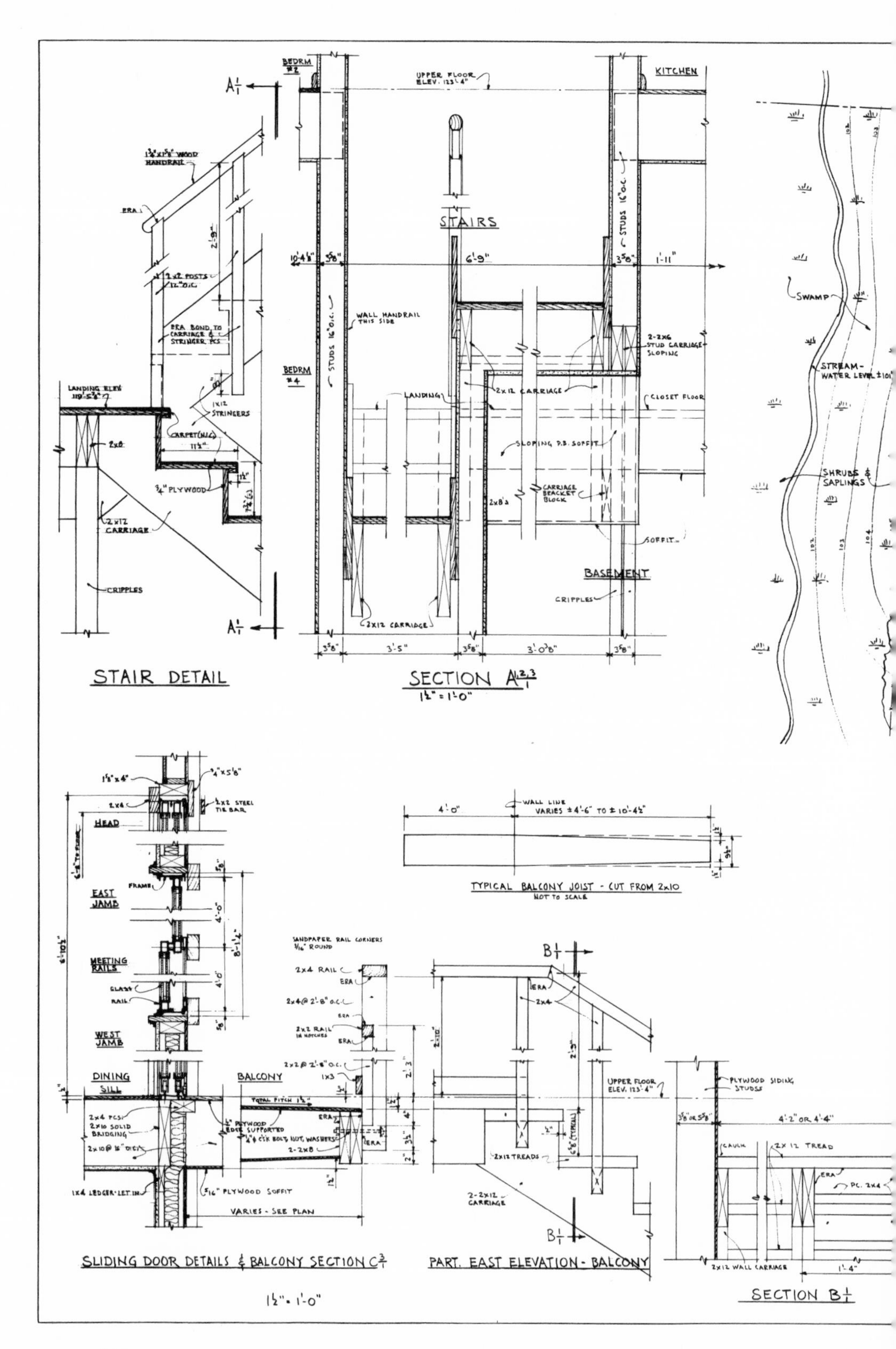

STAIR DETAIL
SECTION A 1,2,3/1
1½" = 1'-0"
STAIRS
UPPER FLOOR ELEV. 123'-4"
BEDRM #2
KITCHEN
BEDRM #4
BASEMENT
LANDING
WALL HANDRAIL THIS SIDE
2x12 CARRIAGE
SLOPING P.B. SOFFIT
CLOSET FLOOR
CRIPPLES
SOFFIT
1x12 STRINGERS
¾" PLYWOOD
CARPET (N.I.C.)
2x2 POSTS 12" O.C.
ERA
SWAMP
STREAM - WATER LEVEL ±101'
SHRUBS & SAPLINGS
TYPICAL BALCONY JOIST - CUT FROM 2x10
NOT TO SCALE
WALL LINE VARIES ±4'-6" TO ±10'-4½"
HEAD
EAST JAMB
MEETING RAILS
WEST JAMB
DINING SILL
BALCONY
SANDPAPER RAIL CORNERS 1/16" ROUND
2x4 RAIL
2x2 RAIL IN NOTCHES
VARIES - SEE PLAN
SLIDING DOOR DETAILS & BALCONY SECTION C 3/1
PART. EAST ELEVATION - BALCONY
2x12 TREADS
2-2x12 CARRIAGE
UPPER FLOOR ELEV. 123'-4"
PLYWOOD SIDING STUDS
2x12 TREAD
2x12 WALL CARRIAGE
SECTION B 1/1
1½" = 1'-0"

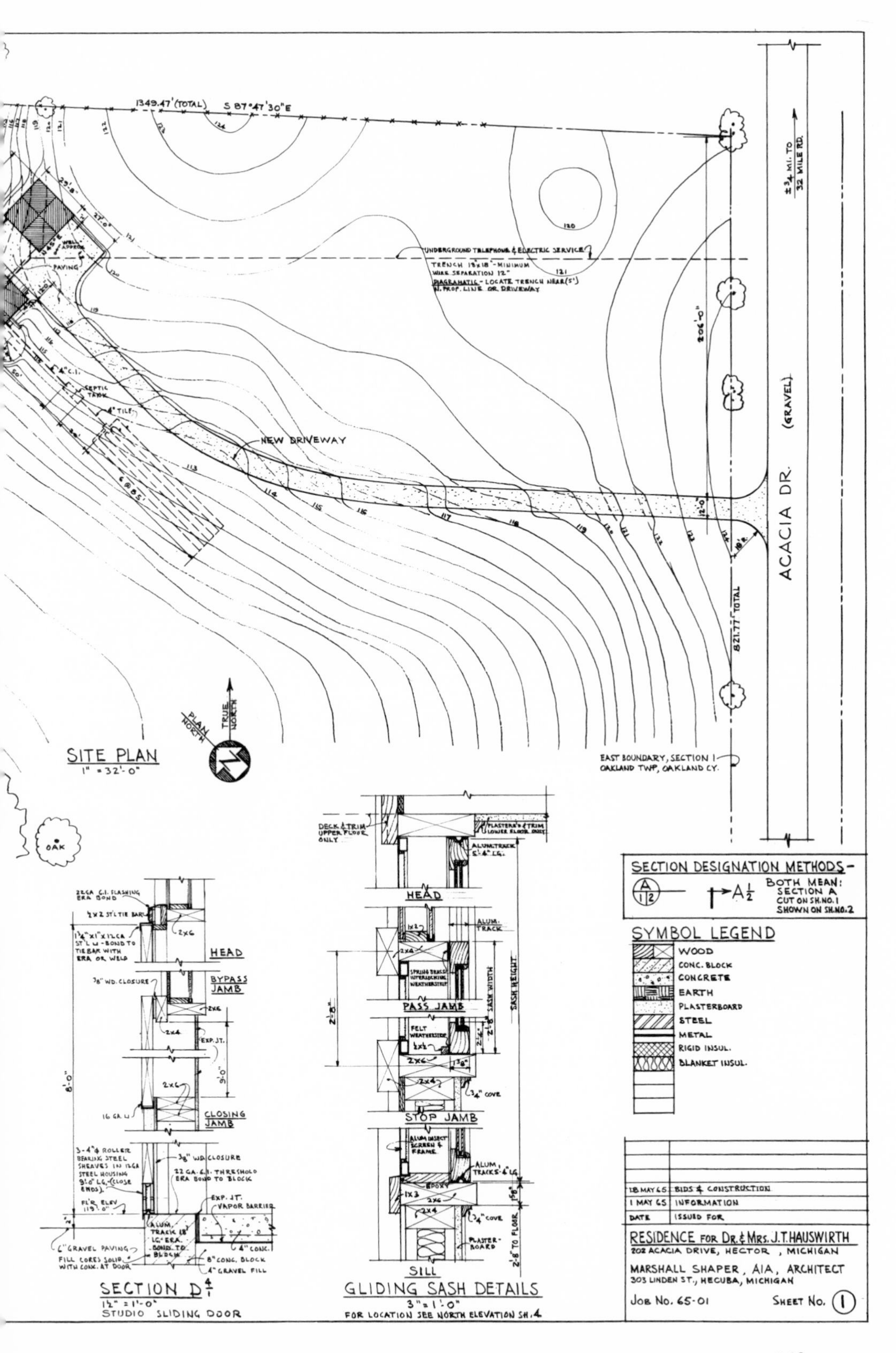

1349.47' (TOTAL) S 87°47'30"E
UNDERGROUND TELEPHONE & ELECTRIC SERVICE
TRENCH 18"x18" - MINIMUM WIRE SEPARATION 12"
DIAGRAMATIC - LOCATE TRENCH NEAR (5') N. PROP. LINE OR DRIVEWAY
±3/4 MI. TO 32 MILE RD.
206'-0"
NEW DRIVEWAY
PAVING
SEPTIC TANK
4" TILE
(GRAVEL)
ACACIA DR.
821.77' TOTAL
SITE PLAN
1" = 32'-0"
TRUE NORTH
PLAN NORTH
EAST BOUNDARY, SECTION 1 OAKLAND TWP, OAKLAND CY.
OAK
SECTION DESIGNATION METHODS -
BOTH MEAN: SECTION A CUT ON SH.NO.1 SHOWN ON SH.NO.2
SYMBOL LEGEND
WOOD
CONC. BLOCK
CONCRETE
EARTH
PLASTERBOARD
STEEL
METAL
RIGID INSUL.
BLANKET INSUL.
HEAD
BYPASS JAMB
CLOSING JAMB
SECTION D 4/1
1 1/2" = 1'-0"
STUDIO SLIDING DOOR
DECK & TRIM UPPER FLOOR ONLY
PLASTERBD & TRIM LOWER FLOOR ONLY
HEAD
PASS JAMB
STOP JAMB
SILL
SASH WIDTH
SASH HEIGHT
GLIDING SASH DETAILS
3" = 1'-0"
FOR LOCATION SEE NORTH ELEVATION SH. 4
18 MAY 65 BIDS & CONSTRUCTION
1 MAY 65 INFORMATION
DATE ISSUED FOR
RESIDENCE FOR DR. & MRS. J.T. HAUSWIRTH
202 ACACIA DRIVE, HECTOR, MICHIGAN
MARSHALL SHAPER, AIA, ARCHITECT
303 LINDEN ST., HECUBA, MICHIGAN
JOB NO. 65-01
SHEET NO. 1

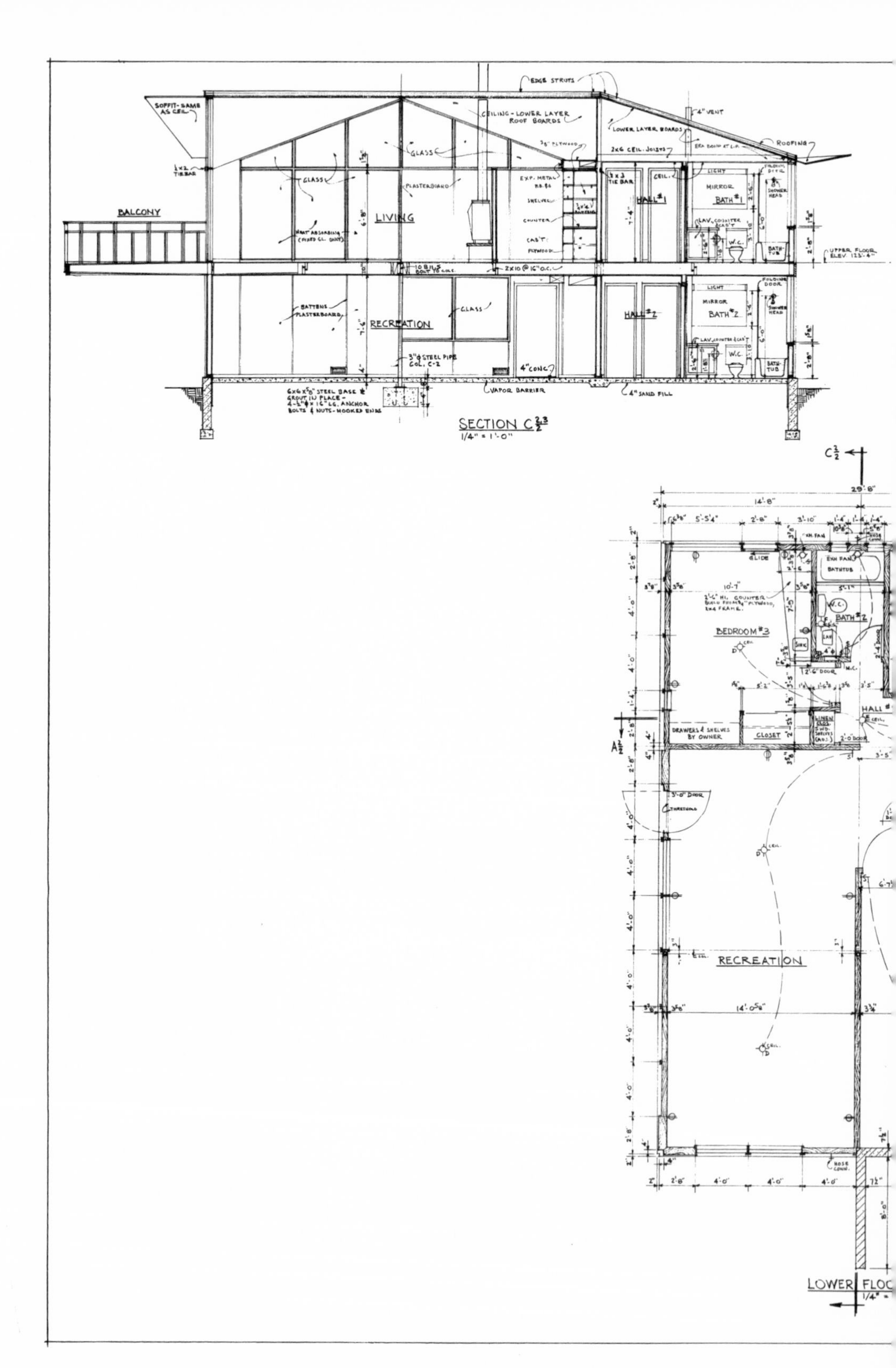
SECTION C 2 3/2
1/4" = 1'-0"
BALCONY
LIVING
RECREATION
HALL #1
HALL #2
BATH #1
BATH #2
EDGE STRUTS
CEILING - LOWER LAYER ROOF BOARDS
LOWER LAYER BOARDS
4" VENT
ROOFING
SOFFIT - SAME AS CEIL.
GLASS
PLASTERBOARD
VAPOR BARRIER
4" SAND FILL
4" CONC
BEDROOM #3
CLOSET
DRAWERS & SHELVES BY OWNER
LOWER FLOO

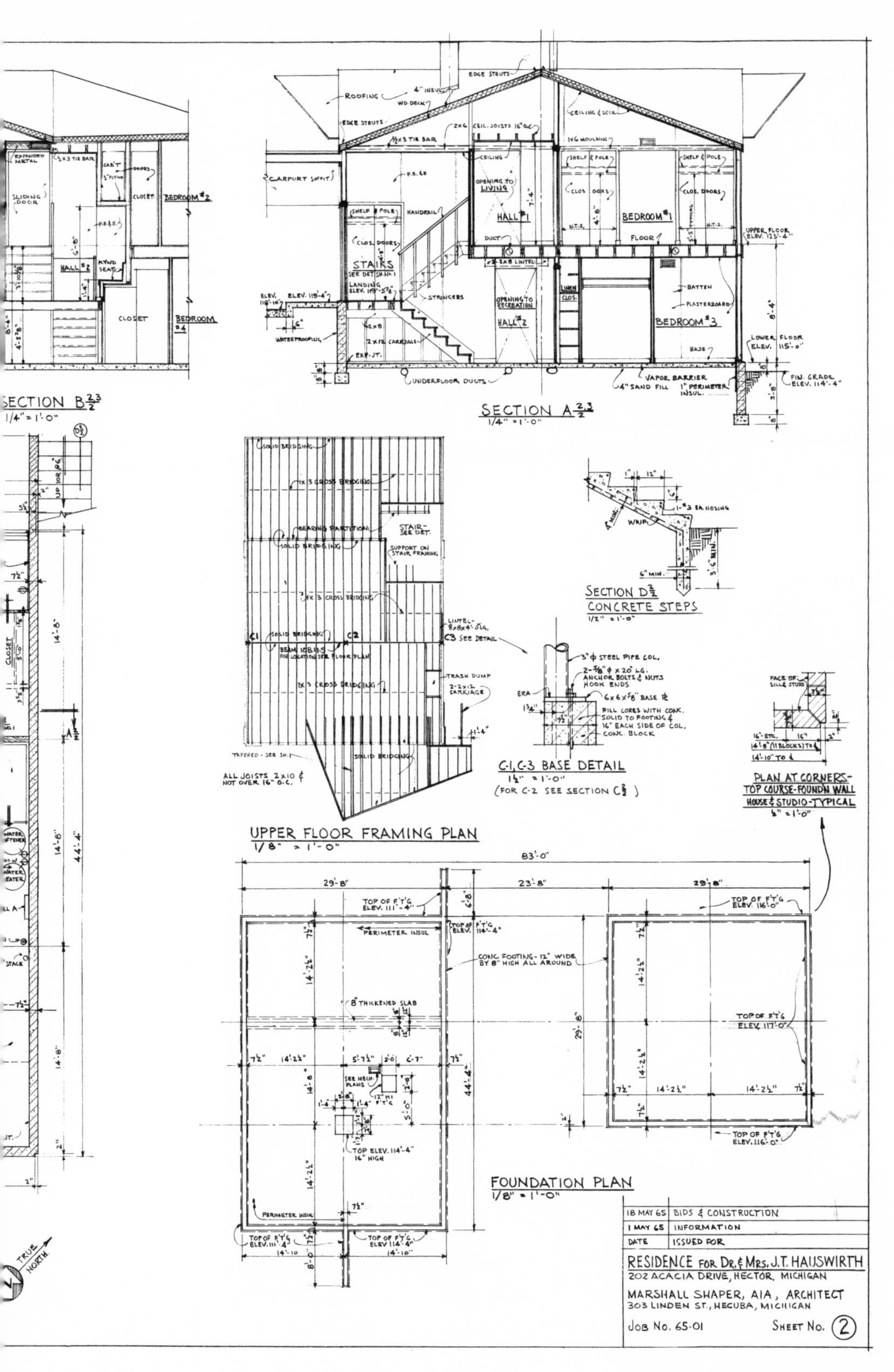
SECTION B 2,3/2
1/4" = 1'-0"
SECTION A 2,3/2
1/4" = 1'-0"
BEDROOM #2
BEDROOM #4
HALL #2
CLOSET
SLIDING DOOR
EDGE STRUTS
ROOFING
WD. DECK
4" INSUL.
2x6 CEIL. JOISTS 16" O.C.
CEILING & DECK
1x6 MOULDING
CARPORT SOFFIT
SHELF & POLE
CLOS. DOORS
HANDRAIL
STAIRS
SEE DET. SH. No. 1
LANDING
ELEV. 119'-5 7/8"
STRINGERS
OPENING TO LIVING
HALL #1
DUCT
2x8 LINTEL
OPENING TO RECREATION
HALL #2
LINEN CLOS.
BEDROOM #1
FLOOR
BEDROOM #3
BATTEN
PLASTERBOARD
BASE
UPPER FLOOR ELEV. 123'-4"
LOWER FLOOR ELEV. 115'-0"
FIN. GRADE ELEV. 114'-4"
VAPOR BARRIER
4" SAND FILL
1" PERIMETER INSUL.
UNDERFLOOR DUCTS
WATERPROOFING
EXP. JT.
2x12 CARRIAGE
UPPER FLOOR FRAMING PLAN
1/8" = 1'-0"
SOLID BRIDGING
1x3 CROSS BRIDGING
BEARING PARTITION
STAIR- SEE DET.
SUPPORT ON STAIR FRAMING
LINTEL- 8x8x4·5 LG.
C3 SEE DETAIL
BEAM 18B11.5 FOR LOCATION SEE FLOOR PLAN
TRASH DUMP
2-2x12 CARRIAGE
TAPERED - SEE SH. 1
ALL JOISTS 2x10 & NOT OVER 16" O.C.
SECTION D 3/2
CONCRETE STEPS
1/2" = 1'-0"
1-#3 EA. NOSING
WWF
6" MIN.
3'-6" MIN.
3" φ STEEL PIPE COL.
2-5/8" φ x 20" LG. ANCHOR BOLTS & NUTS HOOK ENDS
6x6x5/8" BASE ℄
FILL CORES WITH CONC. SOLID TO FOOTING & 16" EACH SIDE OF COL.
CONC. BLOCK
C-1, C-3 BASE DETAIL
1 1/2" = 1'-0"
(FOR C-2 SEE SECTION C 3/2)
FACE OF SILL & STUDS
14'-10" TO ℄
PLAN AT CORNERS-
TOP COURSE-FOUND'N WALL
HOUSE & STUDIO-TYPICAL
1/2" = 1'-0"
83'-0"
29'-8"
23'-8"
TOP OF F'T'G ELEV. 111'-4"
TOP OF F'T'G ELEV. 114'-4"
TOP OF F'T'G ELEV. 116'-0"
TOP OF F'T'G ELEV. 117'-0"
PERIMETER INSUL.
CONC. FOOTING - 12" WIDE BY 8" HIGH ALL AROUND
8" THICKENED SLAB
SEE MECH. PLANS
TOP ELEV. 114'-4" 16" HIGH
44'-4"
FOUNDATION PLAN
1/8" = 1'-0"
TRUE NORTH
18 MAY 65 | BIDS & CONSTRUCTION
1 MAY 65 | INFORMATION
DATE | ISSUED FOR
RESIDENCE FOR DR. & MRS. J.T. HAUSWIRTH
202 ACACIA DRIVE, HECTOR, MICHIGAN
MARSHALL SHAPER, AIA, ARCHITECT
303 LINDEN ST., HECUBA, MICHIGAN
JOB No. 65-01
SHEET No. 2

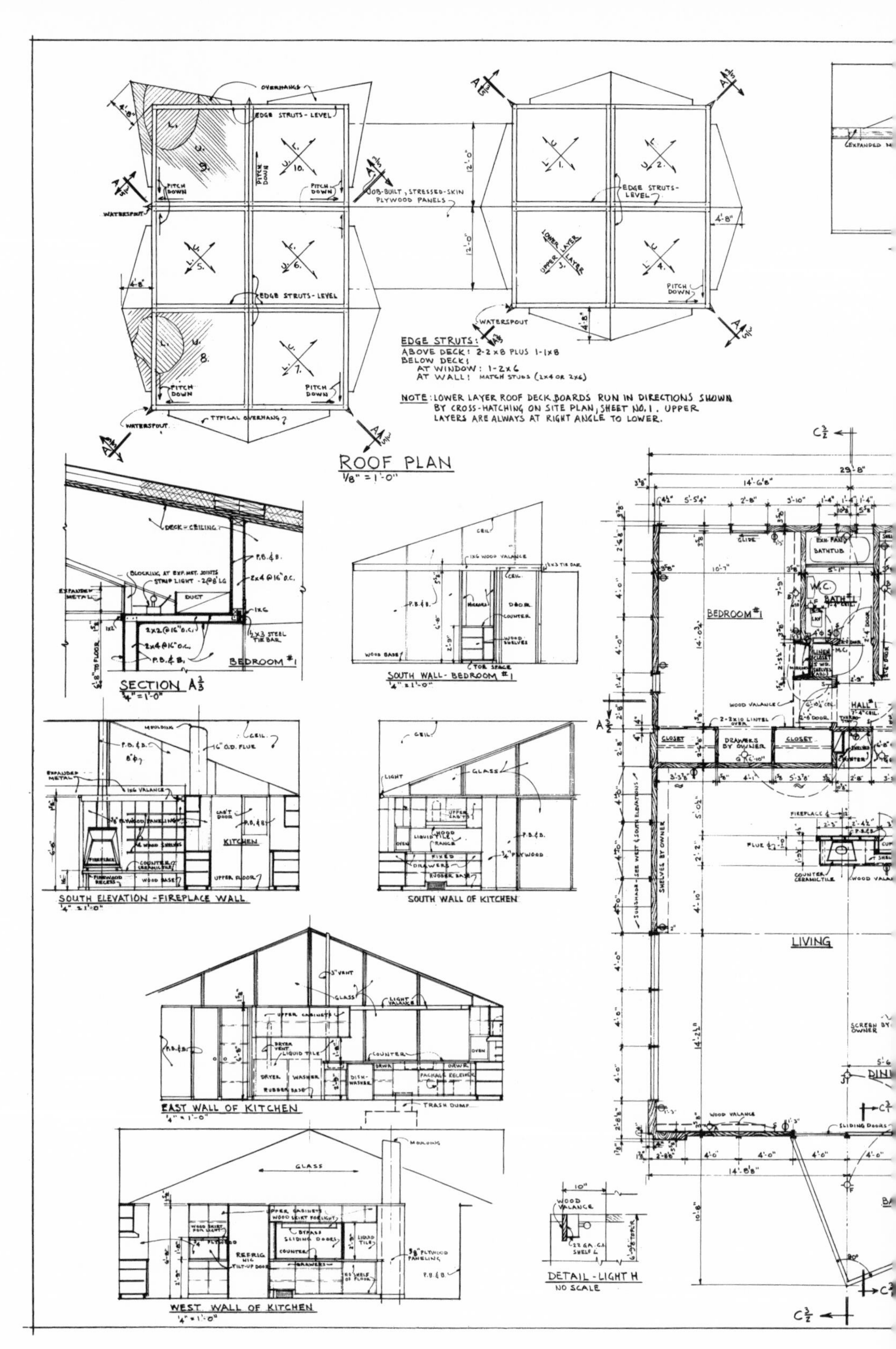
ROOF PLAN
1/8" = 1'-0"
OVERHANGS
EDGE STRUTS - LEVEL
JOB-BUILT, STRESSED-SKIN PLYWOOD PANELS
PITCH DOWN
WATERSPOUT
TYPICAL OVERHANG
EDGE STRUTS:
ABOVE DECK: 2-2x8 PLUS 1-1x8
BELOW DECK:
AT WINDOW: 1-2x6
AT WALL: MATCH STUDS (2x4 OR 2x6)
NOTE: LOWER LAYER ROOF DECK BOARDS RUN IN DIRECTIONS SHOWN BY CROSS-HATCHING ON SITE PLAN, SHEET NO. 1. UPPER LAYERS ARE ALWAYS AT RIGHT ANGLE TO LOWER.
SECTION A 3/3
1/4" = 1'-0"
BEDROOM #1
SOUTH WALL - BEDROOM #1
1/4" = 1'-0"
SOUTH ELEVATION - FIREPLACE WALL
1/4" = 1'-0"
KITCHEN
SOUTH WALL OF KITCHEN
EAST WALL OF KITCHEN
1/4" = 1'-0"
TRASH DUMP
WEST WALL OF KITCHEN
1/4" = 1'-0"
DETAIL - LIGHT H
NO SCALE
BEDROOM #1
BATH #1
HALL #1
CLOSET
LIVING
EXPANDED METAL

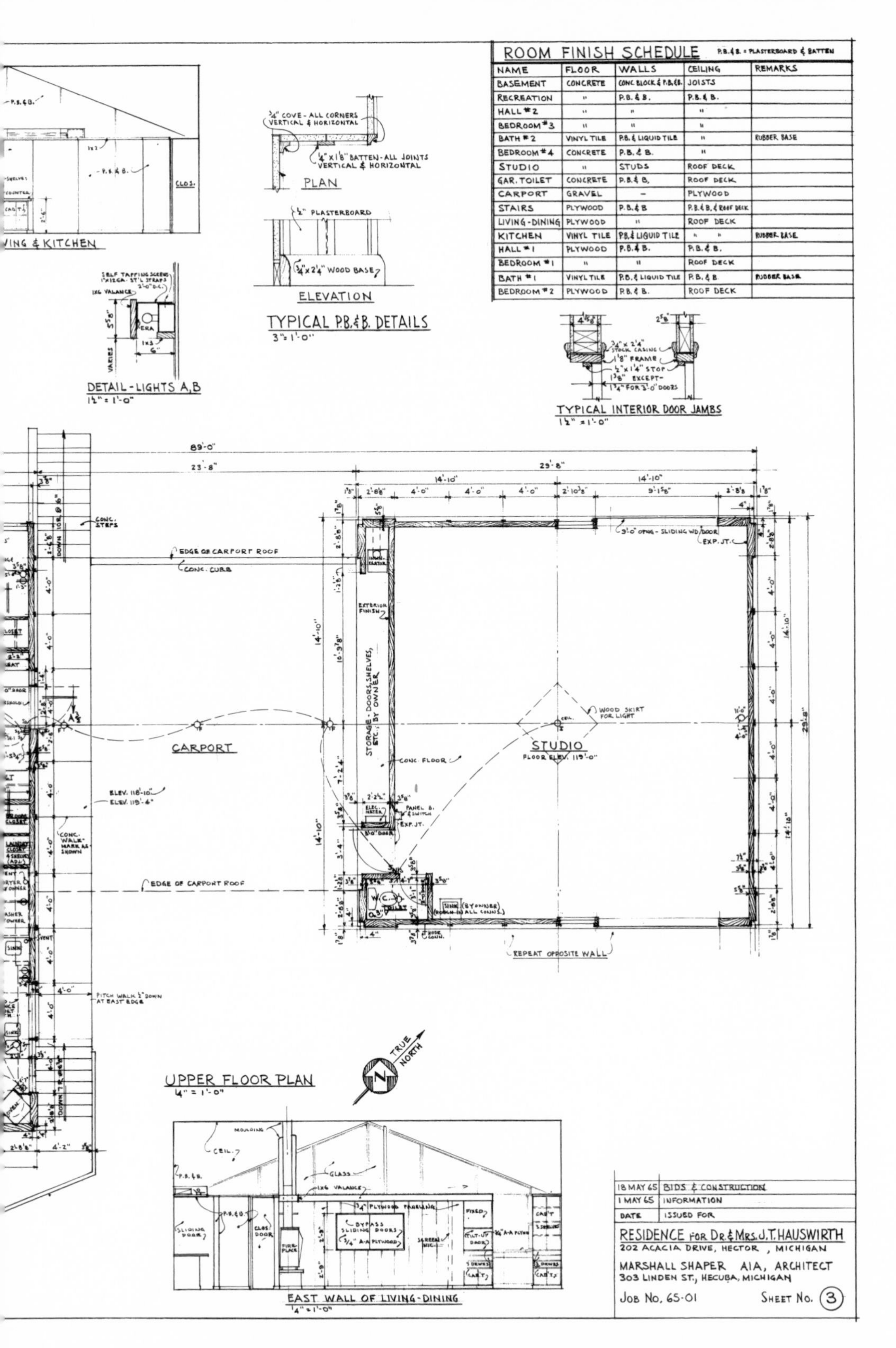

ROOM FINISH SCHEDULE P.B.&B. = PLASTERBOARD & BATTEN

NAME	FLOOR	WALLS	CEILING	REMARKS
BASEMENT	CONCRETE	CONC. BLOCK & P.B.&B.	JOISTS	
RECREATION	"	P.B. & B.	P.B. & B.	
HALL #2	"	"	"	
BEDROOM #3	"	"	"	
BATH #2	VINYL TILE	P.B. & LIQUID TILE	"	RUBBER BASE
BEDROOM #4	CONCRETE	P.B. & B.	"	
STUDIO	"	STUDS	ROOF DECK	
GAR. TOILET	CONCRETE	P.B. & B.	ROOF DECK	
CARPORT	GRAVEL	–	PLYWOOD	
STAIRS	PLYWOOD	P.B. & B	P.B. & B. & ROOF DECK	
LIVING-DINING	PLYWOOD	"	ROOF DECK	
KITCHEN	VINYL TILE	P.B. & LIQUID TILE	" "	RUBBER BASE
HALL #1	PLYWOOD	P.B. & B.	P.B. & B.	
BEDROOM #1	"	"	ROOF DECK	
BATH #1	VINYL TILE	P.B. & LIQUID TILE	P.B. & B	RUBBER BASE
BEDROOM #2	PLYWOOD	P.B. & B.	ROOF DECK	

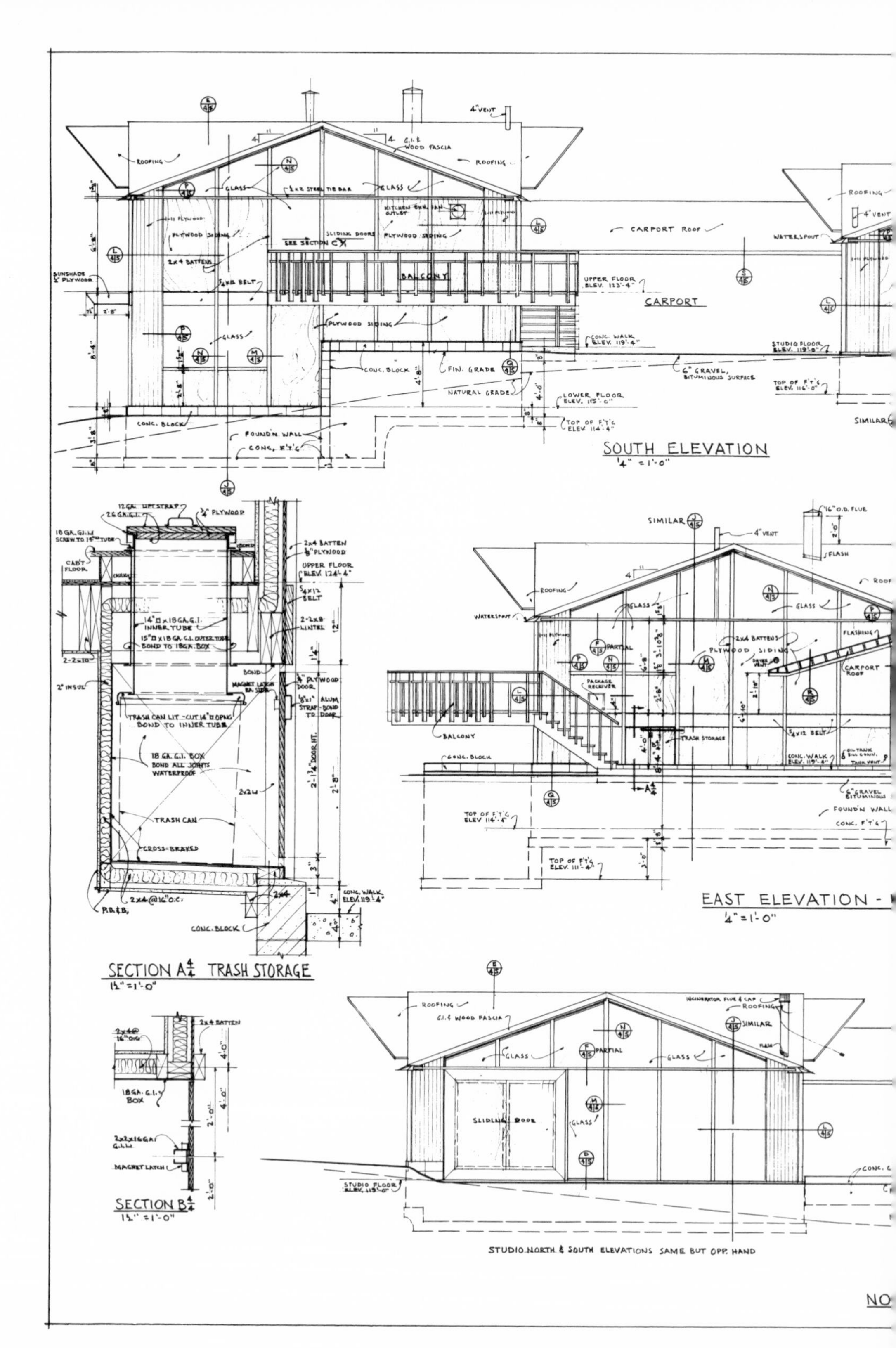
SOUTH ELEVATION
¼" = 1'-0"
CARPORT
BALCONY
CARPORT ROOF
SECTION A 4/4 TRASH STORAGE
1½" = 1'-0"
SECTION B 4/4
1½" = 1'-0"
EAST ELEVATION
¼" = 1'-0"
STUDIO NORTH & SOUTH ELEVATIONS SAME BUT OPP. HAND

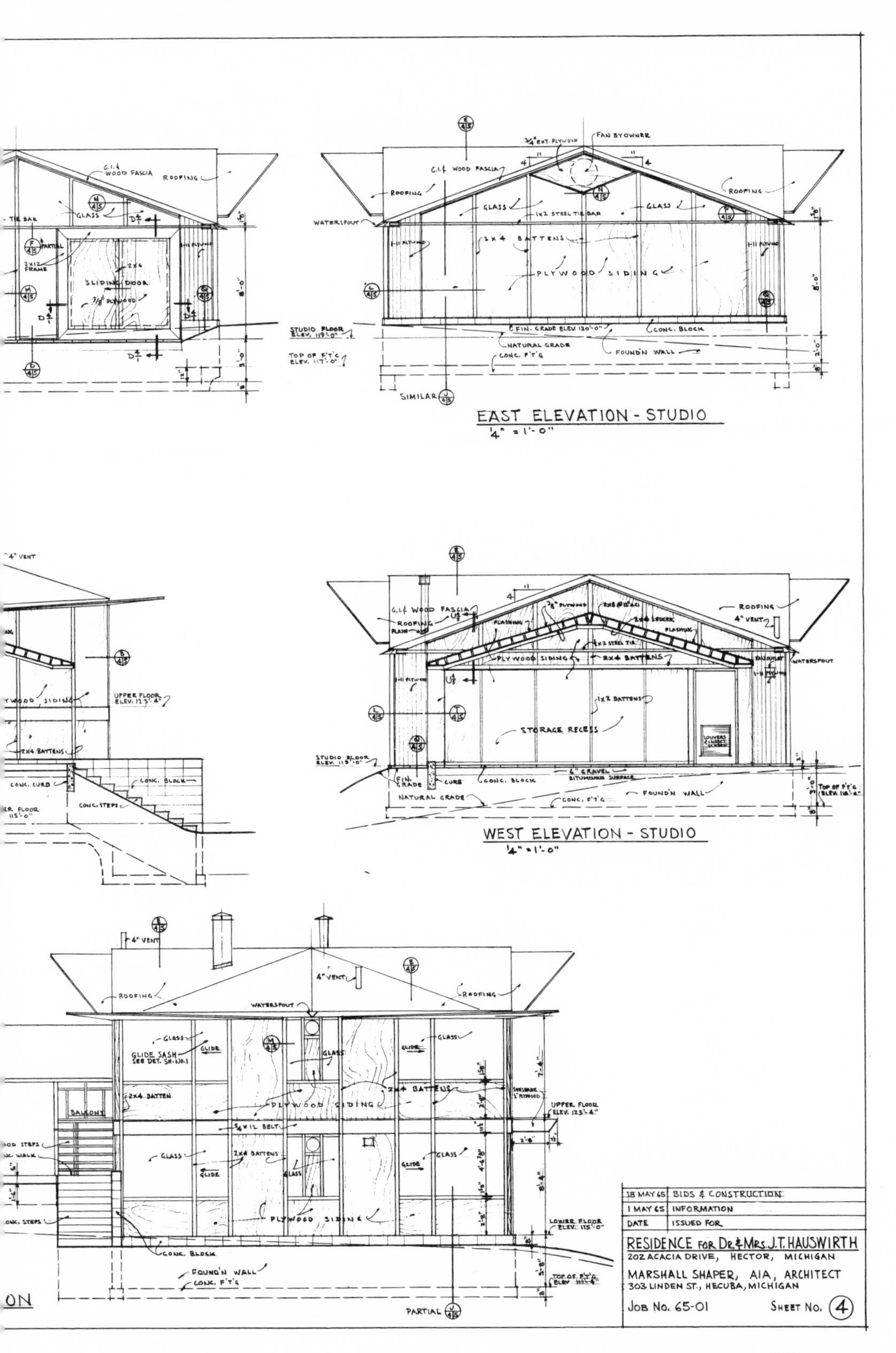
EAST ELEVATION - STUDIO
¼" = 1'-0"
WEST ELEVATION - STUDIO
¼" = 1'-0"
ON
18 MAY 65 BIDS & CONSTRUCTION
1 MAY 65 INFORMATION
DATE ISSUED FOR
RESIDENCE FOR Dr. & Mrs. J.T. HAUSWIRTH
202 ACACIA DRIVE, HECTOR, MICHIGAN
MARSHALL SHAPER, AIA, ARCHITECT
303 LINDEN ST., HECUBA, MICHIGAN
JOB No. 65-01
SHEET No. 4

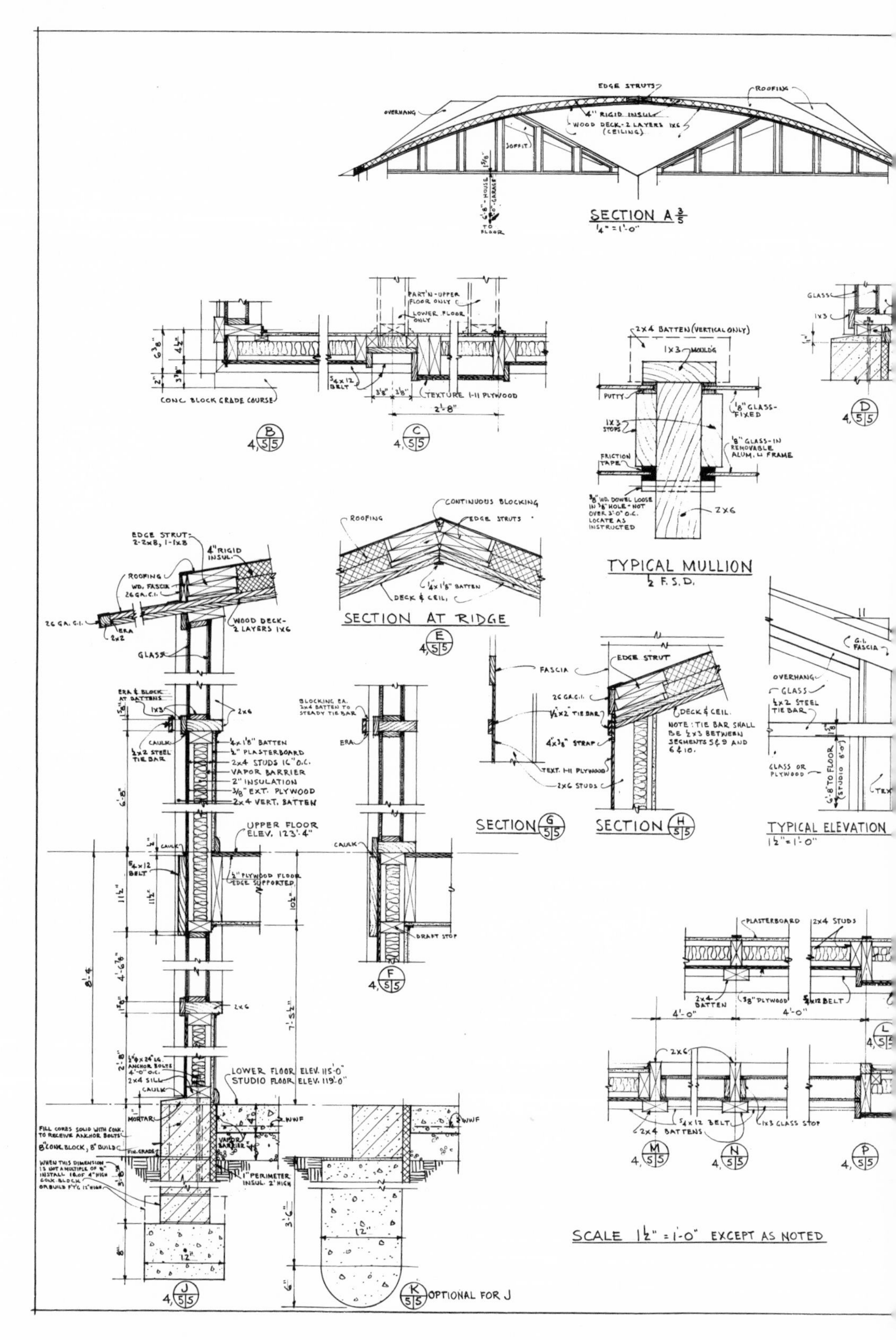

EDGE STRUTS
ROOFING
OVERHANG
4" RIGID INSUL.
WOOD DECK - 2 LAYERS 1x6 (CEILING)
SOFFIT
TO FLOOR
SECTION A 3/5
1/4" = 1'-0"
PART'N - UPPER FLOOR ONLY
LOWER FLOOR ONLY
5/4 x 12 BELT
TEXTURE 1-11 PLYWOOD
CONC BLOCK GRADE COURSE
2'-8"
4, B 5|5
4, C 5|5
2x4 BATTEN (VERTICAL ONLY)
1x3 MOULD'G
PUTTY
1x3 STOPS
1/8" GLASS - FIXED
1/8" GLASS - IN REMOVABLE ALUM. L FRAME
FRICTION TAPE
3/8" WD. DOWEL LOOSE IN 1/2" HOLE - NOT OVER 3'-0" O.C. LOCATE AS INSTRUCTED
2x6
TYPICAL MULLION
1/2 F.S.D.
GLASS
1x3
4, D 5|5
CONTINUOUS BLOCKING
ROOFING
EDGE STRUTS
1/4 x 1 1/8" BATTEN
DECK & CEIL.
SECTION AT RIDGE
4, E 5|5
EDGE STRUT: 2-2x8, 1-1x8
4" RIGID INSUL.
ROOFING
WD. FASCIA
26 GA. G.I.
ERA
2x2
WOOD DECK - 2 LAYERS 1x6
GLASS
ERA & BLOCK AT BATTENS
1x3
2x6
CAULK
1/2 x 2 STEEL TIE BAR
1/4 x 1 1/8" BATTEN
1/2" PLASTERBOARD
2x4 STUDS 16" O.C.
VAPOR BARRIER
2" INSULATION
3/8" EXT. PLYWOOD
2x4 VERT. BATTEN
UPPER FLOOR ELEV. 123'-4"
5/4 x 12 BELT
3/4" PLYWOOD FLOOR EDGE SUPPORTED
LOWER FLOOR ELEV. 115'-0"
STUDIO FLOOR ELEV. 119'-0"
2x4 SILL
MORTAR
FILL CORES SOLID WITH CONC. TO RECEIVE ANCHOR BOLTS
8" CONC. BLOCK, 8" BUILD'G
FIN. GRADE
VAPOR BARRIER
WWF
1" PERIMETER INSUL. 2' HIGH
12"
4, J 5|5
K 5|5 OPTIONAL FOR J
BLOCKING EA. 2x4 BATTEN TO STEADY TIE BAR
ERA
CAULK
DRAFT STOP
4, F 5|5
FASCIA
TEXT. 1-11 PLYWOOD
SECTION G 5|5
EDGE STRUT
26 GA. G.I.
1/2 x 2" TIE BAR
4" x 3/8" STRAP
2x6 STUDS
DECK & CEIL.
NOTE: TIE BAR SHALL BE 1/2 x 3 BETWEEN SEGMENTS 5 & 9 AND 6 & 10.
SECTION H 5|5
G.I. FASCIA
OVERHANG
GLASS
1/2 x 2 STEEL TIE BAR
GLASS OR PLYWOOD
6'-8" TO FLOOR (STUDIO 8'-0")
TYPICAL ELEVATION
1 1/2" = 1'-0"
PLASTERBOARD
2x4 STUDS
2x4 BATTEN
3/8" PLYWOOD
5/4 x 12 BELT
4'-0"
4'-0"
2x6
2x4 BATTENS
5/4 x 12 BELT
1x3 GLASS STOP
4, L 5|5
4, M 5|5
4, N 5|5
4, P 5|5
SCALE 1 1/2" = 1'-0" EXCEPT AS NOTED

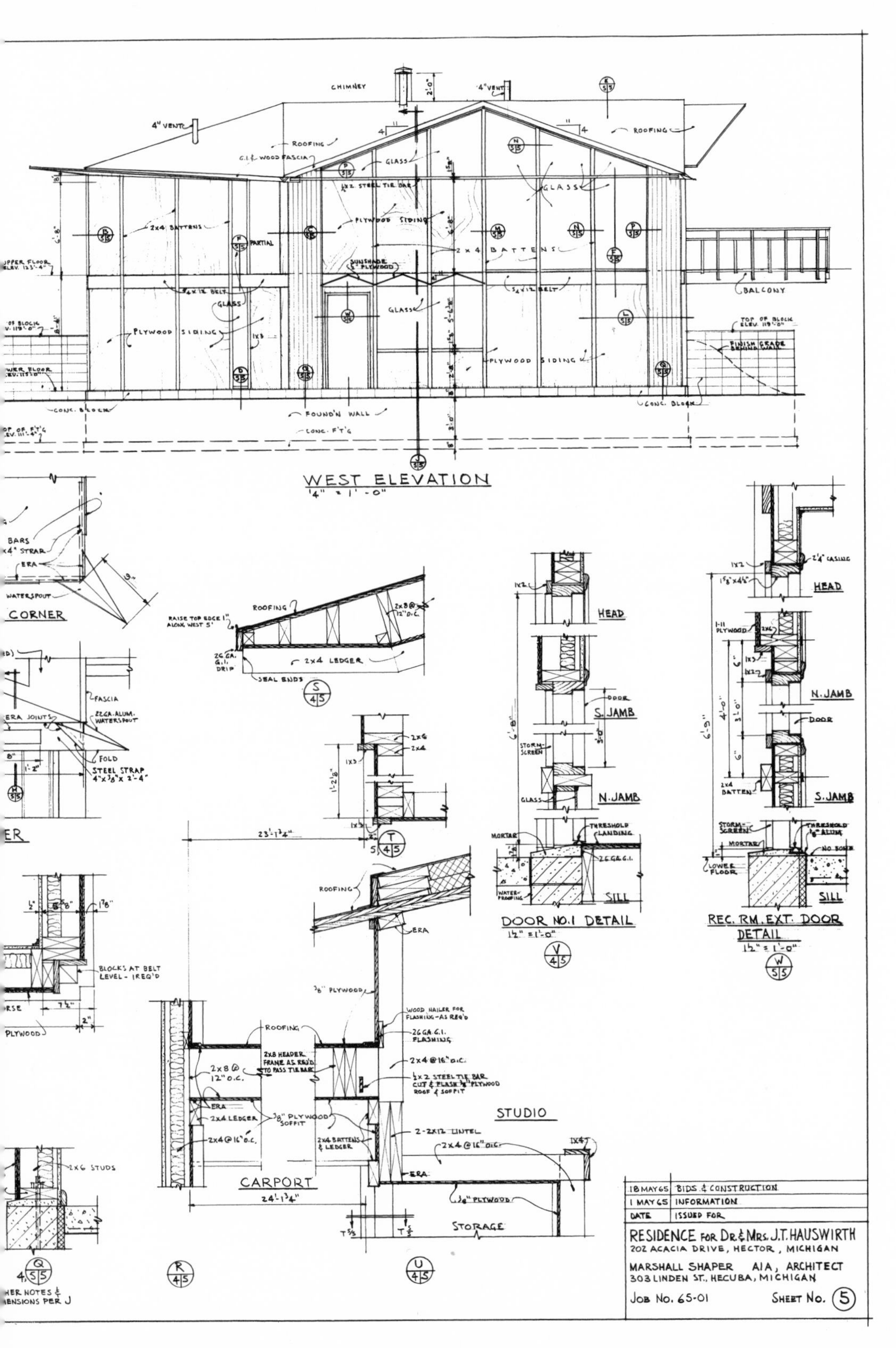

WEST ELEVATION
1/4" = 1'-0"
CHIMNEY
4" VENT
ROOFING
G.I. & WOOD FASCIA
GLASS
1/2 x 2 STEEL TIE BAR
PLYWOOD SIDING
2x4 BATTENS
PARTIAL
SUNSHADE
5/4 x 12 BELT
1x3
BALCONY
TOP OF BLOCK ELEV. 119'-0"
FINISH GRADE
CONC. BLOCK
FOUND'N WALL
CONC. F'T'G
CORNER
BARS
WATERSPOUT
FASCIA
22 GA. ALUM. WATERSPOUT
FOLD
STEEL STRAP
RAISE TOP EDGE 1" ALONG WEST 5'
26 GA. G.I. DRIP
2x4 LEDGER
SEAL ENDS
2x6
2x4
HEAD
S. JAMB
N. JAMB
DOOR
STORM-SCREEN
MORTAR
THRESHOLD
LANDING
26 GA. G.I.
WATER-PROOFING
SILL
DOOR NO. 1 DETAIL
1 1/2" = 1'-0"
2 1/4" CASING
1-11 PLYWOOD
2x4 BATTEN
LOWER FLOOR
REC. RM. EXT. DOOR DETAIL
1 1/2" = 1'-0"
BLOCKS AT BELT LEVEL - 1 REQ'D
PLYWOOD
23'-1 3/4"
3/8" PLYWOOD
WOOD NAILER FOR FLASHING - AS REQ'D
26 GA. G.I. FLASHING
2x4 @ 16" O.C.
2x8 HEADER FRAME AS REQ'D TO PASS TIE BAR
1/2 x 2 STEEL TIE BAR CUT & FLASH 3/8" PLYWOOD ROOF & SOFFIT
2x8 @ 12" O.C.
ERA
2x4 LEDGER
3/8" PLYWOOD SOFFIT
2x4 @ 16" O.C.
2x4 BATTENS & LEDGER
2-2x12 LINTEL
STUDIO
CARPORT
24'-1 3/4"
STORAGE
2x6 STUDS
OTHER NOTES & DIMENSIONS PER J
18 MAY 65 BIDS & CONSTRUCTION
1 MAY 65 INFORMATION
DATE ISSUED FOR
RESIDENCE FOR DR. & MRS. J.T. HAUSWIRTH
202 ACACIA DRIVE, HECTOR, MICHIGAN
MARSHALL SHAPER AIA, ARCHITECT
303 LINDEN ST., HECUBA, MICHIGAN
JOB NO. 65-01
SHEET NO. 5

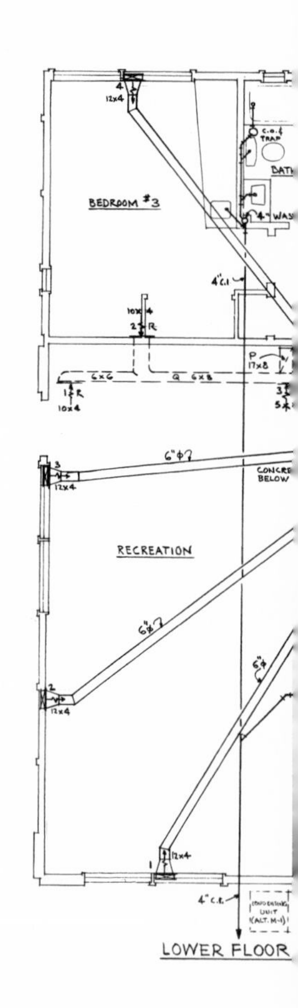
BEDROOM #3
RECREATION
LOWER FLOOR

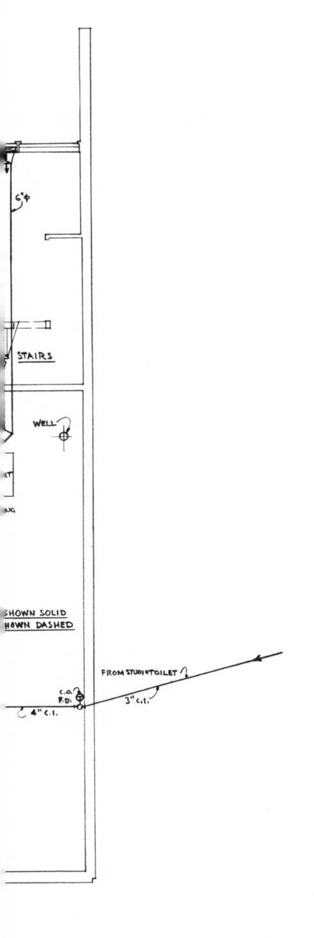

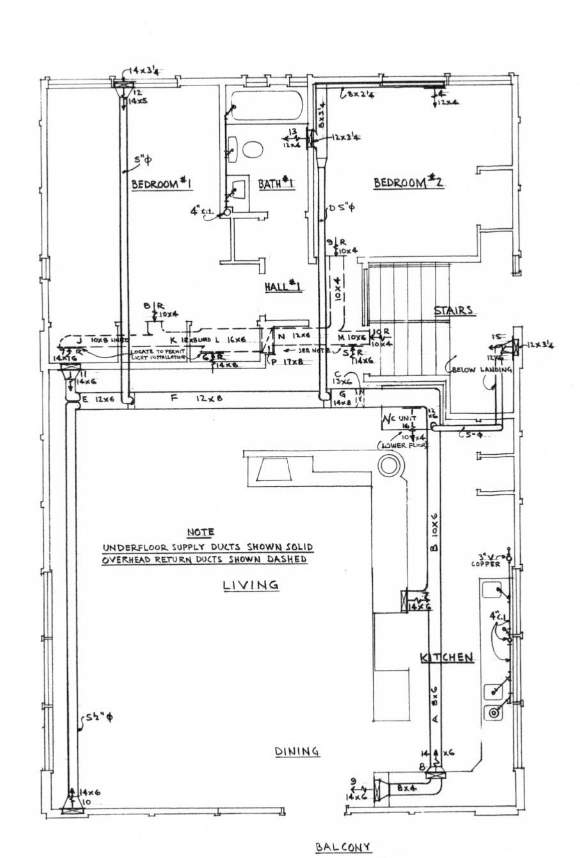

UPPER FLOOR DISTRIBUTION

DUCT & DRAINAGE PLANS

1/4" = 1'-0"

18 MAY 65	BIDS & CONSTRUCTION
1 MAY 65	INFORMATION
DATE	ISSUED FOR

RESIDENCE FOR DR. & MRS. J. T. HAUSWIRTH
202 ACACIA DRIVE, HECTOR, MICHIGAN
MARSHALL SHAPER, AIA, ARCHITECT
303 LINDEN ST., HECUBA, MICHIGAN
JOB NO. 65-01 SHEET NO. 6

On a particular job it may also be necessary to include some conditions not covered in the standard form. On a remodeling job, for instance, if the contractor will be required to pursue his work in such a way that normal operation of the building is not interrupted, the details of this requirement would be a special general condition. The owner of a building project might wish to prohibit the taking of unauthorized photographs during construction, and this prohibition would also be a special condition. The architect often feels it unnecessary to distinguish between special and supplementary general conditions. Then he will probably group them under a single heading, and they, along with the standard general conditions, will comprise the conditions of the Contract.

AGREEMENT BETWEEN OWNER AND CONTRACTOR

The last Contract Document to be considered here is the Agreement between owner and contractor. Earlier I said I would call it simply the Contract. Like the conditions, it is often a standard form. It is short, and consists of articles that necessarily vary with every job. It names the owner and contractor (the parties), states the date of the Contract and time of completion of construction, manner of payment, and Contract amount. It also lists the other Contract Documents.

CONTRACT DOCUMENTS IN GENERAL

To summarize, the Contract Documents include:

1. Contract (Agreement Between Owner and Contractor).
2. Conditions: General, Supplementary, and Special.
3. Specifications.
4. Drawings.

In the sample, *General Conditions, Article 2* says "The Contract Documents are complementary, and what is called for by any one shall be as binding as if called for by all. The intention of the documents is to include all labor and materials, equipment and transportation necessary for the proper execution of the work." Later in the same article appears an important but obscurely worded sentence which should be clearly understood. It says, in effect, that the contractor must supply materials and labor even if nowhere shown on the drawings or called for in the specifications if such materials or labor are necessary to accomplish the intended results. If, for instance, the drawings show a bathtub, the contractor must connect it to the water and drainage piping, whether or not such connection is explicitly called for, because otherwise the obvious intent of the bathtub could not be accomplished.

YOUR APPROVAL OF CONTRACT DOCUMENTS

Although working drawings and specifications mainly amplify and augment the preliminary design, some new questions will arise during their preparation. Most of these questions are technical, and the architect will seek the answers in manufacturers' literature, or manuals, or he will consult specialists or his own judgment. Some questions, however, he will refer to you. These will have to do with minor improvements or difficulties that prolonged contact with the design has brought to mind. Aside from answering such questions, you will have little to do with the job during this stage.

When the drawings and specifications are nearly finished, they will be reproduced and a set or two forwarded for your approval. (The specifications and conditions will probably be in typed-draft form.) As these documents embody, among other things, thousands of esoteric decisions whose wisdom you cannot be expected to evaluate, you may well wonder just what your approval is supposed to signify.

Your approval does not relieve the architect of any of his professional obligations. He remains responsible for such things as structural adequacy and conformity of the design to local laws. He also remains responsible for carrying out your instructions. If some of your instructions conflicted, of course, this means the latest of the conflicting ones. Your instructions include the original program, the approved preliminary design, and any subsequent additions or changes you may have communicated to the architect.

Your approval of the Contract Documents, therefore, means that you have no further instructions for the architect before the job is put out for contractors' bids. It means, furthermore, that in any matter where professional competence permits the architect a choice, and where you have indicated no preference, you ratify the architect's decision. He may, for instance, choose 1⅜-inches-thick wood doors on the grounds that they are cheaper than 1¾-inch doors, or he may choose 1¾-inch doors on the grounds that they are sturdier than 1⅜-inch doors. If you express no preference, you accept his decision, whichever he chose.

If you have, in fact, given the architect all the instructions you wish to give him, then perhaps you could approve the working drawings and specifications sight unseen. You could, but I don't recommend it. There are at least three good reasons for reviewing the Contract Documents. If you hesitate because you fear you won't be able to make head or tail of them, you exaggerate. Anyone can make some sense of these documents, and most people can read them all, given enough time and motivation.

One reason to study the Contract Documents is that it will expose you to all those little decisions, such as door thickness, made by the architect in the absence of instructions from you. You may find you want some of these decisions changed, and now is the time to do it, or at least discuss them with the architect. After construction begins, some changes will become expensive or impossible to make. A second reason for reviewing the architect's work is that he may have misunderstood, failed to receive, or even forgotten some of your instructions. Even if the slip is his fault, that will be cold comfort later. A third reason for familiarizing yourself with the Contract Documents is that the construction period will then be pleasanter and more interesting for you. The more advance knowledge you have of the complex of processes, elements, and subassemblies involved in the physical growth of the building, the more rewarding will be your experiences as you watch that growth take place, and the better able you will be to make intelligent decisions on the occasional questions that will arise during that growth.

The arguments for studying the Contract Documents apply to all of them, but some of the general conditions demand attention even if you read nothing else. Most of the conditions state duties of the contractor and rights of the owner, but some of them, conversely, describe rights of the contractor and duties (or options) of the owner. These you should know about.

Surveys, Permits, Etc. Article 11: requires that you secure and pay for all necessary surveys as discussed in Chapter 8.

Contractor's Right to Stop Work or Terminate Contract, Article 23: gives the contractor the right to quit if you fail to pay him in the agreed installments, or if the local authorities close down the job for legal violations not the fault of the contractor. If, for example, despite following the excavation specifications, the contractor's digging began to undermine an adjacent building, the building inspector might order the work stopped. After thirty days of stoppage the contractor could rescind the Contract.

Fire Insurance, Etc., Article 29: You, the contractor, and subcontractors are all susceptible to loss from fire at the job site, but if each party maintains separate fire insurance, the premium costs are greater and settlement of claims more complicated than if just one policy exists. As you usually have the largest single interest in the uncompleted building, it is fitting that you buy the fire insurance, and act as trustee for the interests of all parties concerned.

Two other articles in the general conditions grant you certain options, and you must decide how to exercise them.

Owner's Liability Insurance, Article 28: If a delinquent youth is injured while playfully breaking your new windows some night, or if an unauthorized visitor stumbles over a concealed brick, he—or his heirs—may bring suit against not only the contractor but also the architect and you. Even if you are not responsible for the accident, you may have the expense of defending yourself in or out of court. The apparent trend of the times in liability cases strongly suggests that you protect yourself with adequate insurance.

Guaranty Bonds, Article 30: You can require the contractor to furnish a bond guaranteeing satisfactory performance of his work. The bonding company (the surety), in return for a premium, obligates itself to take over the completion of the Contract if the contractor becomes insolvent, or for any reason not your fault fails to do the work. The bonding company will not do the work itself in this case, but will either refinance your contractor or get another one. You will, of course, pay the bonding company the unpaid balance of the original Contract amount. Performance bonds cost about 1 percent of the Contract amount on the first $100,000 and about 0.65 percent on the balance. In dollars this amount may seem high, but viewed as a percentage of project cost it is small. As building contracting is a risky business, causing many contractors to fail, I recommend performance bonds on all but the smallest jobs. Even an old, established contractor, loaded with assets, tends to be more chary of your interests, I think, if his reputation with a bonding company is at stake.

Before construction begins, you should read *Architect's Status, Article 38* and the second paragraph of *Article 15, Changes in the Work.* Note that the architect is the interpreter of the meaning of the Contract Documents; and is authorized to make minor changes not involving changes in cost, and under certain circumstances, to stop the work. He has no other authority over the contractor unless you specifically grant it. Article 38 also obligates the architect to protect the contractor's rights as well as your own, under the Contract. This provision, in reality, serves your interests. Contractors will bid lower than otherwise if they are assured in advance that the provisions of the Contract will be interpreted and enforced by the architect, who is both familiar with construction work and also intimately aware of the contents of the drawings and specifications.

TIMELY COMPLETION

Everyone involved with a construction job tends to benefit if the work goes speedily. The contractor will have less overhead and earn quicker profits. The architect will save work by having to make fewer visits to the site. You will be able to move in sooner, which may permit earlier profit from operation of the building, may reduce carrying charges on the construction loan, may reduce cost of other quarters, and which always satisfies your natural impatience to occupy the building you have been nursing along for so many months. Besides, if construction is slow after groundbreaking, there is more opportunity for deterioration of the uncompleted work from weather, vandalism, and so forth.

Opposing everyone's desire for speed are certain vagaries of modern commerce. Let's take an exaggerated case. The architect specifies a light fixture with a plastic lens. You approve. Eight weeks before they are needed in the building, the electrical subcontractor orders the fixtures from the supplier, giving himself a two-week cushion on the normal six-weeks delivery time. The supplier forwards the order to the distributor, who, having none in stock, orders the fixture from the manufacturer. The factory then schedules a production run and orders the lenses from the plastics manufacturer, who happens to be out of the dye used to tint the lenses and so orders some from Sweden. Two weeks later the plastics firm learns from the Swedish firm that the dye will arrive FOB New York in two months. It has already been two months since the electrical subcontractor placed his order. Meanwhile, back on the job, the plasterers can't start because the light fixture frames must be installed before ceilings can be plastered. Many long-distance telephone calls later the architect learns enough of the story to recommend substituting a different fixture. You approve. Six weeks later they arrive. Eventually the rescheduled plasterers return, and the job has suffered a net delay of several weeks. No one is really to blame, or perhaps what amounts to the same thing, everyone is somewhat to blame.

In any job a few things go astray in shipment. Other delays are caused by the occasional acts of carelessness, ignorance, or miscalculation among the hundreds of persons upon whose prompt, intelligent action rapid construction depends. Inclement weather may hold up the work. Add to these some delays that will probably occur as a result of changes you will order during construction, and you can understand why a job is almost never completed when it "should" be.

To minimize delay, there are a couple of Contract devices, either of which you may use. The first is a liquidated-damages clause. You calculate how much each week's or month's delay will cost you in lost profits, increased rent, increased carrying charges, and so forth. Then have the architect insert a clause in the conditions stating that the contractor agrees that delay of completion will damage the owner, and agrees to liquidate such damages by deducting them from the Contract amount. Elsewhere a "time of completion" is stated.

The other device for speeding contruction is the penalty-bonus clause. It will state that for every month of late completion the contractor will pay you so much (to be deducted from the Contract amount), but that for every month of early completion you will pay the contractor an equal amount (to be added to the Contract amount). A penalty-bonus clause is thus a sort of sporting arrangement and permits you to collect compensation for lateness without having to show that the lateness entailed actual financial loss. Often, especially when the job is your own house, the dollar loss to you of late completion seems less important than the annoyance caused by delay. In this case a penalty-bonus arrangement is more appropriate than liquidating damages.

If you will now review *Delays and Extensions of Time, Article 18,* you will see that neither Contract provision we have discussed can assure you either of timely completion or that you will be paid money for all delays. Choose a good contractor, and try not to fret too much about delays that can't be helped, or that could have been avoided if human beings were perfect.

LEGAL ADVICE

It is always appropriate to consult your lawyer on the wisdom and wording of delay-compensation provisions, or on any questions that occur to you in connection with the general conditions and Contract. Unlike the drawings and specifications, the rest of the Contract Documents are in the lawyer's field as well as the architect's.

CONCLUSION

After you have discussed and agreed on the Contract Documents with the architect, you can approve them. Then the job can be put out for bids. The next few weeks may be a period of not unpleasant suspense.

HAUSWIRTH RESIDENCE, JOB NO. 65-01 TITLE PAGE

SPECIFICATIONS*

DIVISION TITLE	DIV.	PAGES
AGREEMENT BETWEEN OWNER & CONTRACTOR		
GENERAL CONDITIONS....................		1-10
SUPPLEMENTARY GENERAL CONDITIONS.....		1-5
GENERAL REQUIREMENTS.................	1	1-2
SITE WORK............................	2	1-3
CONCRETE.............................	3	1-4
MASONRY..............................	4	1-4
METALS: STRUCTURAL & MISCELLANEOUS...	5	1-2
ROUGH CARPENTRY......................	6A	1-2
ROOF CARPENTRY.......................	6B	1-3
FINISH CARPENTRY.....................	6C	1-3
MOISTURE PROTECTION..................	7	1-4
DOORS, WINDOWS, AND GLASS............	8	1-5
FINISHES.............................	9	1-6
SPECIALTIES..........................	10	1-4
EQUIPMENT (NOT USED).................	11	
FURNISHINGS (NOT USED)...............	12	
SPECIAL CONSTRUCTION (NOT USED)......	13	
CONVEYING SYSTEMS (NOT USED).........	14	
MECHANICAL...........................	15	1-9
ELECTRICAL...........................	16	1-5
ALTERNATE NO. 1......................		1

*For further notes see page 203.

THE AMERICAN INSTITUTE OF ARCHITECTS

AIA DOCUMENT A101
SEPT. 1963 ED.

THE STANDARD FORM OF AGREEMENT BETWEEN OWNER AND CONTRACTOR

WHERE THE BASIS OF PAYMENT IS A

STIPULATED SUM

THIS FORM TO BE USED ONLY WITH THE LATEST EDITION OF AIA DOCUMENT A201, GENERAL CONDITIONS OF THE CONTRACT

THIS AGREEMENT

made this 23RD day of JUNE in the year Nineteen Hundred and SIXTY FIVE

BY AND BETWEEN

JOHN T. HAUSWIRTH AND
HARRIET HAUSWIRTH, HIS WIFE, hereinafter called the Owner, and

ARCADIA BUILDING COMPANY hereinafter called the Contractor,

WITNESSETH,

that the Owner and the Contractor for the considerations hereinafter named agree as follows:

ARTICLE 1. SCOPE OF THE WORK

The Contractor shall furnish all of the materials and perform all of the work shown on the Drawings and described in the Specifications entitled: (Here insert the caption descriptive of the work as used on other contract documents.)

RESIDENCE FOR DR. AND MRS. JOHN T. HAUSWIRTH

prepared by: MARSHALL SHAPER, REGISTERED ARCHITECT

acting as and in these Contract Documents entitled the Architect; and shall do everything required by this Agreement, the General Conditions of the Contract, the Specifications and the Drawings.

ARTICLE 2. TIME OF COMPLETION

The work to be performed under this Contract shall be commenced and completed as follows:
(Here insert stipulation as to liquidated damages, if any.)

THE WORK SHALL BE COMMENCED IMMEDIATELY AND SHALL BE COMPLETED NOT LATER THAN 30 NOVEMBER 1965.

ARTICLE 3. THE CONTRACT SUM

The Owner shall pay the Contractor for the performance of the Contract, subject to additions and deductions provided therein, in current funds as follows: (State here the lump sum amount, unit prices, or both, as desired.)

FIFTY THREE THOUSAND ONE HUNDRED FIFTY THREE AND NO/100S DOLLARS ($53,153.00)

Where the quantities originally contemplated are so changed that application of the agreed unit price to the quantity of work performed is shown to create a hardship to the Owner or the Contractor, there shall be an equitable adjustment of the Contract to prevent such hardship.

ARTICLE 4. PROGRESS PAYMENTS

The Owner shall make payments on account of the Contract as provided therein, as follows:

On or about the TENTH day of each month NINETY per cent of the value, based on the Contract prices of labor and materials incorporated in the work and per cent of materials suitably stored at the site thereof or at some other location agreed upon in writing by the parties up to the FIRST day of that month, as estimated by the Architect, less the aggregate of previous payments; and upon Substantial Completion of the entire work, a sum sufficient to increase the total payments to NINETY per cent of the Contract price.

(Insert here any provision made for limiting or reducing the amount retained after the work reaches a certain stage of completion.)

ARTICLE 5. ACCEPTANCE AND FINAL PAYMENT

Final payment shall be due TEN days after Substantial Completion of the work provided the work be then fully completed and the contract fully performed.

Upon receipt of written notice that the work is ready for final inspection and acceptance, the Architect shall promptly make such inspection, and when he finds the work acceptable under the Contract and the Contract fully performed he shall promptly issue a final certificate, over his own signature, stating that the work provided for in this Contract has been completed and is accepted by him under the terms and conditions thereof, and that the entire balance found to be due the Contractor, and noted in said final certificate, is due and payable.

Before issuance of final payment the Contractor shall submit evidence satisfactory to the Architect that all payrolls, material bills, and other indebtedness connected with the work have been paid or otherwise satisfied.

If after the work has been Substantially Completed, full completion thereof is materially delayed through no fault of the Contractor, and the Architect so certifies, the Owner shall, upon certificate of the Architect, and without terminating the Contract, make payment of the balance due for that portion of the work fully completed and accepted. Such payment shall be made under the terms and conditions governing final payment, except that it shall not constitute a waiver of claims.

ARTICLE 6. THE CONTRACT DOCUMENTS

The General Conditions of the Contract, the Supplementary General Conditions, the Specifications and the Drawings, together with this Agreement, form the Contract, and they are as fully a part of the Contract as if hereto attached or herein repeated. There follows an enumeration of the Contract Documents:

DRAWINGS NO. 1 THROUGH 6

SPECIFICATIONS AS LISTED ON THE TITLE PAGE THEREOF INCLUDING: ALL CONDITIONS, DIVISIONS, AND ALTERNATE NO. 1., EXCEPT THAT IN DOORS, WINDOWS, AND GLASS, DIVISION 8., THERMOPANE IS CHANGED TO TWINPANE IN ACCORDANCE WITH CONTRACTOR'S PROPOSAL.

IN WITNESS WHEREOF

the parties hereto have executed this Agreement, the day and year first above written.

Harriet Hauswirth

Owner John T. Hauswirth

JOHN T. HAUSWIRTH
HARRIET HAUSWIRTH

Contractor Gerald Framer

GERALD FRAMER FOR
ARCADIA BUILDING COMPANY

THE AMERICAN INSTITUTE OF ARCHITECTS

AIA DOCUMENT A201
SEPT. 1963 ED.

THE GENERAL CONDITIONS OF THE CONTRACT FOR THE CONSTRUCTION OF BUILDINGS

INDEX TO THE ARTICLES

ARTICLE 1

DEFINITIONS

a) The Contract Documents consist of the Agreement, the General Conditions of the Contract, the Supplementary General Conditions, the Drawings and Specifications, including all modifications thereof incorporated in the documents before their execution. These form the Contract.

b) The Owner, the Contractor and the Architect are those mentioned as such in the Agreement. They are treated throughout the Contract Documents as if each were of the singular number and masculine gender.

c) The term Subcontractor, as employed herein, includes only those having a direct contract with the Contractor and it includes one who furnishes material worked to a special design according to the Drawings or Specifications of this work, but does not include one who merely furnishes material not so worked.

d) Written notice shall be deemed to have been duly served if delivered in person to the individual or to a member of the firm or to an officer of the corporation for whom it is intended, or if delivered at or sent by registered mail to the last business address known to him who gives the notice.

e) The term "work" of the Contractor or Subcontractor includes labor or materials or both.

f) All time limits stated in the Contract Documents are of the essence of the Contract.

g) The law of the place of building shall govern the construction of the Contract.

h) The date of substantial completion of a project or specified area of a project is the date when construction is sufficiently completed, in accordance with Contract Documents, as modified by any change orders agreed to by the parties, so that the Owner can occupy the project or specified area of the project for the use it was intended.

ARTICLE 2

EXECUTION, CORRELATION AND INTENT OF DOCUMENTS

The Contract Documents shall be signed in duplicate by the Owner and the Contractor. In case either the Owner or the Contractor or both fail to sign the General Conditions, Supplementary General Conditions, Drawings or Specifications, the Architect shall identify them.

The Contract Documents are complementary, and what is called for by any one shall be as binding as if called for by all. The intention of the documents is to include all labor and materials, equipment and transportation necessary for the proper execution of the work. Materials or work described in words which so applied have a well-known technical or trade meaning shall be held to refer to such recognized standards.

It is not intended, that work not covered under any heading, section, branch, class or trade of the Specifications, shall be supplied unless it is shown on Drawings or is reasonably inferable therefrom as being necessary to produce the intended results.

ARTICLE 3

DETAIL DRAWINGS AND INSTRUCTIONS

The Architect shall furnish with reasonable promptness, additional instructions by means of drawings or otherwise, necessary for the proper execution of the work. All such drawings and instructions shall be consistent with the Contract Documents, true developments thereof, and reasonably inferable therefrom.

The work shall be executed in conformity therewith and the Contractor shall do no work without proper drawings and instructions.

Immediately after being awarded the Contract the Contractor shall prepare an estimated Progress Schedule and submit it for Architect's approval. It shall indicate the dates for the starting and completion of the various stages of construction.

ARTICLE 4

COPIES FURNISHED

Unless otherwise provided in the Contract Documents the Contractor will be furnished, free of charge, all copies of drawings and specifications reasonably necessary for the execution of the work.

ARTICLE 5

SHOP DRAWINGS

The Contractor shall check and verify all field measurements and shall submit with such promptness as to cause no delay in his own work or in that of any other Contractor, three copies, checked and approved by him, of all shop or setting drawings and schedules required for the work of the various trades. The Architect shall check and approve, with reasonable promptness, such schedules and drawings only for conformance with the design concept of the Project and compliance with the information given in the Contract Documents. The Contractor shall make any corrections required by the Architect, file with him two corrected copies and furnish such other copies as may be needed. The Architect's approval of such drawings or schedules shall not relieve the Contractor from responsibility for deviations from Drawings or Specifications, unless he has in writing called the Architect's attention to such deviations at the time of submission, and secured his written approval, nor shall it relieve him from responsibility for errors in shop drawings or schedules.

ARTICLE 6

DRAWINGS AND SPECIFICATIONS ON THE WORK

The Contractor shall keep one copy of all Drawings and Specifications on the work, in good order, available to the Architect and to his representative.

ARTICLE 7

OWNERSHIP OF DRAWINGS

All Drawings, Specifications and copies thereof furnished by the Architect are his property. They are not to be used on other work, and, with the exception of the signed Contract set, are to be returned to him on request, at the completion of the work.

ARTICLE 8

SAMPLES

The Contractor shall furnish for approval, with such promptness as to cause no delay in his own work or in that of any other Contractor, all samples as directed by the Architect. The Architect shall check and approve such samples, with reasonable promptness, only for conformance with the design concept of the Project and for compliance with the information given in the Contract Documents. The work shall be in accordance with approved samples.

ARTICLE 9

MATERIALS, APPLIANCES, EMPLOYEES

Unless otherwise stipulated, the Contractor shall provide and pay for all materials, labor, water, tools, equipment, light, power, transportation and other facilities necessary for the execution and completion of the work.

Unless otherwise specified all materials shall be new and both workmanship and materials shall be of good quality. The Contractor shall, if required, furnish satisfactory evidence as to the kind and quality of materials.

The Contractor shall at all times enforce strict discipline and good order among his employees, and shall not employ on the work any unfit person or anyone not skilled in the work assigned to him.

ARTICLE 10

ROYALTIES AND PATENTS

The Contractor shall pay all royalties and license fees. He shall defend all suits or claims for infringement of any patent rights and shall save the Owner harmless from loss on account thereof, except that the Owner shall be responsible for all such loss when a particular process or the product of a particular manufacturer or manufacturers is specified, but if the Contractor has information that the process or article specified is an infringement of a patent, he shall be responsible for such loss unless he promptly gives such information to the Architect or Owner.

ARTICLE 11

SURVEYS, PERMITS, LAWS, TAXES AND REGULATIONS

The Owner shall furnish all surveys unless otherwise specified.

Permits and licenses necessary for the prosecution of the work shall be secured and paid for by the Contractor. Easements for permanent structures or permanent changes in existing facilities shall be secured and paid for by the Owner, unless otherwise specified.

The Contractor shall give all notices and comply with all laws, ordinances, rules and regulations bearing on the conduct of the work as drawn and specified. If the Contractor observes that the Drawings and Specifications are at variance therewith, he shall promptly notify the Architect in writing and any necessary changes shall be adjusted as provided in the Contract for changes in the work. If the Contractor performs any work knowing it to be contrary to such laws, ordinances, rules and regulations, and without such notice to the Architect, he shall bear all costs arising therefrom.

Wherever the law of the place of building requires a sales, consumer, use, or other similar tax, the Contractor shall pay such tax.

ARTICLE 12

PROTECTION OF WORK AND PROPERTY

The Contractor shall continuously maintain adequate protection of all his work from damage and shall protect the Owner's property from injury or loss arising in connection with the Contract. He shall make good any such damage, injury or loss, except such as may be directly due to errors in the Contract Documents or caused by agents or employees of the Owner, or due to causes beyond the Contractor's control and not to his fault or negligence. He shall adequately protect adjacent property as provided by law and the Contract Documents.

The Contractor shall take all necessary precautions for the safety of employees on the work, and shall comply with all applicable provisions of Federal, State, and Municipal safety laws and building codes to prevent accidents or injury to persons on, about or adjacent to the premises where the work is being performed. He shall erect and properly maintain at all times, as required by the conditions and progress of the work, all necessary safeguards for the protection of workmen and the public and shall post danger signs warning against the hazards created by such features of construction as protruding nails, hoists, well holes, elevator hatchways, scaffolding, window openings, stairways and falling materials; and he shall designate a responsible member of his organization on the work, whose duty shall be the prevention of accidents. The name and position of any person so designated shall be reported to the Architect by the Contractor.

In an emergency affecting the safety of life or of the work or of adjoining property, the Contractor, without special instruction or authorization from the Architect or Owner, is hereby permitted to act, at his discretion, to prevent such threatened loss or injury; and he shall so act, without appeal, if so authorized or instructed. Any compensation, claimed by the Contractor on account of emergency work, shall be determined by agreement or arbitration.

ARTICLE 13

ACCESS TO WORK

The Architect and his representatives shall at all times have access to the work wherever it is in preparation or progress and the Contractor shall provide proper facilities for such access and so that the Architect may perform his functions under the Contract Documents.

If the Specifications, the Architect's instructions, laws, ordinances or any public authority require any work to be specially tested or approved, the Contractor shall give the Architect timely notice of its readiness for observation by the Architect or inspection by another authority, and if the inspection is by another authority, of the date fixed for such inspection, required certificates of inspection being secured by the Contractor. Observations by the Architect shall be promptly made, and where practicable at the source of supply. If any work should be covered up without approval or consent of the Architect, it must, if required by the Architect, be uncovered for examination at the Contractor's expense.

Re-examination of questioned work may be ordered by the Architect and if so ordered the work must be uncovered by the Contractor. If such work be found in accordance with the Contract Documents the Owner shall pay the cost of re-examination and replacement. If such work be found not in accordance with the Contract Documents the Contractor shall pay such cost, unless it be found that the defect in the work was caused by a Contractor employed as provided in Article 35, and in that event the Owner shall pay such cost.

ARTICLE 14

CONTRACTOR'S SUPERINTENDENCE AND SUPERVISION

The Contractor shall keep on his work, during its progress, a competent superintendent and any necessary assistants, all satisfactory to the Architect. The superintendent shall not be changed except with the consent of the Architect, unless the superintendent proves to be unsatisfactory to the Contractor and ceases to be in his employ. The superintendent shall represent the Contractor in his absence and all directions given to him shall be as binding as if given to the Contractor. Important directions shall be confirmed in writing to the Contractor. Other directions shall be so confirmed on written request in each case. The Architect shall not be responsible for the acts or omissions of the superintendent or his assistants.

The Contractor shall give efficient supervision to the work, using his best skill and attention. He shall carefully study and compare all Drawings, Specifications and other instructions and shall at once report to the Architect any error, inconsistency or omission which he may discover, but he shall not be liable to the Owner for any damage resulting from any errors or deficiencies in the Contract Documents or other instructions by the Architect.

ARTICLE 15

CHANGES IN THE WORK

The Owner, without invalidating the Contract, may order extra work or make changes by altering, adding to or deducting from the work, the Contract Sum being adjusted accordingly. All such work shall be executed under the conditions of the original Contract except that any claim for extension of time caused thereby shall be adjusted at the time of ordering such change.

In giving instructions, the Architect shall have authority to make minor changes in the work, not involving extra cost, and not inconsistent with the purposes of the building, but otherwise, except in an emergency endangering life or property, no extra work or change shall be made unless in pursuance of a written order from the Owner signed or countersigned by the Architect, or a written order from the Architect stating that the Owner has authorized the extra work or charge, and no claim for an addition to the Contract Sum shall be valid unless so ordered.

The value of any such extra work or change shall be determined in one or more of the following ways:
a) By estimate and acceptance in a lump sum.
b) By unit prices named in the Contract or subsequently agreed upon.
c) By cost and percentage or by cost and a fixed fee.

If none of the above methods is agreed upon, the Contractor, provided he receives an order as above, shall proceed with the work. In such case and also under case (c), he shall keep and present in such form as the Architect may direct, a correct account of the cost, together with vouchers. In any case, the Architect shall certify to the amount, including reasonable allowance for overhead and profit, due to the Contractor. Pending final determination of value, payments on account of changes shall be made on the Architect's certificate.

Should conditions encountered below the surface of the ground be at variance with the conditions indicated by the Drawings and Specifications the Contract Sum shall be equitably adjusted upon claim by either party made within a reasonable time after the first observance of the conditions.

ARTICLE 16

CLAIMS FOR EXTRA COST

If the Contractor claims that any instructions by drawings or otherwise involve extra cost under the Contract, he shall give the Architect written notice thereof within a reasonable time after the receipt of such instructions, and in any event before proceeding to execute the work, except in emergency endangering life or property, and the procedure shall then be as provided for changes in the work. No such claim shall be valid unless so made.

ARTICLE 17

DEDUCTIONS FOR UNCORRECTED WORK

If the Architect and Owner deem it inexpedient to correct work injured or done not in accordance with the Contract, an equitable deduction from the Contract Sum shall be made therefor.

ARTICLE 18

DELAYS AND EXTENSION OF TIME

If the Contractor be delayed at any time in the progress of the work by any act or neglect of the Owner or the Architect, or of any employee of either, or by any separate Contractor employed by the Owner, or by changes ordered in the work, or by labor disputes, fire, unusual delay in transportation, unavoidable casualties or any causes beyond the Contractor's control, or by delay authorized by the Architect pending arbitration, or by any cause which the Architect shall decide to justify the delay, then the time of completion shall be extended for such reasonable time as the Architect may decide.

No such extension shall be made for delay occurring more than seven days before claim therefor is made in writing to the Architect. In the case of a continuing cause of delay, only one claim is necessary.

If no schedule or agreement stating the dates upon which drawings shall be furnished is made, then no claim for delay shall be allowed on account of failure to furnish drawings until two weeks after demand for such drawings and not then unless such claim be reasonable.

This article does not exclude the recovery of damages for delay by either party under other provisions in the Contract Documents.

ARTICLE 19

CORRECTION OF WORK BEFORE SUBSTANTIAL COMPLETION

The Contractor shall promptly remove from the premises all work condemned by the Architect as failing to conform to the Contract, whether incorporated or not, and the Contractor shall promptly replace and re-execute his own work in accordance with the Contract and without expense to the Owner and shall bear the expense of making good all work of other contractors destroyed or damaged by such removal or replacement.

If the Contractor does not remove such condemned work within a reasonable time, fixed by written notice, the Owner may remove it and may store the material at the expense of the Contractor. If the Contractor does not pay the expenses of such removal within ten days' time thereafter, the Owner may, upon ten days' written notice, sell such materials at auction or at private sale and shall account for the net proceeds thereof, after deducting all the costs and expenses that should have been borne by the Contractor.

ARTICLE 20

CORRECTION OF THE WORK AFTER SUBSTANTIAL COMPLETION

The Contractor shall remedy any defects due to faulty materials or workmanship and pay for any damage to other work resulting therefrom, which shall appear within a period of one year from the date of Substantial Completion as defined in these General Conditions, and in accordance with the terms of any special guarantees provided in the Contract. The Owner shall give notice of observed defects with reasonable promptness. All questions arising under this Article shall be decided by the Architect subject to arbitration, notwithstanding final payment.

ARTICLE 21

THE OWNER'S RIGHT TO DO WORK

If the Contractor should neglect to prosecute the work properly or fail to perform any provision of the Contract, the Owner, after three days' written notice to the Contractor may, without prejudice to any other remedy he may have, make good such deficiencies and may deduct the cost thereof from the payment then or thereafter due the Contractor, provided, however, that the Architect shall approve both such action and the amount charged to the Contractor.

ARTICLE 22

OWNER'S RIGHT TO TERMINATE CONTRACT

If the Contractor should be adjudged a bankrupt, or if he should make a general assignment for the benefit of his creditors, or if a receiver should be appointed on account of his insolvency, or if he should persistently or repeatedly refuse or should fail, except in cases for which extension of time is provided, to supply enough properly skilled workmen or proper materials, or if he should fail to make prompt payment to subcontractors or for material or labor, or persistently disregard laws, ordinances or the instructions of the Architect, or otherwise be guilty of a substantial violation of any provision of the Contract, then the Owner, upon the certificate of the Architect that sufficient cause exists to justify such action, may, without prejudice to any other right or remedy and after giving the Contractor, and his surety if any, seven days' written notice, terminate the employment of the Contractor and take possession of the premises and of all materials, tools and appliances thereon and finish the work by whatever method he may deem expedient. In such case the Contractor shall not be entitled to receive any further payment until the work is finished. If the unpaid balance of the Contract Sum shall exceed the expense of finishing the work including compensation for additional architectural, managerial and administrative services, such excess shall be paid to the Contractor. If such expense shall exceed such unpaid balance, the Contractor shall pay the difference to the Owner. The expense incurred by the Owner as herein provided, and the damage incurred through the Contractor's default, shall be certified by the Architect.

ARTICLE 23

THE CONTRACTOR'S RIGHT TO STOP WORK OR TERMINATE CONTRACT

If the work should be stopped under an order of any court, or other public authority, for a period of thirty days, through no act or fault of the Contractor or of anyone employed by him, then the Contractor may, upon seven days' written notice to the Owner and the Architect, terminate the Contract and recover from the Owner payment for all work executed and any proven loss sustained upon any plant or materials and reasonable profit and damages.

Should the Architect fail to issue any Certificate for Payment, through no fault of the Contractor, within seven days after the Contractor's formal request for payment or if the Owner should fail to pay to the Contractor within seven days of its maturity and presentation, any sum certified by the Architect or awarded by arbitrators, then the Contractor may, upon seven days' written notice to the Owner and the Architect, stop the work or terminate the Contract as set out in the preceding paragraph.

ARTICLE 24

APPLICATIONS FOR PAYMENTS

At least ten days before each payment falls due, the Contractor shall submit to the Architect an itemized application for payment, supported to the extent required by the Architect by receipts or other vouchers, showing payments for materials and labor, payments to subcontractors and such other evidence of the Contractor's right to payment as the Architect may direct.

If payments are made on valuation of work done, the Contractor shall, before the first application, submit to the Architect a schedule of values of the various parts of the work, including quantities, aggregating the total sum of the Contract, divided so as to facilitate payments to subcontractors in accordance with Article 37(e), made out in such form as the Architect and the Contractor may agree upon, and, if required, supported by such evidence as to its correctness as the Architect may direct. This schedule, when approved by the Architect, shall be used as a basis for Certificates for Payment, unless it be found to be in error. In applying for payments, the Contractor shall submit a statement based upon this schedule.

If payments are made on account of materials not incorporated in the work but delivered and suitably stored at the site, or at some other location agreed upon in writing, such payments shall be conditioned upon submission by the Contractor of bills of sale or such other procedure as will establish the Owner's title to such material or otherwise adequately protect the Owner's interest including applicable insurance.

ARTICLE 25

CERTIFICATES FOR PAYMENTS

If the Contractor has made application for payment as above, the Architect shall, not later than the date when each payment falls due, issue a Certificate for Payment to the Contractor for such amount as he decides to be properly due, or state in writing his reasons for withholding a certificate.

No certificate issued nor payment made to the Contractor, nor partial or entire use or occupancy of the work by the Owner, shall be an acceptance of any work or materials not in accordance with the Contract. When advised by the Contractor that the work is substantially completed, the Architect and the Contractor shall within a reasonable time make a joint inspection of the work and if the Architect shall determine that the work is substantially completed, he shall then prepare a Certificate of Substantial Completion, which shall be submitted to the Owner and the Contractor for their execution. The making and acceptance of the final payment shall constitute a waiver of all claims by the Owner, other than those arising from unsettled liens, from faulty work appearing after Substantial Completion or from failure to comply with Drawings and Specifications and the terms of any special guarantees specified in the Contract and of all claims by the Contractor, except those previously made and still unsettled.

Should the Owner fail to pay the sum named in any Certificate for Payment issued by the Architect or in any award by arbitration, upon demand when due, the Contractor shall receive, in addition to the sum named in the Certificate for Payment, interest thereon at the legal rate in force at the place of building.

ARTICLE 26

PAYMENTS WITHHELD

The Architect may withhold or, on account of subsequently discovered evidence, nullify the whole or a part of any certificate to such extent as may be necessary in his reasonable opinion to protect the Owner from loss on account of:

a) Defective work not remedied.

b) Claims filed or reasonable evidence indicating probable filing of claims.

c) Failure of the Contractor to make payments properly to subcontractors or for material or labor.

d) A reasonable doubt that the Contract can be completed for the balance then unpaid.

e) Damage to another Contractor.

When the above grounds are removed payment shall be made for amounts withheld because of them.

ARTICLE 27

CONTRACTOR'S LIABILITY INSURANCE

The Contractor shall maintain such insurance as will protect him from claims under workmen's compensation acts and other employee benefits acts; from claims for damages because of bodily injury, including death, to his employees and all others; and from claims for damages to property—any or all of which may arise out of or result from the Contractor's operations under the Contract, whether such operations be by himself or by any subcontractor or anyone directly or indirectly employed by either of them. This insurance shall be written for not less than any limits of liability specified as part of the Contract. Certificates of such insurance shall be filed with the Owner and Architect.

ARTICLE 28

OWNER'S LIABILITY INSURANCE

The Owner shall be responsible for and at his option may maintain such insurance as will protect him from his contingent liability to others for damages because of bodily injury, including death, which may arise from operations under the Contract, and any other liability for damages which the Contractor is required to insure under any provision of the Contract.

ARTICLE 29

FIRE INSURANCE WITH EXTENDED COVERAGE

Unless otherwise provided, the Owner shall effect and maintain fire insurance with extended coverage upon the entire structure on which the work of the Contract is to be done to one hundred per cent of the insurable value thereof, including items of labor and materials connected therewith whether in or adjacent to the structure insured, materials in place or to be used as part of the permanent construction including surplus materials, shanties, protective fences, bridges, temporary structures, miscellaneous materials and supplies incident to the work, and such scaffoldings, stagings, towers, forms, and equipment as are not owned or rented by the Contractor, the cost of which is included in the cost of the work. EXCLUSIONS: This insurance does not cover any tools owned by mechanics, any tools, equipment, scaffolding, staging, towers, and forms owned or rented by the Contractor, the capital value of which is not included in the cost of the work, or any cook shanties, bunk houses or other structures erected for housing the workmen. The loss, if any, is to be made adjustable with and payable to the Owner as Trustee for the insureds and Contractors and subcontractors as their interests may appear, except in such cases as may require payment of all or a proportion of said insurance to be made to a mortgagee as his interests may appear.

Certificates of such insurance shall be filed with the Contractor if he so requires. If the Owner fails to effect or maintain insurance as above and so notifies the Contractor, the Contractor may insure his own interests and that of the subcontractors and charge the cost thereof to the Owner. If the Contractor is damaged by failure of the Owner to maintain such insurance or to so notify the Contractor he may recover as stipulated in the Contract for recovery of damages. If other special insurance not herein provided for is required by the Contractor, the Owner shall effect such insurance at the Contractor's expense by appropriate riders to his fire insurance policy. The Owner, Contractor, and all subcontractors waive all rights, each against the others, for damages caused by fire or other perils covered by insurance provided under the terms of this article, except such rights as they may have to the proceeds of insurance held by the Owner as Trustee.

The Owner shall be responsible for and at his option may insure against loss of use of his existing property, due to fire or otherwise, however caused. If required in writing by any party in interest, the Owner as Trustee shall, upon the occurrence of loss, give bond for the proper performance of his duties. He shall deposit any money received from insurance in an account separate from all his other funds and he shall distribute it in accordance with such agreement as the parties in interest may reach, or under an award of arbitrators appointed, one by the Owner, another by joint action of the other parties in interest, all other procedure being as provided elsewhere in the Contract for arbitration. If after loss no special agreement is made, replacement of injured work shall be ordered and executed as provided for changes in the work.

The Trustee shall have power to adjust and settle any loss with the insurers unless one of the Contractors interested shall object in writing within three working days of the occurrence of loss, and thereupon arbitrators shall be chosen as above. The Trustee shall in that case make settlement with the insurers in accordance with the directions of such arbitrators, who shall also, if distribution by arbitration is required, direct such distribution.

ARTICLE 30

GUARANTY BONDS

The Owner shall have the right, prior to the signing of the Contract, to require the Contractor to furnish bond covering the faithful performance of the Contract and the payment of all obligations arising thereunder, in such form as the Owner may prescribe and with such sureties as he may approve. If such bond is required by instructions given previous to the submission of bids, the premium shall be paid by the Contractor; if subsequent thereto, it shall be paid by the Owner.

ARTICLE 31

DAMAGES

Should either party to the Contract suffer damages because of any wrongful act or neglect of the other party or of anyone employed by him, claim shall be made in writing to the party liable within a reasonable time of the first observance of such damage and not later than the final payment, except as expressly stipulated otherwise in the case of faulty work or materials, and shall be adjusted by agreement or arbitration.

ARTICLE 32

LIENS

Neither the final payment nor any part of the retained percentage shall become due until the Contractor, if required, shall deliver to the Owner a complete release of all liens arising out of the Contract, or receipts in full in lieu thereof and, if required in either case, an affidavit that so far as he has knowledge or information the releases and receipts include all the labor and material for which a lien could be filed; but the Contractor may, if any subcontractor refuses to furnish a release or receipt in full, furnish a bond satisfactory to the Owner, to indemnify him against any lien. If any lien remains unsatisfied after all payments are made, the Contractor shall refund to the Owner all moneys that the latter may be compelled to pay in discharging such a lien, including all costs and a reasonable attorney's fee.

ARTICLE 33

ASSIGNMENT

Neither party to the Contract shall assign the Contract or sublet it as a whole without the written consent of the other, nor shall the Contractor assign any moneys due or to become due to him hereunder, without the previous written consent of the Owner.

ARTICLE 34

MUTUAL RESPONSIBILITY OF CONTRACTORS

Should the Contractor cause damage to any separate contractor on the work the Contractor agrees, upon due notice, to settle with such contractor by agreement or arbitration, if he will so settle. If such separate contractor sues the Owner on account of any damage alleged to have been so sustained, the Owner shall notify the Contractor, who shall defend such proceedings at the Owner's expense and, if any judgment against the Owner arise therefrom, the Contractor shall pay or satisfy it and pay all costs incurred by the Owner.

ARTICLE 35

SEPARATE CONTRACTS

The Owner reserves the right to let other contracts in connection with this work under similar General Conditions. The Contractor shall afford other contractors reasonable opportunity for the introduction and storage of their materials and the execution of their work, and shall properly connect and cordinate his work with theirs.

If any part of the Contractor's work depends for proper execution or results upon the work of any other contractor, the Contractor shall inspect and promptly report to the Architect any defects in such work that render it unsuitable for such proper execution and results. Failure of the Contractor so to inspect and report shall constitute an acceptance of the other contractor's work as fit and proper for the reception of his work, except as to defects which may develop in the other contractor's work after the execution of his work.

To insure the proper execution of his subsequent work the Contractor shall measure work already in place and shall at once report to the Architect any discrepancy between the executed work and the Drawings.

ARTICLE 36

SUBCONTRACTS

As soon as practicable and before awarding any subcontracts, the Contractor shall notify the Architect in writing of the names of the subcontractors proposed for the principal parts of the work, and for such other parts as the Architect may direct, and shall not employ any to whom the Architect or the Owner may have a reasonable objection.

If before or after the execution of the Contract a change of any subcontractor on such list is required by the Architect or by the Owner prior to the award of the relevant contract, the Contract Sum shall be increased or decreased by the difference in cost occasioned by such change.

The Contractor shall not be required to employ any subcontractor against whom he has a reasonable objection.

The Architect shall, on request, furnish to any subcontractor, wherever practicable, evidence of the amounts certified on his account.

The Contractor agrees that he is as fully responsible to the Owner for the acts and omissions of his subcontractors and of persons either directly or indirectly employed by them, as he is for the acts and omissions of persons directly employed by him.

Nothing contained in the Contract Documents shall create any contractual relation between any subcontractor and the Owner.

ARTICLE 37

RELATIONS OF CONTRACTOR AND SUBCONTRACTOR

The Contractor agrees to bind every Subcontractor and every Subcontractor agrees to be bound by the terms of the Agreement, the General Conditions of the Contract, the Supplementary General Conditions, the Drawings and Specifications as far as applicable to his work, including the following provisions of this article, unless specifically noted to the contrary in a subcontract approved in writing as adequate by the Owner or Architect.

The Subcontractor agrees—

a) To be bound to the Contractor by the terms of the Agreement, General Conditions of the Contract, the Supplementary General Conditions, the Drawings and Specifications, and to assume toward him all the obligations and responsibilities that he, by those documents, assumes toward the Owner.

b) To submit to the Contractor applications for payment in such reasonable time as to enable the Contractor to apply for payment under Article 24 of the General Conditions.

c) To make all claims for extras, for extensions of time and for damages for delays or otherwise, to the Contractor in the manner provided in the General Conditions of the Contract and the Supplementary General Conditions for like claims by the Contractor upon the Owner, except that the time for making claims for extra cost is one week.

The Contractor agrees—

d) To be bound to the Subcontractor by all the obligations that the Owner assumes to the Contractor under the Agreement, General Conditions of the Contract, the Supplementary General Conditions, the Drawings and Specifications, and by all the provisions thereof affording remedies and redress to the Contractor from the Owner.

e) To pay the Subcontractor, upon the payment of certificates, if issued under the schedule of values described in Article 24 of the General Conditions, the amount allowed to the Contractor on account of the Subcontractor's work to the extent of the Subcontractor's interest therein.

f) To pay the Subcontractor, upon the payment of certificates, if issued otherwise than as in (e), so that at all times his total payments shall be as large in proportion to the value of the work done by him as the total amount certified to the Contractor is to the value of the work done by him.

g) To pay the Subcontractor to such extent as may be provided by the Contract Documents or the subcontract, if either of these provides for earlier or larger payments than the above.

h) To pay the Subcontractor on demand for his work or materials as far as executed and fixed in place, less the retained percentage, at the time the Certificate for Payment should issue, even though the Architect fails to issue it for any cause not the fault of the Subcontractor.

j) To pay the Subcontractor a just share of any fire insurance money received by him, the Contractor, under Article 29 of the General Conditions.

k) To make no demand for liquidated damages or penalty for delay in any sum in excess of such amount as may be specifically named in the subcontract.

l) That no claim for services rendered or materials furnished by the Contractor to the Subcontractor shall be valid unless written notice thereof is given by the Contractor to the Subcontractor during the first ten days of the calendar month following that in which the claim originated.

m) To give the Subcontractor an opportunity to be present and to submit evidence in any arbitration involving his rights.

n) To name as arbitrator under arbitration proceedings as provided in the General Conditions the person nominated by the Subcontractor, if the sole cause of dispute is the work, materials, rights or responsibilities of the Subcontractor; or, if of the Subcontractor and any other subcontractor jointly, to name as such arbitrator the person upon whom they agree.

The Contractor and the Subcontractor agree that—

o) In the matter of arbitration, their rights and obligations and all procedure shall be analogous to those set forth in this Contract; provided, however, that a decision by the Architect shall not be a condition precedent to arbitration.

Nothing in this article shall create any obligation on the part of the Owner to pay or to see to the payment of any sums to any subcontractor.

ARTICLE 38

ARCHITECT'S STATUS; ARCHITECT'S SUPERVISION

The Architect shall be the Owner's representative during the construction period. The Architect will make periodic visits to the site to familiarize himself generally with the progress and quality of the work and to determine in general if the work is proceeding in accordance with the Contract Documents. He will not be required to make exhaustive or continuous on-site inspections to check the quality or quantity of the work and he will not be responsible for the Contractor's failure to carry out the construction work in accordance with the Contract Documents. During such visits and on the basis of his observations while at the site, he will keep the Owner informed of the progress of the work, will endeavor to guard the Owner against defects and deficiencies in the work of Contractors, and he may condemn work as failing to conform to the Contract Documents. He shall have authority to act on behalf of the Owner only to the extent expressly provided in the Contract Documents or otherwise in writing, which shall be shown to the Contractor. He shall have authority to stop the work whenever such stoppage may be necessary in his reasonable opinion to insure the proper execution of the Contract.

The Architect shall be, in the first instance, the interpreter of the conditions of the Contract and the judge of its performance. He shall side neither with the Owner nor with the Contractor, but shall use his powers under the Contract to enforce its faithful performance by both.

In case of the termination of the employment of the Architect, the Owner shall appoint a capable and reputable Architect against whom the Contractor makes no reasonable objection, whose status under the contract shall be that of the former Architect; any dispute in connection with such appointment shall be subject to arbitration.

ARTICLE 39

ARCHITECT'S DECISIONS

The Architect shall, within a reasonable time, make decisions on all claims of the Owner or Contractor and on all other matters relating to the execution and progress of the work or the interpretation of the Contract Documents.

The Architect's decision, in matters relating to artistic effect, shall be final, if within the terms of the Contract Documents.

Except as above or as otherwise expressly provided in the Contract Documents, all the Architect's decisions are subject to arbitration.

If, however, the Architect fails to render a decision within ten days after the parties have presented their evidence, either party may then demand arbitration. If the Architect renders a decision after arbitration proceedings have been initiated, such decision may be entered as evidence but shall not disturb or interrupt such proceedings except where such decision is acceptable to the parties concerned.

ARTICLE 40

ARBITRATION

All disputes, claims or questions subject to arbitration under the Contract shall be submitted to arbitration in accordance with the provisions, then obtaining, of the Standard Form of Arbitration Procedure of The American Institute of Architects, and the Agreement shall be specifically enforceable under the prevailing arbitration law, and judgment upon the award rendered may be entered in the court of the forum, state or federal, having jurisdiction. It is mutually agreed that the decision of the arbitrators shall be a condition precedent to any right of legal action that either party may have against the other.

The Contractor shall not cause a delay of the work during any arbitration proceedings, except by agreement with the Owner.

Notice of the demand for arbitration of a dispute shall be filed in writing with the other party to the Contract, and a copy filed with the Architect. The demand for arbitration shall be made within a reasonable time after the dispute has arisen; in no case, however, shall the demand be made later than the time of final payment, except as otherwise expressly stipulated in the Contract.

The arbitrators, if they deem that the case requires it, are authorized to award to the party whose contention is sustained, such sums as they or a majority of them shall deem proper to compensate him for the time and expense incident to the proceeding and, if the arbitration was demanded without reasonable cause, they may also award damages for delay. The arbitrators shall fix their own compensation, unless otherwise provided by agreement, and shall assess the costs and charges of the proceedings upon either or both parties.

ARTICLE 41

CASH ALLOWANCES

The Contractor shall include in the Contract Sum all allowances named in the Contract Documents and shall cause the work so covered to be done by such contractors and for such sums as the Architect may direct, the Contract Sum being adjusted in conformity therewith. The Contractor declares that the Contract Sum includes such sums for expenses and profit on account of cash allowances as he deems proper. No demand for delivery costs, expenses or profit other than those included in the Contract Sum shall be allowed. The Contractor shall not be required to employ for any such work persons against whom he has a reasonable objection.

ARTICLE 42

USE OF PREMISES

The Contractor shall confine his apparatus, the storage of materials and the operations of his workmen to limits indicated by law, ordinances, permits or directions of the Architect and shall not unreasonably encumber the premises with his materials.

The Contractor shall not load or permit any part of the structure to be loaded with a weight that will endanger its safety.

ARTICLE 43

CUTTING, PATCHING

The Contractor shall do all cutting, fitting or patching of his work that may be required to make its several parts come together properly and fit it to receive or be received by work of other contractors shown upon, or reasonably implied by, the Drawings and Specifications for the completed structure, and he shall make good after them as the Architect may direct.

Any cost caused by defective or ill-timed work shall be borne by the party responsible therefor.

The Contractor shall not endanger any work by cutting, excavating or otherwise altering the work and shall not cut or alter the work of any other contractor save with the consent of the Architect.

ARTICLE 44

CLEANING UP

The Contractor shall at all times keep the premises free from accumulation of waste materials or rubbish caused by his employees or work, and at the completion of the work he shall remove all his rubbish from and about the building and all his tools, scaffolding and surplus materials and shall leave his work "broom-clean" or its equivalent, unless more exactly specified. In case of dispute the Owner may remove the rubbish and charge the cost to the several contractors as the Architect shall determine to be just.

HAUSWIRTH RESIDENCE
JOB NO. 65-01

ROUGH CARPENTRY *
DIVISION 6A PAGE 1

1. WORK INCLUDED

PROVIDE ROUGH FRAMING, SIDING, MULLIONS, EXTERIOR BATTENS AND BELT, WALL INSULATION, ROUGH HARDWARE, DRYWALL, WOOD FASCIAS, GLASS STOPS, BALCONY FRAMING, PLYWOOD FLOOR, STAIRS. FURNISH ANCHOR BOLTS FOR INSTALLATION BY OTHERS. FURNISH ALL REQUIRED EPOXY ADHESIVE.

2. WORK NOT INCLUDED

ROOF FRAMING, DECK, AND INSULATION (DIVISION 6B); AND FINISH CARPENTRY (DIVISION 6C).

3. MATERIALS

A. FRAMING LUMBER: STANDARD GRADE DOUGLAS FIR.

B. MULLIONS: CLEAR DOUGLAS FIR.

C. EPOXY ADHESIVE (ERA): EPX-92 AS FORMULATED BY CYANOTIC CHEMICAL CO., ANDROMACHE, MICHIGAN.

D. SIDING:

(1) ON 2x4 STUDS: 3/8" EXTERIOR GRADE A-D PLYWOOD.

(2) ON 2x6 STUDS: EXTERIOR GRADE DFPA A-C TEXTURE ONE-ELEVEN WITH ¼" DEEP GROOVES @ 4" O.C.

E. WALL INSULATION: 3" THICK FIBROUS GLASS WITH VAPOR BARRIER ON INTERIOR SURFACE.

F. WOOD FLOORS: ½" INTERIOR GRADE A-C PLYWOOD, EXCEPT BALCONY FLOOR SHALL BE EXTERIOR GRADE.

G. DRYWALL: ½" GYPSUM WALLBOARD, SQUARE-EDGED.

4. ROUGH HARDWARE

PROVIDE AS SHOWN OR REQUIRED. CLEARLY INDICATE TO CONCRETE AND MASONRY SUBCONTRACTORS THE CORRECT LOCATION OF ALL ANCHOR BOLTS FURNISHED TO THEM FOR INSTALLATION.

*For further notes see page 203.

5. FRAMING

FRAME WALLS AND PARTITIONS WITH 2x4 AND 2x6 STUDS @ 16" O.C. PROVIDE SINGLE SILLS AND PLATES. BRIDGE JOISTS WITH DIAGONAL 1x2S; SUBSTITUTE STRAIGHT METAL BRIDGING WHERE DUCTS OCCUR. DOUBLE FRAMING MEMBERS AROUND OPENINGS 16" OR MORE WIDE. NAIL FRAMING IN ACCORDANCE WITH NLMA'S "MANUAL FOR HOUSE FRAMING." LOCATE BATHROOM STUDS TO RECEIVE FIXTURE AND ACCESSORY MOUNTING SCREWS. PROVIDE NECESSARY WOOD LINTELS. PROVIDE POCKET FOR SLIDING DOOR. WHERE ROOF SOFFIT IS CURVED, WARP WALL PLATES TIGHT AGAINST SOFFIT AND BOND WITH EPOXY.

6. BUCKS

PROVIDE WOOD BUCKS FOR DOOR, WINDOW, AND OTHER OPENINGS.

7. SIDING

INSTALL TEXTURE ONE ELEVEN PLYWOOD WITH 8D. GALVANIZED CASING NAILS 4" O.C. AT EDGES AND 8" O.C. AT INTERMEDIATE SUPPORTS. INSTALL OTHER PLYWOOD SIDING WITH 6D. GALVANIZED CASING NAILS 6" O.C. AT EDGES AND 12" O.C. AT INTERMEDIATE SUPPORTS. NEATLY SHIPLAP TEXTURE ONE ELEVEN HORIZONTAL JOINTS; MAKE ALL OTHER PLYWOOD JOINTS BEHIND BATTENS OR BELT.

8. INSULATION

PROVIDE INSULATION IN ALL EXTERIOR WALL AREA.

9. DRYWALL

MOUNT DRYWALL ON ALL INTERIOR WALL AND PARTITION SURFACES USING THREADED NAILS OR CONTACT CEMENT IN ACCORDANCE WITH MANUFACTURER'S LATEST PRINTED INSTRUCTIONS. SET PANELS VERTICALLY WITH NO HORIZONTAL JOINTS. VERTICAL JOINTS SHALL BE 4' O.C. EXCEPT END JOINT IN WALLS WHOSE LENGTH IS NOT AN EVEN MULTIPLE OF 4'. (VERTICAL JOINTS SHALL BE COVERED BY BATTENS OR OTHER WALL FINISH UNDER DIVISION 6C OR 9.)

10. MULLIONS

VERTICAL MULLIONS SHALL BE ONE-PIECE, CONTINUOUS. SILLS AND HORIZONTAL MULLIONS SHALL BE SEGMENTED.

NOTES ON SPECIFICATIONS TABLE OF CONTENTS

Every piece of paper in the contract documents must be self-identifying, and somewhere all the pieces must be listed. Therefore the documents are itemized on the Contract form and the number of pages in each division of the Specifications is shown on the Title Page.

Division 1, General Requirements, resembles but is not the same as General Conditions. Contents of some of the other divisions is not readily apparent, so the following notes are included for the curious.

Division 3 also includes formwork and reinforcing.

Things like steel beams and columns are "structural metal"; things like stair rails and anchor bolts are "miscellaneous metal."

Moisture Protection includes roofing, waterproofing, and flashing. Finishes include paint, plaster, tile, and so forth. Specialties include towel racks, door knobs, folding partitions, and a number of other things. Special Construction includes swimming pools, luminous ceilings, and a few other wild items.

Elevators, escalators, dumbwaiters, and factory conveyor belts all snuggle under the heading of Conveying Systems.

NOTES ON ROUGH CARPENTRY, DIVISION 6A OF SPECIFICATIONS

The text of each division is arranged to facilitate cost estimating and construction administration, as well as to provide needed information for the field force.

The first two paragraphs of each division allocate all labor and materials required for the project into easily designated portions. Thus each subbidder can offer to "do all work under Division X" and everyone knows exactly what the offer includes. Of course, everybody in the business knows, without being told, most of the items that will occur in any division, but there are enough items the allocation of which varies from job to job to justify listing all included items at the beginning of each division.

The balance of the text in each division is split: First comes a description of materials; next come instructions for their installation. To you and me it would probably seem more logical to describe one material at a time, explain how it was to be installed, and then move on to the next item. The contractor, however, first buys the material, then installs it. He welcomes having the description of materials grouped near the beginning for his order department. The field force, then, concentrates on only the installation instructions, also segregated from the rest of the text.

Chapter 15

THE CONSTRUCTION TEAM

WHENEVER a building is erected, an organization comes into being to do the work. The relations among members of the organization differ from job to job, but certain similarities recur. There will be, first of all, someone in charge. It is normally not the architect. Usually the job is run by a general contractor. Under him will be his own employees, fabricators, and materials suppliers; plus numerous subcontractors, who also have employees, fabricators, and suppliers. In order to appreciate what goes on during construction you need both to recognize the bit players in the cast as well as understand the contractors, who star in the production. To belabor the analogy, the architect can be thought of as the author of the play, and you as the producer. The general contractor is the director and may also be a leading actor.

MATERIALS SUPPLIERS

Firms that sell materials and standard manufactured products for the building are called suppliers. Suppliers of light fixtures and suppliers of electrical wire sell directly to the electrical subcontractors. Suppliers of door hardware, windows, shingles, and so forth, sell directly to the general contractor. Suppliers are sales agents or manufacturers' representatives. They order products from the factory or distributor for delivery to the job site, in most cases, but they may also sell and deliver material to fabricators rather than to the contractor or subcontractors.

FABRICATORS

A fabricator has a shop where he forms and joins raw materials or standard products into custom assemblies for specific building projects. Thus a woodworking or cabinetmaking firm builds special kitchen cabinets, or modifies standard manufactured cabinets, to suit an individual job. A steel fabricator buys standard steel sections from the mill: He cuts them to shape, welds or rivets some of them together, and delivers the results to the job site for field erection.

CONSTRUCTION WORKMEN

Contractors and subcontractors employ both skilled and unskilled workmen: They work at the construction site. Unskilled workmen are designated laborers. They perform hand excavation, transport concrete in wheelbarrows, clean up construction debris, and assist skilled workmen in a variety of jobs as specified in finicky detail by construction workers' unions. Skilled construction workers are all termed mechanics. They include carpenters, bricklayers, plumbers, electricians, caulkers, lathers, plasterers, glaziers, ironworkers, and many others. They earn, with fringe benefits, in the neighborhood of $6 per hour. Laborers earn a little over $4 per hour. The jobs of most construction workmen are temporary: They are hired at the beginning of a project by a contractor and let go when the job is done.

CONTRACTORS

A contractor is a firm that is in the business of doing work under contract. In this context, of course, we mean construction work. A construction firm that has a contract with you is called a prime contractor: A firm that has a contract with a prime contractor is called a subcontractor.

It is common for construction projects to be organized around a single prime contract between you and a so-called general contractor. Under such an arrangement the general contractor will let subcontracts for the mechanical and electrical work, and for any other categories of work that he does not wish to have performed by his own employees. The general contractor assumes complete responsibility to you for the entire project, so obviously his role as construction manager is of primary importance. In fact, in some cases, a general contractor may subcontract all of the construction work and do nothing himself but manage the job. Typically, however, the general contractor hires his own carpenters, masons, and laborers, and subcontracts all work not performed by these workmen. The subcontractors are directly responsible to the general contractor, not to you. The general contractor is normally allowed to choose his subcontractors, but some provisions of the general Contract usually allow you and the architect a measure of control over the selection of subcontractors.

You may, as we shall see in the next chapter, elect to have the work performed by a dozen or so specialized construction firms all working under prime contracts and coordinated by an employee of yours, such as the architect, rather than by a general contractor. In this case the carpentry would be performed by a carpentry contractor, the electrical work by the electrical contractor (not subcontractor), and so forth. This arrangement is rare.

In the balance of this section I will discuss general contractors, but almost everything said here applies equally to the specialized firms that more often work under subcontracts.

A contractor will have field forces and an office force. A field force will consist of one or more laborers and mechanics who may be assisted by apprentices or helpers. If there are enough in any trade, a foreman will be assigned. In charge of a field force will be a job superintendent. He may do some hiring and firing of workmen, and he is responsible for daily scheduling and the layout of the work. He checks to insure that the job is built in accordance with his interpretation of the Contract Documents, and his interpretation will be clarified or corrected from time to time by the architect. A mechanical subcontractor's superintendent will be in charge of the mechanical work, but a general contractor's superintendent will be in charge of the whole job, including all subcontractors' superintendents. Most house jobs require no more than one or two mechanics in each trade, and only a general contractor's superintendent, who will probably also double as a working carpenter or mason.

The office force, aside from clerical staff, includes estimators and administrators. Estimators work independently of the field force. At any one time they will be engaged in calculating required amounts of labor and materials for preparing cost estimates on one or more jobs that are out for bids from various architects' offices. Another office job is negotiating with suppliers and fabricators for purchase of materials and subassemblies that will be required on jobs the firm is under contract to build. The office force prepares progress schedules for each project at the beginning of the work, and should correct these schedules from time to time as the work proceeds. The office force processes applications for payment received from suppliers, fabricators, and subcontractors, and prepares the firm's own applications for payment addressed to you and other owners to whom the firm is under contract. The head of the firm is part of the office force, and he, or his deputies, make periodic visits of inspection to the jobs on which the firm is working, and also make special trips to jobs where the superintendent encounters problems that demand resolution by higher authority.

1. Large Contractors

A construction firm with a president, a vice president or two, one or more estimators, accountants, bookkeepers, and some superintendents who are not let go at the end of each job, is a large construction firm. It can handle millions of dollars worth of work annually. Its offices, and even some of its superintendents, may be graduate professional engineers. A large contractor, like a large architectural firm, will not ordinarily be interested in building a $50,000 house.

2. Small Contractors

The small general contractor usually starts his career as a carpenter or mason. In working on various construction jobs he gradually becomes familiar with the activities of other trades. If he has initiative and intelligence, he will probably be promoted to superintendent. Instead of remaining a superintendent, he may decide, after a few years, to start his own contracting firm.

Typically the one-man contractor is both honest and a good craftsman who takes pride in his work. The fact that he stays in business at all proves he is a competent estimator, because if his estimates were consistently too high, he would get no business, and if they were consistently too low, he would rapidly go broke. Craftsmanship and estimating are not enough, however: The small contractor is all too likely to make such mistakes as keeping his accounts on the backs of envelopes containing unanswered correspondence, or else trying to carry his business around in his head, a brimming pail that spills a little with every step he takes. In short, he is not a trained administrator, and he tends to spend too much time in the field and not enough in the office. Happily he may have a son who graduates from college and joins his father in the business. This advent tends to overcome father's most glaring deficiencies and convert the firm into the potentially best instrument available for small construction jobs.

Another species of small general contractor is a construction manager only. He wears a necktie. He subcontracts everything, including carpentry, masonry, and labor. He tends to be the things an ex-mechanic is not, and he is not skilled at a construction trade or cost-estimating. If he is a good manager and uses good subcontractors he may be a very desirable small-job contractor.

The trouble with good small contractors, of course, is that their ability permits them to grow into good big contractors who no longer can afford to take on small projects. Luckily some first-rate small construction firms prefer to remain small and available for small jobs.

CONCLUSION

The picture of the construction team offered in this chapter has been designed partly to acquaint you with terminology, and partly to provide an orientation helpful in making some of the decisions required during a building project. The problem of selecting a contractor is an obvious case in point, and will be the subject of the next chapter.

There is another observation that can be made now. Contractors are in the business of selling a material product at a profit. They do not sell their services directly. Their services, the labor of their workmen, plus manufactured products and materials are all incorporated into a building, and it is the building that you buy. Contractors are thus unlike doctors, lawyers, and architects, all of whom provide service but not a tangible product.

A peculiarity of the product sold by building contractors, in contrast with typical manufactured products, is that each example is unique (an assertion that is false for mass-produced houses, but this book is not about them). The uniqueness of each building means that its cost depends significantly on guesswork. Unforeseen contingencies, of course, may affect the cost of manufacturing an automobile or a bar of soap, and it is conversely true that past experience provides some indication of the cost of manufacturing a building, but still a relatively high degree of production cost uncertainty characterizes the building industry and makes it a risky business. Therefore a building contractor, even when his work appears to be progressing serenely and profitably, is always trying to cut his production costs as much as possible. He can do so by skill and efficiency, but also by using cheaper products and materials, and by abbreviating the activities of the workmen. No doubt he wants to maintain his reputation as a reliable firm, but he must profit to survive. The conclusion you must draw is that the interests of your building contractor are to an appreciable extent opposed to your own. Bear this in mind as you read the next chapter.

Chapter 16

SELECTING A CONTRACTOR

THE decisions for you to make in the process of selecting a contractor are relatively few but extremely important. This chapter is intended to show that these decisions should largely depend on the architect's recommendations. You will also find that understanding the problems of selecting a contractor provides useful clues to the problems of dealing with contractors both before and after contracts are signed.

One early decision concerns the number of prime contracts you will let in connection with the project. And there are different types of contracts from which to choose. Bidding presents still other problems. Bids, by the way, should not be confused with contracts. A bid is an offer, a contract is an accepted offer.

NUMBER OF PRIME CONTRACTS

It is possible to make the work of each trade division of the specifications the subject of a prime contract. Then you will have a mechanical contractor, electrical contractor, elevator contractor, and so forth. An arrangement of this kind is called the *separate* or *segregated contract system.* At the other extreme you may let just one prime contract, an arrangement called the *single contract system.* There are also intermediate possibilities.

1. Separate Contracts

Under this system there may be twenty or more prime contracts. Its two main advantages can be understood only by contrast with the alternatives.

Under the single contract system the work is coordinated and managed by a general contractor. Much of the actual work, however, will be performed by subcontractors paid by the general contractor. You pay the general contractor enough to cover his payments to subcontractors and an additional amount, which not only covers the cost of managing the subcontractors but also provides the general contractor with a profit on his transactions with the subcontractors. All the firms that would be subcontractors under the single contract system, however, are prime contractors under the separate contract system. An advantage of the separate contract system, therefore, is that by eliminating the general contractor, you save his markup on the subcontractors.

Construction management must be exercised by someone, however, so under the separate contract system you will have to hire someone to do it. Herein lies a second advantage. The project will be managed by someone loyal to your interests rather than to another firm. The problem is whom to hire.

You may be able to engage the architect, for a fee of about 5 percent of construction cost, to manage construction. The advantages of having him are that he is eager to see that the design is accurately borne out in the actual building, and he is also more conversant than anyone else with the meaning of the voluminous content of the Contract Documents. Having him almost constantly at the job site, contrasted with the occasional visits that are all his basic services include, is of great value to you. Unfortunately the architect is not normally an experienced construction manager. Over the years enough knowledge may have rubbed off on him to enable him to run some kinds of projects successfully, but he is prone to make scheduling mistakes that result in delay and perhaps in extra costs. If he feels qualified to manage your job, however, and wants to do it, you are probably well advised to let him take it on. Becoming your construction manager does not turn the architect into a contractor himself. You will still pay the contractors yourself, and the architect will neither take profits from their work nor assume responsibility for the contractor's mistakes. His relation to each of the many contractors remains the same as it would be to the one contractor under the single contract system.

Instead of the architect you might hire a more experienced construction manager, such as a former supervisory employee of a construction firm. It will usually be hard to find a qualified person who is willing to accept the short-term employment of a single project.

Unless the architect has special reasons for advocating it, the separate contract system is not recommended to most readers. It can best be used by corporations and agencies that are constantly building, thus offering steady employment to construction managers and providing a training ground for future managers.

You need not begrudge the general contractor his markup on the subcontractors. He usually earns it.

2. Three Prime Contractors

For certain historical reasons it has not been uncommon in the past to let prime contracts for mechanical, electrical, and general work. Such an arrangement is merely a restricted version of the separate contract system with correspondingly restricted advantages, disadvantages, and problems. The "three prime contract system" seems to be going out of style. The present trend is either to multiply contracts or reduce them to one.

3. Single Contract

Under this system a general contractor assumes responsibility for the entire project. Typically he will use his own employees for about one-fourth to one-half of the work, and subcontract the rest, but he may subcontract all of the work.

General contractors prefer the single contract system because by enlarging the field of their responsibility it increases their potential profits. Architects tend to prefer the single contract system because they are neither particularly willing nor able to manage construction themselves, nor do they often have cause to be confident of the abilities of independent construction managers, who, unlike established construction firms, are likely to have no relevant reputation with the architect. Mechanical, electrical, and some other specialized firms, on the other hand, ordinarily advocate separate contracts for their work. One reason they do so is that they expect fairer treatment from the architect or some other owner-hired manager than past experience leads them to expect from general contractors.

From your point of view the single contract system has another positive advantage. If any of the work is done incorrectly, or damaged during construction, the general contractor must see that it is corrected or repaired at no cost to you. Under the separate contract system, your manager, who can't watch everything simultaneously, in many instances may not be able to establish which contractor is responsible for faults in the work. In these cases the expense of correcting the faults will fall to you.

There is no pat answer to the question of the optimum number of prime contractors. Talk it over with the architect, taking the foregoing considerations into account, and allowing for the peculiarities of your own project. Is a trustworthy construction manager available? What is local practice? You may not find the perfect solution but you will surely find a satisfactory one.

4. Contracts Easily Separated

Often some parts of a project are by their nature easily separable from the main body of work. Well-drilling, landscaping, and septic tank-tile field installation are examples of physical separation. Other work may be separated in time from the main work. Examples include carpeting, curtains, furniture, and so forth. In all these cases separate contracts may be let without producing a need for experienced construction management, although separating contracts will still increase the architect's work.

To speed a job, it is sometimes possible to let a contract for foundations, while drawings and specifications for the rest of the building are still under preparation by the architect. This ploy has negligible value on small jobs, however.

TYPES OF CONSTRUCTION CONTRACT

From here on, for simplicity, I will assume the single contract system. *Contractor* will mean the general contractor, but anything said of him will usually also be true of any prime contractor.

1. Cost-Plus Construction Contract

A cost-plus contract for construction is an arrangement similar to a cost-plus agreement for architectural service. The contractor orders materials, hires workmen, and hires other specialized construction firms for parts of the work. Weekly or monthly the contractor will add up his payments for wages and commitments for materials and services and send you a statement of the total, substantiated by duplicate invoices and time-cards if you so specify. On his statement he will add a previously agreed-to percentage or sum for his overhead and profit. You then pay the contractor and he disburses the necessary amounts to the others. The advantages and disadvantages of a cost-plus contract are the same as those discussed in Chapter 6 with reference to architectural services.

With a cost-plus arrangement the contractor should still give you an estimate of the total construction cost, but this estimate will not be a bid. If the contractor's costs plus profit exceed his estimate you pay the difference.

A refinement of the cost-plus method is the addition of a "guaranteed maximum" provision. The contractor then agrees that if costs exceed the guaranteed maximum, he will pay the excess. It is more common, however, to agree that if costs are either higher or lower than the guaranteed maximum you and the contractor will split the difference. He is thus motivated to bring the job in under the guaranteed maximum because he will then earn a bonus equal to half the saving: If he runs over, however, he will be penalized an amount equal to half the overrun. The advisability of such an arrangement depends on the size of the guaranteed maximum. You can't tell where wisdom lies unless you have a reliable, independent estimate of what the job "should" cost to compare with the maximum that the contractor offers to guarantee.

Cost-plus work is most appropriate when the uniqueness of the project makes accurate cost-estimating impossible or when there is only one available contractor who is capable of doing the job.

2. Lump-Sum Construction Contract

If project cost can be estimated with reasonable accuracy, it is advisable to have one or more contractors prepare estimates and then make firm offers to do the work for a lump sum. A suitable lump-sum contract provides the best assurance that the job can be built for the budgeted amount, and the great majority of construction contracts are of this type. The process of letting a lump-sum contract is called bidding, which is the subject of most of the rest of this chapter.

SINGLE VS. COMPETITIVE BIDS

You can ask a single contractor to give you a bid. He will collect bids from sub-bidders, prepare estimates of the cost of the work he plans to do with his own field force, and then make you an offer. If you accept, his bid becomes the Contract amount and he and his sub-bidders assume the risk for errors and miscalculations in their estimates. The single-bid method is indicated if, because of his reputation or other circumstances, you insist on having the job built by a particular contractor.

A more common method of awarding construction contracts is through competitive bidding. With this system several contractors submit bids, which you open at an appointed time, and then normally let the contract to the low bidder. The method has its pitfalls, of course, and some of them will be considered below, but if they are avoided, your job will go to the firm that best perceives how to do the work inexpensively. The competitive bid method thus tends to minimize construction costs. Hence its popularity with owners.

COMPETITIVE BID METHOD

To recapitulate, we are discussing the process of awarding a single, prime, lump-sum contract on the basis of competitive bids. The usual steps are as follows:

1. Inviting Bids

Make a list of desired bidders. The architect will assemble the list but be sure to tell him of any construction firms you want included or excluded. The architect or you should then telephone to invite the listed firms to bid. You may be surprised at how few are interested. They may be too busy to take on new work, or your project may be the wrong size for them, or there may be something about it that will make accurate cost-estimating too uncertain for them to want to risk bidding. Alternately, especially if construction activity is scarce, every builder for miles around may want to bid, and they will be calling you for permission to do so. Refer them to the architect, if you like, but don't give them permission to bid. The number of bidders should be limited, as we shall see.

Potential bidders will normally want to know who the other bidders are, and they should be given this information for reasons that will appear below.

2. Issue of Contract Documents

The architect will issue sets of Contract Documents so that everyone who needs to consult them will have access to them. Prime bidders usually go to the architect's office and pick up two or three sets apiece. Sub-bidders also need to consult the documents. Sub-bidders include not only firms that may become subcontractors but also suppliers and fabricators. Some sub-bid takeoffs take so much time to prepare that those sub-bidders will need a set of Contract Documents. Other sub-bidders can consult sets in the architect's office or in "plan rooms."

Builders' associations (and the F. W. Dodge Corp.) maintain plan rooms in most cities. Sets of Contract Documents for many projects from many architect's offices are kept there during their bid periods, as in a library. Members who wish to submit bids can use these sets on the premises for the minutes or hours they need to make their takeoffs.

Contract Documents for bidding are issued by the architect on a loan basis. After bids are submitted, all sets should be returned by plan rooms and bidders for eventual reissue to the successful bidders who will use them during construction. To encourage return of Contract Documents by bidders, the architect may require them to make a deposit for each set approximately equal to the cost of reproduction. When sets are returned, deposits are refunded. You keep the deposit for sets not returned.

Efficient bidding for a small house will require about twenty-five sets of Contract Documents. A hundred or more sets may be required for a large job.

3. Instructing Bidders

Bound in the front of the specifications book there will be a page or two headed "Instructions to Bidders" or "Notice to Contractors." Its purpose is to explain the ground rules for bidding. It will tell bidders when and where their bids are due, and include details of bid registry, bonds, separate bids, and so forth, of which more later.

JOB 65-01

NOTICE TO CONTRACTORS

PROJECT: RESIDENCE FOR
DR. AND MRS. J.T. HAUSWIRTH
202 ACACIA DRIVE
HECTOR, MICHIGAN

1. SEALED BIDS WILL BE ACCEPTED AT THE ARCHITECT'S OFFICE UNTIL 2 P.M., TUESDAY, 12 JUNE 1965; AND WILL BE OPENED PRIVATELY BY THE OWNER AND ARCHITECT AT THAT TIME.

2. THE FOLLOWING HAVE BEEN INVITED TO BID ON THE COMPLETE PROJECT. UNINVITED BIDS WILL NOT BE ACCEPTED.

ARCADIA BUILDING COMPANY

DROSSCLAD CONSTRUCTION COMPANY

GILTBILT BUILDERS, INC.

LEVELFIELD AND SON, BUILDERS

3. CONTRACT DOCUMENTS WILL BE ON FILE AT:

ARCHITECT'S OFFICE

BUILDERS AND TRADERS EXCHANGE

4. THE OWNER RESERVES THE RIGHT TO REJECT ANY OR ALL BIDS, TO ACCEPT ANY BID, AND TO WAIVE ANY INFORMALITY IN BIDS.

Marshall Shaper

MARSHALL SHAPER
REGISTERED ARCHITECT
303 LINDEN ST.
HECUBA, MICHIGAN
PH: 666-6666

4. Bid Preparation

From the time of issue of Contract Documents to the time of receipt of bids you should allow about a month. Two weeks might be enough for a small to medium-sized project, but that would be cutting it pretty thin. A very large project might require two months. If many other jobs are "out for bids" in your area, the time should be increased. The architect, probably after consulting some of the bidders, should set the bid due date. As you must approve it, however, you should understand why you can't get bids overnight.

Let us follow a thread of the bidding to see where time flies. Ajax Plumbing Company wants to bid for the plumbing subcontract. Hercules Ajax, the boss, gets a set of Contract Documents and makes a takeoff of labor and materials. For pipe and fittings he may telephone three suppliers and read off his bill of materials to each one. A day or two later each telephones back and quotes a price. Ajax incorporates the lowest of the three prices into his estimate. He would follow the same procedure for plumbing fixtures, but it turns out he doesn't have to: Four plumbing fixture salesmen, each of whom learned from the builders' association that this project was out for bids, have each visited the plan room, made a fixture takeoff, and are now telephoning their prices to all the plumbing firms known (or suspected) to be "figuring the job." Ajax notes the fixture bids, but rejects the low one because the company submitting it has a slow-delivery record. Ajax therefore uses the second-low fixture bid in his own estimate. Eventually he gets prices for all materials and equipment that will be required under the Plumbing Division of the project. He then adds up all the items on his estimate; adds an amount for insurance, overhead, contingencies, and profit; and forwards the final sum as his bid to some or all of the prime bidders.

Each prime bidder, in turn, has been making his own takeoff and also collecting sub-bids from other plumbing contractors, electrical contractors, various manufacturers' representatives, salesmen, fabricators, suppliers, and so forth. Thus scores or hundreds of individuals have to make takeoffs, incorporate them into estimates, produce bids, and forward them up the chain until all the prime bidders have all the information they need for their own bids. It all takes time.

5. Bid Submission

Each prime bidder makes his bid by filling out a proposal form in duplicate, keeping one copy, and mailing or delivering the other in a sealed envelope to you or the architect, whichever the instructions to bidders specifies, on or before the due date. The proposal form is drafted by the architect for your approval and often included near the front of the specifications book. The bidders remove the forms to use them. A sample, filled-in proposal form appears on the following page. Note that bidders, in this example, may compete on the basis of early completion of construction as well as on cost. You might accept someone other than the low bidder if he offered to complete the job a month or two earlier.

The proposal submitted by the Arcadia Building Company to the Hauswirths was the low bid and they accepted it. The high bid was $57,125.00. The owner-contractor agreement form shown in Chapter 14 was then filled in and signed by the Hauswirths and the contractor. Both alternate no. 1 and the proposed substitution of glass were accepted by the owner. The Contract amount was thus $51,680 plus $1,935 minus $462, which equals $53,153.

Work began on 1 July 1965.

6. Bid Receipt

Typically, the morning of the day bids are due, one or more bidders telephone the architect to say they need more time. The architect will check with you. Be realistic. If two of a total of four bidders can't make the deadline, are you better off to wait a day or two and get four bids or hold the line and get only two? Your chagrin at delay and annoyance with the bidders' apparent procrastination should be irrelevant.

If an extension of time is granted, all bidders must immediately be informed by the architect. Any bid arriving after the final deadline should be absolutely refused. To do otherwise would be a serious breach of faith with the other bidders.

7. Bid Opening

Bids may be opened in public, that is in the presence of the bidders. This method is customary in government work, but in other cases there are advantages to private opening. Referring again to the proposal form on the next page, you can see that the bids will differ not only in base cost but also in alternate costs, substitutions, and date of completion of the work. The architect may need to make outside inquiries about substitutions before he can recommend acceptance or rejection of them. Furthermore, you and

JOB 65-01

<u>CONTRACTOR'S PROPOSAL</u>

DR. JOHN T. HAUSWIRTH
1000 GALEN ROAD
VERONA, MICHIGAN

DEAR SIR:

HAVING CAREFULLY EXAMINED CONDITIONS AT THE SITE, WE, THE UNDERSIGNED, PROPOSE TO PERFORM ALL WORK SET FORTH IN THE DRAWINGS AND SPECIFICATIONS PREPARED BY MARSHALL SHAPER AND BEARING HIS JOB NO. 65-01 FOR THE SUM OF:

fifty one thousand six hundred eighty & no/100s dollars ($51,680.00)

WE FURTHER PROPOSE TO PERFORM THE WORK OF ALTERNATE NO. 1 AS SET FORTH IN THE SAME FOR THE ADDITIONAL SUM OF:

one thousand nine hundred thirty five & no/100s dollars ($1,935.00)

WE AGREE TO BE BOUND BY THIS PROPOSAL FOR A PERIOD OF THIRTY DAYS FROM THIS DATE.

WE FURTHER AGREE THAT IF AWARDED THE CONTRACT WE WILL COMPLETE THE WORK NOT LATER THAN November 30, 1965

THIS PROPOSAL IS BASED ON PROVIDING MATERIALS AND EQUIPMENT NAMED IN THE DRAWINGS AND SPECIFICATIONS. IF ANY OF THE FOLLOWING SUBSTITUTIONS IS ACCEPTED WE AGREE TO MAKE THE CORRESPONDING ADDITIONS OR DEDUCTIONS FROM THE ABOVE-PROPOSED AMOUNT.

SUBSTITUTION	ADD/DEDUCT
Twinpane instead of Thermopane glass – deduct	$462.00

SUBMITTED BY:

ARCADIA BUILDING COMPANY

SIGNED BY:

Gerald Framer

DATE June 21, 1965

he may need a few hours to consider and discuss the other variations before deciding which bid, if any, it will best serve your interests to accept. The tensions in a room full of eager bidders are not conducive to either dispassionate thought or frank discussion.

8. Negotiating With Low Bidder

A great deal of past effort has been aimed at insuring that you can, after discerning the low (or "best") bidder, lift the telephone and ask him to drop around to sign the Contract. If all the recommendations of this book are followed, you can probably do just that. Unfortunately it is still possible that all the bids will be too high.

In such a pickle you can try to negotiate a reduction of the low bid. Merely informing the low bidder that unless he knocks off a few thousand dollars you can't proceed will probably get you nowhere. Preferably you and the architect should meet with the low bidder and explore possible changes in construction or design that would permit reduction of the bid. The low bidder, as he has hitherto attacked this project strictly from the point of view of cost, may have ideas for savings that have occurred to neither you nor the architect. If enough such changes can be agreed to, the architect will describe them in an addendum to the Contract Documents, the bidder's proposal can be modified, and the Contract then signed.

PITFALLS AND SAFEGUARDS OF COMPETITIVE BIDDING

We have traced the steps in bidding partly because you will be directly involved in the process, but also partly because a knowledge of the mechanics of bidding seems like a necessary foundation for full comprehension of certain other related problems. These other problems are taken up below. They concern the selection of bidders, the number of bidders, bid-shopping, collusion among bidders, and bid bonds.

1. Selecting Bidders

The purpose of competitive bidding is to get your building built at least cost. The method is to award the construction Contract to the firm that offers to do the work for the lowest price, but why does one firm bid lower than another? One hopes it is for one or more of the following reasons:

(a) The firm's skill and experience, developed in past work, enable it to build efficiently and hence cheaply.

(b) By ingenuity the firm perceives inexpensive ways of building your particular project.

(c) The firm is willing to work for moderate profit.

There are, however, other reasons that a firm may bid low. One of these is estimating error. An estimator, through simple carelessness, may leave out some part of the work. ("Great Scott! I forgot the roof!") Or he may underestimate the amount of labor or materials involved in such operations as the construction of concrete forms or the erection of stud walls or something else. (If he overestimates, always a possibility, he will of course tend to bid high and not get the job.) For brevity, if not with complete justification, let us call all erring bidders ninnies.

Another way that a construction firm may bid low is by planning to cheat. For brevity, and with complete justice, let us call such bidders scoundrels.

On first consideration you may think that the Contract Documents will protect you if you enter into a Contract with a ninny or a scoundrel. All that careful drafting, those compendious specifications, and ironbound conditions will surely keep the contractor on a strait path. These notions are reasonable but false.

The architect or his representative is present on the construction site, at best, hardly more than 20 percent of the time. A contractor who is determined to cheat can cut a lot of corners and cover them up during the remaining 80 percent of the time. He can place footings on loose earth, thus saving a little on excavation and concrete costs. He can throw wood scraps in the backfill, thus saving a little on excavation and cleanup costs. He may get away with using fewer nails or lower quality wood than specified. He may leave gaps in the insulation. He may apply only two coats of paint where three are specified. There are scores of possibilities for the scoundrel. The architect will undoubtedly catch some of these discrepancies but not all of them. As construction is not an exact science, some of these faults may never show themselves; others will not become apparent for years. Those that show up fairly soon may be uncorrectable, and the contractor may by then have quietly dissolved his corporation and gone into business under another name so you can't even find anyone to sue. The possibilities for cheating that are open to the scoundrel are also tempting to the ninny. The inexperienced firm that errs in its estimate may be faced with the prospect of losing its shirt on the job. It will certainly try every way it can to cut costs. Its morale will be poor and its workmanship of the lowest quality, and quality of workmanship is something almost impossible to pin down precisely in specifications.

The conclusion that must be drawn from the foregoing, and from actual experience, is not an unfamiliar one: A contract is no better than the abilities and intentions of the contracting parties. If a contractor is a ninny, his mistakes will cost you money, delay your job, reduce its quality, or more likely, all three. If he is a scoundrel, you will suffer, no matter what the Contract Documents say. A building contract, like fire insurance, mitigates disaster but does not preclude loss. To get good work you need a contractor who views the Contract Documents as an instrument to organize and facilitate sound construction, not as a target in which to shoot holes.

In competitive bidding, the nature of the faults we have been discussing tend to make their practitioners the low bidders. Therefore, to insure that your job is built by able firms with good intentions, the ninnies and the scoundrels must not be allowed to bid in the first place. You, or the architect, or the two of you together, should investigate the qualifications of potential bidders and then invite only firms you have reason to believe will protect their reputations by doing conscientious work, firms that also exhibit a combination of acumen and experience. Any firm that has been successful for many years is probably able, but note its record on jobs similar in type and size to your own: Your job may be too far removed from the firm's experience. To help in selection, you can turn a proposed list of bidders over to a reputable bonding company and inform them you will want them to write a performance bond on the successful bidder. The bonding company will then conduct its own inquiries and may tell you that they will not stand surety on certain of the proposed bidders. Any bidder the bonding company will not bond is one you had better not allow to bid.

Do not, however, make the mistake with construction firms that I warned about with architects: Don't make it impossible for new construction firms to get started. Every new firm must sometime do its first job, and will tend to bid low to get it. If the backgrounds of the heads of the new firm are satisfactory, let them bid, even on jobs somewhat larger than they have yet done. If owners create a climate in which new contractors cannot succeed, the tendency is for established firms, deprived of fresh competition, to become decadent, their work overpriced, and their methods antiquated.

The final list of bidders should be such that you are willing, without reservation, to enter into a Contract with any one of them should he be the low bidder.

2. Number of Bidders

If to any group of bidders you add one, there is always some chance that the added one will bid lower than any of the original group. It is therefore mathematically probable that if the number of bidders is increased, the low bid will be reduced. These statements, however, ignore other factors which begin to supervene as the number of bidders is increased.

In any locale there is a limited number of high caliber construction firms. Increasing the number of bidders thus increases the chance that the overeager and the semihonest will begin to creep into the list. Their presence will have an adverse effect on the good guys. A good firm wants to compete with other good firms on the basis of skill, experience, ingenuity, and profit expectation. It does not want to compete with bad firms because it can succeed only by employing their chiseling tactics. Good firms will therefore refuse to bid if the list includes some sour apples. Furthermore, if the number of bidders is very large, the good firms will either know or be forced to assume that one or more of the other bidders is a ninny or a scoundrel. The good firm's refusal to bid against a large or partly shoddy group of other bidders can take two forms. The firm may politely tell you it does not care to bid, but an outright refusal might offend you or the architect, who after all may have future work to let. As an alternative the firm may therefore agree to bid, but instead of spending the many hours of work required for a careful construction cost estimate, the firm will rough out a hasty estimate with plenty of padding and incorporate it into a bid. They know this bid is so high that if by some miracle it is accepted the firm can't lose money. It is called a *courtesy bid,* but it's no favor to you.

If you have at least three bidders, then the degree of competition is usually adequate to produce at least one bid that is about as low as practical. If there are more than about six bidders, the better firms will begin to lose interest.

3. Bid-Shopping

There is a pernicious practice, which it is in your interest to avoid. A rascally bidder may look over his sub-bids, such as for lumber, and note that Lumber Company A is low. So the bidder telephones Lumber Company B, tells him A's bid, and invites B to bid a little lower. If B agrees to a lower figure, the rascal then telephones C, tells him B's bid, and again invites a still lower bid. He may continue this process through D and E and even back to A. This method of reducing costs by auctioning one's subcontracts is called bid-shopping. Prime bidders may shop their sub-bids; sub-bidders may shop their sub-sub-bids, and so forth.

When construction work is scarce, even good firms are tempted either to indulge in or acquiesce in bid-shopping, reasoning that it is better to have profitless work than no work at all. And as the subcontract amount is forced downward, the pressure to cheat rises, and you are exposed to the severe headaches of advanced construction gamesmanship.

One way to reduce bid-shopping is to require that all sub-bids, and perhaps even sub-sub-bids, be submitted to you directly or through the architect, rather than to the prime bidders. You then select the low bidder in each category with the understanding that the low prime bidder will accept each of the low sub-bidders as subcontractors. The result is still a single prime contract, but based on separate bids. A minor drawback of separate bids is the sheer labor of inviting, receiving, and evaluating up to a hundred sub-bids, which is a larger number than any prime bidder would normally have to deal with. A more serious snag in the system of separate bids arises from the history of relations among primes and subs in any locality. Jones Roofing Company, for instance, has learned from bitter experience that Brown Builders can't maintain a construction schedule, so Jones invariably has to pay overtime wages when working under Brown. Brown, in turn, has learned that Robinson Tile is so well managed that the firm needs no supervision by the general contractor, which reduces the general's overhead and permits him to lower his bid. In this situaton both general and sub-bidders, not knowing with whom they may end up working, will tend to bid high.

There is a refinement to the separate bid system which seems to overcome the disadvantages outlined above. It is called the *bid-registry system.* The sub-bid submission deadline is set a day or more before the prime bid deadline. Sub-bids are submitted in duplicate to a disinterested agent, such as the builders' association or the architect. Each sub-bidder submits a separate bid for each prime bidder, but only to those prime bidders to whom he cares to bid, and he can bid different amounts to each prime bidder if he wishes. After the sub-bid deadline the prime bidders pick up all bids addressed to them, and the prime bidders are then free to use whichever of the sub-bids addressed to them they prefer, whether low or not. Meanwhile the duplicates of all sub-bids remain in the hands of the disinterested party who first received them. The prime bidders now complete their own bids and submit them to you. When you select the successful prime bidder, he informs you which sub-bidders he has accepted, and the disinterested agent turns over their bids to the architect and destroys the rest. After you sign the Contract, and your contractor then signs his subcontracts, any subcontractor who finds his subcontract amount is less than his bid can prove it by reference to the duplicates held by the architect, which would convict the contractor of fraud. (I am oversimplifying the legal aspects of the matter.) Bid-registry is a fairly new practice and seems to be gaining favor. It seems worth trying because it promises advantages without disadvantages, aside from a tolerable amount of red tape. If the system is used the "Notice to Contractors" becomes long and makes dull reading (those legal aspects), so I have not based the sample in this chapter on bid-registry.

4. Collusion

One hears tales of how all the local construction firms confer secretly prior to bid deadlines, and agree among themselves as to who shall bid low. They set the low bid generously high, of course, and take turns being low bidder. Everyone shares the gravy equally. It is impossible to say to what extent such illicit combinations exist. The more firms involved, no doubt, the sooner they are betrayed, but if there are only two painting contractors, for instance, or three lumber companies in a given area, the temptation to collude may prove irresistible. There are at least two ways to discourage this kind of cheating. One is to permit the fresh competition of new firms, as recommended earlier in this chapter. Another is to invite a bid or two from firms that, perhaps because of geographical separation, are likely to be outside the ring of cheaters.

5. Bid Bonds

When bids are opened, and bidders are all informed of the amounts of all bids, and the low bidder finds himself a great deal lower than the others, he is likely to think he made a mistake and want to withdraw his bid. To prevent him from doing so, or to indemnify you if his withdrawal forces you to accept a higher bid, you can require all bids to be accompanied by a bid bond or certified check, usually equal to about 5 percent of the bid, and forfeitable if the bidder withdraws after bids are opened. If the bidder actually erred, however, it is probably not a good idea to force him into a contract, nor does it really seem fair to charge him 5 percent of his bid for an honest error. In fact, if the bidder can prove he made serious mistakes of omission or calculation in his bid, he may succeed legally in withdrawing his bid without forfeiting the bid bond. For these reasons bid bonds are not recommended unless there are special circumstances.

A PAIR OF UNKNOWN QUANTITIES

In England they have people called *quantity surveyors* who work independently or for architects. Quantity surveyors make careful, professional takeoffs from the Contract Documents, and their takeoffs are distributed to all bidders. All bids are then required to be based on the takeoff made by the quantity surveyor. This procedure tends to eliminate a large fraction of bidding errors and is held to have other advantages too. The practice is almost unheard of in the United States, but there are a few quantity surveyors in this country. You can take up the matter with your architect if you wish.

Recently I heard some one toss out for discussion the notion that the competitive bidding system should be based on acceptance of the *second*-lowest bid, not the lowest. At first I thought the fellow was drunk, but on thinking over the idea, I began to see that it had its attractions. In the first place it would automatically shut out the erroneously lowest bid, but more significantly it would seem to compel bidders to strive for accuracy and make bid-shopping quite unattractive. To my knowledge it has never been tried. You may be the first.

AFTER CONTRACT, BEFORE CONSTRUCTION

Ordinarily the architect will write to each bidder informing him of the amounts of the bids, and thanking him for submitting a bid. It is thus unnecessary for you to thank the bidders, which makes it all the more appreciated if you do.

Before the contractor moves onto the site, you should be sure to have the necessary fire coverage. A certificate of this insurance should be forwarded to the contractor. If you intend to purchase owner's contingent liability insurance, delay no more. Before he starts work the contractor should submit certificates of all insurance he is required to provide. He should also furnish you with a certified copy of the performance bond, if he is so required. If you are buying the bond from the surety yourself, now is the time to do it.

The Contract Documents usually provide that the contractor obtain and pay for all municipal permits required in connection with the work. These will include the building permit, plumbing and electrical permits, and perhaps others. Their cost will have been included in the contractor's original bid, of course.

You may now have to apply for utility service. Sometimes these applications can be made by the contractor, but often the utility companies prefer to deal directly with you, who are the true, ultimate customer.

SUMMARY

It is the recommendation of this chapter that most conventional construction projects be performed by a single, prime contractor, and that the Contract be awarded on the basis of lump-sum competitive bids by from three to six bidders. Separate Contracts may be advisable for site work, landscaping, furnishing, and other naturally separable parts of the project.

Because a Contract is likely to be no better than the ability and intention of the parties to it, only reputable construction firms should be allowed to bid. To minimize the abuse known as bid-shopping, the system of bid-registry shows promise and may be worth trying.

Chapter 17

THE PROJECT REPRESENTATIVE

LONG before ground-breaking, you ought to consider the advisability of hiring a *project representative.* He used to be called a *clerk-of-the-works,* but his job, in parallel with construction itself, has become increasingly complex in recent years and demands someone of more stature than is implied by the term *clerk.*

The project representative works for and is paid by you. In general his duty is to be present at the construction site whenever work is in progress in order to observe it and insure that it conforms to the Contract Documents. He also assists the contractor to understand the intent of the documents, and provides liaison between the architect and contractor. The last is especially important if the architect's office is a long-distance telephone call away from the job site. The contractor's superintendent is usually loath to run up his boss's telephone bill with calls to the architect, but you can and should give your project representative carte blanche for such calls. The errors they will avert will far more than compensate for their cost.

To explore more fully the role of the project representative, you should first review the sample Owner-Architect Agreement, Article 3.4, which describes the architect's duties during construction. Then read the sample "Suggested Instructions to Full-Time Project Representative" at the end of this chapter. Note how his duties supplement and augment those of the architect.

Although he works for you, the project representative should unquestionably be a person proposed by or at least acceptable to the architect. The project representative's duties should be agreed on in advance, and should resemble, or duplicate, those listed in the sample instruction. You should not interfere with his work, which should be supervised by the architect on your behalf.

Don't confuse the role of project representative with that of a construction manager or superintendent: The contractor will manage the job. The project representative has no authority except the right of access to the work. Nevertheless his presence polices the contractor. With a project representative continuously on the site, it is extremely difficult for the scoundrel to succeed or the ninny to escape detection.

The pre-eminently desirable qualities of a project representative are incorruptibility and maturity. He must be capable of protecting your interests against the contractor's errors (or villainy) despite close, daily association with the contractor's employees, and at the same time do his job without antagonizing the contractor, all of which will require firmness, fairness, and tact.

The project representative must also be intelligent enough to be able to read the Contract Documents and understand that the job is to be built in accordance with them, not according to any other ideas he or the contractor may have. This requirement for the work to conform to the Contract may seem too obvious to be worth mentioning, but it is astounding, not to say maddening, how often some mechanic or superintendent on the job thinks of a "better way" to build something and goes ahead without bothering to inform the architect. It is quite true that workmen at the site often find better ways than the drawings or specifications indicate for accomplishing some part of the work, and workmen should be encouraged to put forth their ideas, but unless the architect can review them carefully, what seems like a good idea too often turns out to have disasterous, unforeseen side-effects. The project representative prevents these unauthorized divergences from the Contract Documents, but transmits all ideas of the architect so that he can take steps to incorporate the sound ones into the work.

Finally, the project representative should know as much as possible about construction work. This, too, may seem obvious, but I want to emphasize that his knowledge of construction, although desirable, is a low-priority attribute. He is not a builder. The project representative's job is to observe, record, and communicate.

The time to consider hiring a project representative is shortly after approval of the preliminary design. Before that it is difficult to know if one will be needed, but if you wait very long after that, it will be hard to find and hire a good one before construction begins. The job is a temporary one, and that always makes it harder to find applicants. Possibilities include (but are not limited to) a draftsman on loan from an architect or engineer's office, a retired contractor, or even a mature college student. You can expect to pay him from $2.50 to $5.00 per hour, depending on his age and experience. His wages for a six-month job will thus range from $2,500 to $5,000. At a bit over the lowest rate a project representative, it can be seen, would add about 3 percent to the cost of a $100,000 project, and the percentage tends to decline as project size increases. I believe a project representative is a wise investment on any project costing over $100,000, but many architects would set the figure at $500,000, and some architects would not recommend a project representative on any job.

Once hired, your project representative should be furnished with two or three complete sets of the Contract Documents, and a library of reference material such as manuals, manufacturers's literature, and standard specifications relevant to the project. He should have office space with a desk, a couple of chairs, filing cabinet, and telephone; all of which it is most practical to have the contractor provide, along with a safety helmet, by inserting a suitable clause in the special general conditions.

In summary and conclusion, it is more desirable to have a project representative (1) the further the job is from the architect's office, (2) the more complicated or unusual the design or construction of the project is, (3) the less you can rely on the ability and goodwill of the prime and subcontractors, (4) the higher the project cost, and (5) the more conservative you are, in general, about taking chances. Among other things, a project representative is like an insurance policy tending to protect you against certain kinds of unforeseeable incidents involved in construction projects.

THE AMERICAN INSTITUTE OF ARCHITECTS
AIA DOCUMENT B352
SEPT. 1963 ED.

SUGGESTED INSTRUCTIONS TO FULL-TIME PROJECT REPRESENTATIVE

RECOMMENDED AS AN EXHIBIT TO THE OWNER-ARCHITECT AGREEMENT WHEN A FULL-TIME PROJECT REPRESENTATIVE IS EMPLOYED

1 **EXPLAIN CONTRACT DOCUMENTS:** Assist the Contractor via the Contractor's Superintendent to understand the intent of the Contract Documents.

2 **OBSERVATIONS:** Conduct on-site observations and spot checks of the work in progress as a basis for determining conformance of work, materials and equipment with the Contract Documents.

3 **ADDITIONAL INFORMATION:** Obtain from the Architect additional details or information if, and when, required at the job site for proper execution of the work.

4 **MODIFICATIONS:** Consider and evaluate suggestions or modifications which may be submitted by the Contractor to the Architect; and report them with recommendations to the Architect for final decision.

5 **CONSTRUCTION SCHEDULE AND COMPLETION:** Be alert to the completion date and to conditions which may cause delay in completion, and report same to the Architect. When the construction work has been completed in accordance with the Contract Documents, advise the Architect that the work is ready for general inspection and acceptance.

6 **LIAISON:** Serve as liaison between Contractor and the Architect and maintain relationship with the Contractor and all subcontractors on the job only through the Contractor's job superintendent. Protect against the Owner issuing instructions to the Contractor or his employees.

7 **JOB CONFERENCES:** Attend and report to the Architect on all required conferences held at the job site.

8 **OBSERVE TESTS:** See that tests which are required by the Contract Documents are actually conducted; observe, record and report to the Architect all details relative to the test procedures; and advise the Architect's office in advance of the schedules of tests.

9 **INSPECTIONS BY OTHERS:** If inspectors, representing local, state or federal agencies, having jurisdiction over the Project, visit the job site, accompany such inspectors during their trips through the Project, record the outcome of these inspections and report same to the Architect's office.

10 **SAMPLES:** Receive samples which are required to be furnished at the job site; record date received and from whom, notify the Architect of their readiness for examination; record Architect's approval or rejection; and maintain custody of approved samples.

11 **RECORDS:**
a) Maintain at the job site orderly files for (1) correspondence, (2) reports of job conferences, (3) shop drawings and (4) reproductions of original contract documents including all addenda, change orders and additional drawings issued subsequent to the award of the contract.
b) Keep a daily diary or log book, recording hours on the job site, weather conditions, list of visiting officials and jurisdiction, daily activities, decisions, observations in general, and specific observations in more detail as in the case of observing test procedures.
c) Record names, addresses and telephone numbers of all contractors and subcontractors.

12 **SHOP DRAWINGS:** Do not permit the installation of any materials and equipment for which shop drawings are required unless such drawings have been duly approved and issued by the Architect.

13 **CONTRACTOR'S REQUISITIONS FOR PAYMENT:** Review with all concerned the requisitions for payment as submitted by the Contractor and forward them with recommendations to the Architect for disposition.

14 **LIST OF ITEMS FOR CORRECTION:** After Substantial Completion, make a list of items for correction before final inspection, and check each item as it is corrected.

15 **OWNER'S OCCUPANCY OF THE BUILDING:** If the Owner occupies (to any degree) the building prior to actual completion of the work by the Contractor, be especially alert to possibilities of claims for damage to completed work prior to the acceptance of the building.

16 **OWNER'S EXISTING OPERATION:** In the case of additions to, or renovations of an existing facility, which must be maintained as an operational unit, be alert to conditions on the job site which may have an effect on the Owner's existing operation.

17 **GUARANTEES, CERTIFICATES, MAINTENANCE AND OPERATION MANUALS:** During the course of the work, collect Guarantees, Certificates and Maintenance Operation Manuals and Keying Schedule, and at the acceptance of the Project, assemble this material and deliver it to the Architect for forwarding to the Owner.

18 **LIMITATIONS OF AUTHORITY:** Do not become involved in any of the following areas of responsibility unless specific exceptions are established by written instructions issued by the Architect:
a) Do not authorize deviations from the Contract Documents.
b) Avoid conducting any tests personally.
c) Do not enter into the area of responsibility of the Contractor's field superintendent.
d) Do not expedite job for Contractor.
e) Do not advise on, or issue directions relative to, any aspect of the building technique or sequence, unless a specific technique or sequence is called for in the specifications.
f) Do not approve shop drawings or samples.
g) Do not authorize, or advise, the Owner to occupy the Project, in whole, or in part, prior to the final acceptance of the building.
h) Do not issue a Certificate for Payment.

AIA DOC. B352 SEPT. 1963 ED.

Chapter 18

CONSTRUCTION

EVERYONE has seen houses under construction. The superficial aspects of the process are well known. First the builder digs a hole, then puts in the basement walls of block or concrete. Next the carpenters frame up the stud walls and add the rafters or trusses of the roof. Then the roof deck and wall sheathing go on, followed by shingles and siding, or masonry veneer, and doors and windows. Inside the floor deck is installed, partitions are framed, and the rough piping and wiring are done. After the walls and roof are insulated, the finish work begins, and includes the plaster or plasterboard walls and ceiling, painting, flooring, cabinets and shelving, trim, plumbing and lighting fixtures, completion of the air-conditioning system, door hardware, and so forth.

Buildings other than houses proceed in the same general way. In approximate chronological order the typical steps are: excavation, footings, foundation walls, structural frame, roof and floor decks, exterior walls and windows, rough mechanical and electrical work, insulation, interior surfacing, doors, and finish work. For fairly obvious reasons there is little latitude in the course of events. Everything is supported by something else and therefore cannot be installed until that something is there for it to be sat upon or hung from. Also, finished interior work cannot begin until the shell of the building is substantially weatherproof.

A lifetime of sidewalk superintending, however, will still leave you in the dark about some of the events that vitally affect the construction process. A lot goes on besides the tangible multiplication of sticks and bricks that all can see.

ARCHITECT'S INSPECTIONS

The architect, or one of his "field men" will visit nearby projects about two or three times a week and spend an hour or two at the site. If the project is far from the architect's office, he will probably visit it only about once a week but will spend a full day when he does, and weekly visits will be supplemented by telephone calls.

One purpose of the architect's visits is to inspect the work done since the preceding visit and attempt to ascertain that it has been done in conformance to the Contract provisions. These inspections are rather more thorough than the term *spot-check* suggests, but they are not by any means exhaustive inspections. For instance, the architect will inspect just before concrete is cast. He will view the formwork and may notice an error of configuration or a loose board, but he will not measure everything to insure that the dimensions are correct. Doing so is the contractor's job. The architect should look more carefully at the sizes and spacing of reinforcing rods, however, because they will be covered by concrete, which will forever hide any error in their placement, whereas if a wall is out of place the mistake can eventually be discovered and corrected. Any discrepancy the architect finds between the actual work and the drawings and specifications he will call to the contractor's attention on the spot, and the contractor must correct it, although usually he should be allowed to do so at his own convenience, unless waiting would protract a hazardous condition, or expose work to theft or undesirable weathering. As interpreter of the Contract Documents, it is the architect who rules whether or not work conforms to the Contract. If the contractor fails or refuses to correct defective work, you are authorized to withhold payment or even to terminate the Contract. In practice, however, you will probably not be faced with decisions of such extremity. What usually happens when the architect points out a discrepancy in the work is that the contractor reviews the pertinent parts of the drawings and specifications, realizes he has erred, and readily, if morosely, makes amends. On the other hand, if the contractor feels his original interpretation was correct he will argue. Even so, if the architect has the shadow of justice on his side and remains adamant, the contractor will normally acquiesce, unless by so doing he stands to obligate himelf to an unforeseen outlay large enough to take an appreciable bite out of his anticipated profits. The architect, however, knows that if the contractor is convinced he is being unfairly treated he will tend to be uncooperative and retaliate with a certain amount of poor workmanship later in the project, justifying himself by recalling the present "unfairness." Neither party, in short, wants to antagonize the other.

Disagreements on the meaning of the details of the Contract Documents are rare because their meaning is usually plain enough if you look in the right place. The drawings and specifications, however, contain so much information in such concentrated form that the contractor occasionally misses some of it. If he argues when the architect points out the oversight, it is because the contractor merely wants to leave no stone unturned in what he strongly suspects is a vain attempt to evade the extra expense of ripping out a piece of X to install an overlooked Y that should have been put in before X was built in the first place.

ARCHITECT'S MISTAKES

There is always a likelihood of error in the drawing and specifications. A dimension may be wrong. There may be inconsistency if, for instance, the plan notes ceramic tile in some room but the finish schedule in the specifications calls for rubber tile in the same room. There may be omission, as when there is no mention of a water heater in the specifications, but the plan shows a circle labeled *water heater*. In fact, most architects will agree that a perfect set of drawings and specifications is so rare that one automatically assume some errors exist in any set.

Some errors tend to be self-resolving. Dimensioning is similar to double-entry bookkeeping. If one dimension is wrong, it will be manifest to anyone trying to lay out the work. When the contractor discovers such an error, he should get in touch with the architect who will soon tell him where the error lies and correct it. Dimensioning errors are usually the result of a draftsman's faulty arithmetic. One has to sympathize with the drudge who must add up long strings of numerals; such as 3⅝″, 2¼″, 1′-0½″; and allow that he will occasionally add or lose a fraction. Dimensioning errors, and some others, amount in most cases to a minor nuisance to the contractor and architect, but it is a nuisance with which they are used to dealing.

Another class of errors may involve you. Take the missing water heater specification. If any of the bidders for the mechanical subcontract had noticed the water heater shown on the plan and failed to find a specification for it, they would have telephoned the architect, who would quickly have issued a "bulletin" to all bidders informing them what the water heater specification should be. If none noticed the circle on the plan, however, then none of them, including the one who has since become the present mechanical subcontractor, allowed any money in his estimate for it. Now, when the architect points out the labeled circle on the plan, the mechanical subcontractor is suddenly stuck with providing a water heater. No two ways about it: There it is in black and white—*water heater*. Grinding his teeth in chagrin, the plumber admits that he will have to furnish it, and as the general conditions say everything for the project must be new, he is barred from putting in some old wreck he has lying around his shop, but as there is no other specification—just the words *water heater*—the plumber is going to put in the cheapest he can find. The architect, however, thinks you should have a water heater of greater capacity and higher quality than the sleazy product inadvertent omission of a detailed specification permits the plumber to furnish. So the architect asks the plumber how much extra a proper water heater will cost. The answer, say $50, is inevitably somewhat padded because the plumber is trying to recoup some of the money he is losing by not having included any money for a water heater in his original bid, but the architect will probably decide that it will best serve your interests for you to accept the $50 extra and take the better water heater. He will get in touch with you, explain the circumstances, and make his recommendation. In this example you come out ahead either way: You get a low-quality water heater for nothing, or a good one for $50; a bargain.

Now let us revise the example by assuming that a water heater was neither shown on the plan nor mentioned in the specifications. As you must still have one, the architect, when the omission is detected, asks the mechanical subcontractor to quote an extra for providing one. In effect this quotation will be a "single bid," and thus probably somewhat higher than the lowest of competitive bids. You could get competitive bids, if you wanted them, because the Contract normally provides that the owner can have extra work performed by outside contractors (General Conditions, Article 35), but the potential saving on one water heater will not be worth the trouble of taking competitive bids. Thus if the architect errs by leaving something out of the Contract Documents, the true cost of his error is not the amount bid for the item but the difference between that bid and the hypothetical low bid you would have received through competitive bidding. In this example, if the plumber offers to provide the water heater for $100, but competitive bidding would have produced a low bid of $90 for the same equipment, then the cost of the architect's error is $10, the difference between $100 and $90.

There is another possibility in connection with that pesky water heater. If the plumbing was installed before the absence of a water heater was noticed, then it may be necessary, at some extra expense, to undo some of the piping work in order to connect the heater. In this case the cost of the architect's error will also include the extra cost of reworking the piping.

As the architect's errors have cost you money, you may have a case for demanding that he pay for them himself. No one can determine precisely the cost of the errors, but if you feel like making such a demand, the architect may accede to it if the amount is small and the issue clear. If we consider other cases, however, with increasing amounts of money involved, or with increasing uncertainty as to whether the architect actually erred, then a point will be reached beyond which the architect will choose to let a court determine the degree, if any, of his liability for error. All this is mere cold logic; there are other ways to view the situation.

By the time the job is under construction, you and the architect should have become friendly. It is well that you do because his ability to serve your interests is enhanced the better he understands them, and he can understand them better if he is sympathetic. On purely selfish grounds, therefore, it is worth something to you to maintain friendly relations by paying for minor extras caused by his possible errors, than to fall out over a demand that he pay for them himself. The matter of degree must naturally be considered. If his aggregate errors start adding up to around, say 2 percent of the project cost, they may outweigh the value of his good will and justify you in demanding compensation. As 2 percent of project cost is one-fourth or more of the architect's fee, however, the two of you will undoubtedly fail to agree, and the matter will have to be referred to lawyers and perhaps a court. Professional service is a broad concept, and although clear-cut negligence occasionally occurs, merely proving that an architect's judgment was less than perfect is rarely enough to win your case. Of course, the architect wants to retain your good will too. His future depends on satisfied clients. He may decide to pay for errors you think he has committed, even if he believes you are wrong, rather than fight about it.

Don't assume from this discussion of controversy that it characterizes the construction period and amounts to a contant headache. On the contrary, although no project lacks one or two arguments, they are few and far between in the vast majority of jobs.

The photographs on page 237 show the Hauswirths' residence a month and a half after construction began. The boards that look like roof rafters (except that they vary in pitch) are temporary formwork: They are the straight-line generators of the hy-pars. The bent boards that will constitute the permanent structure can be seen on the nearest segment of the studio roof in the second photograph. Only the lower layer is in place. The ends will be trimmed after the upper layer is added. After the upper layer and edge struts have been installed, the temporary "rafters" will be removed.

The architect thought that the most economical way for the contractor to build the roof would be to construct one segment at a time, then reuse the same form boards on the next segment. The contractor, however, was building another house a few miles away. He ordered the floor joists for the other house earlier than needed, had them delivered to the Hauswirth job, and used them to form all ten segments of roof at once. When he took the formwork down, he trucked it to the other house and installed it for floor joists. No architect was involved in the construction of the other house, so it seems unlikely that the owner ever learned that his floor joists were second-hand.

OWNER-ARCHITECT-CONTRACTOR RELATIONSHIP

Before construction began, the relationship between you and the architect was, in a sense, quite simple. The two of you were jointly engaged in solving complex problems, it is true, but each of you had an easily defined role, and your relationhip was one of cooperation. The advent of the contractor severely complicates things. Where you and the architect had a joint interest, the contractor now introduces an interest to some extent opposed to yours, and the architect assumes an obligation to protect the contractor's interest as well as your own. To the extent that the architect may have made mistakes in the drawings and specifications, he also acquires an interest in self-protection that may be opposed to both you and the contractor.

As a result of the high potential for conflict during the construction period, everyone involved should take pains to accommodate the others and be ready to make compromises. A spirit of give-and-take should prevail. Actually, the complexity of relationships during construction is not extraordinary. Almost any businessman's daily affairs are of equal or greater intricacy and require as much or more compromise. But when the businessman, and especially his wife, get involved in the construction arena, they may be at a double disadvantage. In the first place they are neophytes, while the architect and contractor are old hands. Secondly, an owner may have been lulled into a false sense of ease by the serenity of the design period. Suddenly he is immersed in mundane bickering with the profit motive blazing on all sides. Don't let the architect's occasional grim demeanor or the contractor's occasional screams of outrage ruffle your calm. Those two may just be feeling each other out. Affairs will probably adjust themselves if you let them.

One thing in particular that you should guard against is any attempt by the contractor to circumvent the architect and deal directly with you. Some sharpies in the trade are quite skillful at getting you aside and insinuating that they can save you great sums if only certain of the architect's details can be modified, some materials changed, and some silly formalities omitted from the Contract conditions. It is true that you yourself are the best judge of what will best serve some of your interests, but the architect is a better judge of what will best serve others, and any proposal by the contractor should be submitted for thorough evaluation by the architect. He has nothing to gain by letting the quality of your building diminish, whereas a contractor who wants you to let him make changes without consulting the architect is unquestionably trying to pull a fast one. If the contractor claims some change will save you a thousand dollars, rest assured it will save him two thousand. Let the architect provide you with the protection for which you are paying him.

DESIGN CHANGES

The number of buildings completed without a few changes in design made during construction is negligible. The contractor and the workmen, all of whom have fresh eyes and new points of view, will generate suggestions for improvements, some of which the architect and you will agree are worthy of adoption. As the work proceeds, you and the architect will, furthermore, perceive relationships in the actual building that may have been so obscure in the drawings that they weren't noticed before: Some of these conditions, you will decide, can be improved. Finally, mere continued contact with the job invites new ideas. Here are examples of some of the kinds of changes one might decide to make during construction. Procedures for accomplishing them are important, and will be described.

1. Change in Design, No Change in Contract Amount

The mason subcontractor may ask the architect for permission to use a proprietary mortar-mix instead of site-mixing separately purchased sand and cement as described in the specifications. The architect, if satisfied that the proprietary product is equal in quality or better than what was specified, will probably authorize the substitution. The authorization will first be vocal, and should then be confirmed by a written report or bulletin from architect to contractor, with copy to you. There are several things to notice in this little incident.

Article 15, of the General Conditions gives the architect authority to grant requests like the foregoing, and he will grant or deny many others like it in the course of the work. He will not refer each small job-site query to you for an answer. If he did, you would be inundated by a sea of trivia demanding immediate action, and would have to spend as much time at the site as the architect does. In the case of the mortar mix, you are no expert, and there is no point in consulting you. If the decision involved a change of facility or appearance of the building, the architect would consult you before giving orders to the contractor. Borderline cases will arise, and perhaps once or twice the architect will choose not to bother you when, had you known what was up, you would like to have inserted an oar, but such is the modest price for the benefits of delegating authority in large enterprises.

Sometimes minor changes actually cost a little extra or save a few dollars, but the job runs more smoothly if everyone tacitly assumes that small pluses and minuses will so nearly cancel each other out that the red tape of formal change orders can be avoided.

Minor changes should normally be recorded, but some may not be. Perhaps the contractor has some fabricated metal bridging for floor joists left over from a previous job, and he would like to get rid of it. The architect gives permission to substitute it for some of the specified wood bridging, but may feel it unnecessary in this case to promulgate the change on paper.

2. Change in Design, Plus Change in Contract Amount

Walking through the uncompleted building one day, you may decide that a certain doorway should be widened and the door omitted. As the partition has already been framed, this change will entail an extra cost for revising the framing, but it will produce a credit for omitting the door (and its hardware). You should, of course, discuss the change with the architect before resolving on it.

The contractor may report that the ceramic tile specified for the bathroom floors is a style recently discontinued by the manufacturer, and hence not available. Another style will have to be chosen and it may cost, in the aggregate, substantially more or less than the original one.

The architect may get a bright idea for improving the efficiency of the kitchen by a rearrangement and enlargement of some of the cabinetry. It may cost several hundred dollars to accomplish, but you may agree that the improvement is worth the cost.

In these three examples the proposed change in design will entail a change in the cost of the project. The change in kitchen cabinets will also require additional drafting by the architect.

Once you have tentatively decided to change the design, the first step is for the architect to draw up, or write up, an exact description of the proposed change. He submits this description to the contractor with the request that the contractor propose an amount to be added to or deducted from the Contract amount as compensation for the extra or reduced costs. This request is another invitation for a single bid. When the contractor's answer comes back, it will probably not be what you would call "generous," but it should be "fair," meaning perhaps 10 percent higher than it would be if based on competitive bids. There is rarely any practical way to reduce the amount: You could have the work done cost-plus (General Conditions, Article 15, alternative c), but even though this method might eliminate some of the padding, if any, in the contractor's proposal, it probably won't unless you have a project representative to keep track of the time and materials required for the change. If the architect thinks the contractor's proposal is fantastically high, however, the change had better be dropped, or deferred until after the job is completed and then done by another contractor, or done cost-plus now with someone hired to keep track of the time and materials expended.

Once the cost of the proposed change is determined, you can decide intelligently whether to proceed with it or not. If you decide against it the matter drops. If you decide to go ahead, the architect should prepare a formal change order. A sample is shown on the next page. Note that it amounts to a set of instructions for revising the Contract Documents, not for revising the work itself. Each holder of a set of drawings and specifications is meant to incorporate the described revisions into his own

AIA FORM G-701

CHANGE ORDER

OWNER'S COPY

If this order is satisfactory, the owner is requested to please sign and return Contractor's and Architect's copies to the Architect.

ARCHITECT'S JOB No. 65-01

CHANGE ORDER No. 1

ISSUED DATE 21 AUGUST 19 65

AMOUNT (Plus ~~or Minus~~) $ 25

TO ARCADIA BUILDING COMPANY CONTRACTOR

FOR GENERAL CONSTRUCTION IN CONNECTION WITH

HAUSWIRTH RESIDENCE

FOR OWNER DR. AND MRS. JOHN T. HAUSWIRTH

YOUR PROPOSAL FOR MAKING THE FOLLOWING CHANGES HAS BEEN ACCEPTED:

ON SHEET NO. 2, LOWER FLOOR PLAN, SOUTH WALL:
ADD NEW WINDOW IN 4'-0" WIDE SPACE EAST OF AND ADJACENT TO THE TWO WINDOWS SHOWN.

ON SHEET NO. 4, SOUTH ELEVATION:
ADD NEW WINDOW AS NOTED ABOVE; HEAD AND SILL HEIGHTS SHALL MATCH THOSE OF ADJACENT WINDOWS. CHANGE SECTION DESIGNATION M-4/5 TO N-4/5, AND SHIFT DESIGNATION M-4/5 4'-0" EASTWARD.

THE AMOUNT OF THE CONTRACT WILL BE (INCREASED) (~~DECREASED~~) IN THE SUM OF:

TWENTY FIVE DOLLARS ($ 25)

WITH (~~INCREASE~~) (~~DECREASE~~) (NO CHANGE) IN THE CONTRACT TIME OF ~~DAYS~~

OWNER'S APPROVAL J.T. Hauswirth

DATE 22 AUGUST 19 65

MARSHALL SHAPER ARCHITECT

By Marshall Shaper

set by making hand-written notes. Thus the current design is always reflected in the drawings and specifications, and no one needs to consult additional papers to discover how the building is to be built. Some architects handle change orders differently, but the method illustrated is the one I prefer.

The change order shown above not only describes the change, but is also the owner's acceptance of the contractor's offer to modify the Contract. The contractor's offer was embodied in his letter quoting a price for the proposed change. Letter and order taken together, therefore, constitute a supplementary Contract Document.

The architect will prepare the change order for your and his signatures. Each of you keeps a copy and he then gives the contractor two copies, one for office and one for field. If a project representative is involved, he too should receive a copy of all change orders.

Design changes involving additional work, as we have seen, tend to cost a little more than the same work would have cost had it been incorporated early enough to be included in the original competitive bids. We have violated the slogan, *plan ahead.* Design changes involving omission of work also cost extra. If the contractor allowed $50 in his bid for that door you now want to omit, he will probably credit you with only $45 or less for the omission. Part or all of the $5 or more he retains merely covers his overhead for the work of original estimating and present omission: He has to write the architect, change his order to the door manufacturer, correct his prints, and so forth.

Sometimes the changes you want to make require more than simple additions to or omissions from the work. They require ripping down or tearing out work already contructed. If you decide to raise the ceiling after the roof has been built, the contractor may have to rebuild the roof, and relocate wiring and ductwork that is already in place. Changes of this kind waste money. As far as you are concerned, of course, the only criterion is whether a given change is worth the cost, regardless of waste, but the extra cost of changes of any kind when they are made during construction is a strong argument for thoughtful evaluation of the design before construction begins.

3. A General Problem of Construction Changes

You may recall my contention that small changes to the preliminary design sometimes have far-reaching and surprisingly numerous effects on the design as a whole. This effect of change is more serious after construction begins. If a doorway is moved during the preliminary design, the movement affects only the two spaces joined by the doorway. After working drawings and specifications are completed, however, movement of a doorway affects not only the adjacent rooms, but also may affect electric lights, switches, outlets, ductwork, wiring, door schedule, hardware schedule, and perhaps other things. As human beings are what they are (fallible), the architect is more prone to overlook some side-effect of a design change if that change is made late rather than early in the design period. Assuming he carefully chases down and deals with all effects of the change, however, his basic fee does not sufficiently compensate him for the time required. Hence Article 4.3 of the owner-architect agreement provides for extra payment for the work involved in design changes.

PAYMENTS TO THE CONTRACTOR

Shortly after the Contract is signed, the contractor will give the architect a breakdown showing how the Contract amount will be distributed to pay for the various parts of the work: so many dollars for glazing, so many for masonry, and so forth. The architect satisfies himself that the allocations are reasonable: If bid-registry was used the duplicate sub-bids indicate how the Contract amount will be distributed. Thereafter this breakdown will occupy the first two columns of the contractor's periodic applications for payment, a sample of which appears on the next page.

If the Contract calls for monthly payments, then about the first of each month the contractor will receive from each subcontractor a statement of the amount of money that subcontractor claims to have earned to date, expressed as a percentage of his total subcontract amount. These percentages are entered in the "%" column of the application. Alternately the subcontractors may bill the contractor so many dollars for their labor, and so many dollars for materials; and these amounts will be entered in the "Labor" and "Materials" columns of the application. The contractor enters amounts and percentage for his own work and the work of his employees in the same manner that he enters subcontract work. The "Completed to Date" column is either the sum of the labor and materials columns, or the percentage multiplied by the subcontract amount. "Balance to Finish" is the difference between the "Contract Amount" entries and the "Completed to Date" entries. The columns are totaled. The sum of the "Contract Amount" entries is, of course, the total Contract amount. The sum

AIA FORM G-702

APPLICATION FOR PAYMENT

OWNER'S COPY

CONTRACTOR'S APPLICATION NO. 3

ARCHITECT'S JOB No. 65-01 PERIOD FROM 1 SEP 65 TO 30 SEP 65

TO DR. AND MRS. JOHN T. HAUSWIRTH OWNER. APPLICATION IS MADE FOR PAYMENT, AS SHOWN BELOW, IN CONNECTION WITH THE GENERAL CONSTRUCTION WORK FOR YOUR RESIDENCE PROJECT

DESCRIPTION OF WORK	CONTRACT AMOUNT	THIS APPLICATION		COMPLETED		BALANCE TO FINISH
		LABOR	MATERIALS	%	TO DATE	
1. GENERAL CONDITIONS	2880			70	2016	864
2. SITEWORK	1620			65	1052	568
3. CONCRETE	1330			80	1064	266
4. MASONRY	1724			100	1724	0
5. METALS	480			100	480	0
6A. ROUGH CARPENTRY	6400			90	5760	640
6B. ROOF CARPENTRY	5200			100	5200	0
6C. FINISH CARPENTRY	6948			0	0	6948
7. MOISTURE PROTECTION	3144			90	2830	314
8. DOORS, WDWS, GLASS	4883			50	2441	2442
9. FINISHES	3281			10	328	2953
10. SPECIALTIES	936			10	94	842
15A. AIR CONDITIONING	3783			75	2840	943
15B. PLUMBING	7800			60	4680	3120
16. ELECTRICAL	2744			50	1372	1372
CHANGE ORDER NO. 1	25			100	25	0
TOTAL	53178				31906	21272

THIS IS TO CERTIFY THAT THE WORK AS LISTED ABOVE HAS BEEN COMPLETED IN ACCORDANCE WITH THE CONTRACT DOCUMENTS. THAT ALL LAWFUL CHARGES FOR LABOR, MATERIALS, ETC., COVERED BY PREVIOUS CERTIFICATES FOR PAYMENT HAVE BEEN PAID AND THAT A PAYMENT IS NOW DUE IN THE AMOUNT OF

THIRTY ONE THOUSAND NINE HUNDRED SIX DOLLARS ($ 31906)

FROM WHICH RETAINAGE OF 10 % AS SET OUT IN THE CONTRACT DOCUMENTS SHALL BE DEDUCTED.

ARCADIA BUILDING COMPANY CONTRACTOR

DATE 30 SEPTEMBER 19 65 PER Gerald Framer

AIA FORM G-703

CERTIFICATE FOR PAYMENT

OWNER'S COPY

ARCHITECT'S JOB No. 65-01

TO DR. JOHN T. HAUSWIRTH OWNER

CERTIFICATE No. 3

DATE 1 OCT 1965

THIS IS TO CERTIFY THAT IN ACCORDANCE WITH YOUR CONTRACT DATED 23 JUN 1965

ARCADIA BUILDING COMPANY CONTRACTOR

FOR GENERAL CONSTRUCTION IS ENTITLED TO THE THIRD PAYMENT

WHICH IS FOR THE PERIOD 1 SEPTEMBER 1965 THROUGH 30 SEPT. 1965 IN THE AMOUNT OF:

TEN THOUSAND FOUR HUNDRED FIFTY TWO DOLLARS ($ 10452)

THE PRESENT STATUS OF THE ACCOUNT FOR THE ABOVE CONTRACT IS AS FOLLOWS:

ORIGINAL CONTRACT SUM . . . . $ 53153

CHANGE ORDERS APPROVED IN PREVIOUS MONTH'S BY OWNER		TOTAL	ADDITIONS	DEDUCTIONS
CHANGE ORDER No. 1	APPROVED 22 AUG	1965	$ 25	$
CHANGE ORDER No.	APPROVED	19		
CHANGE ORDER No.	APPROVED	19		
CHANGE ORDER No.	APPROVED	19		
CHANGE ORDER No.	APPROVED	19		
CHANGE ORDER No.	APPROVED	19		
TOTALS			$ 25	$

TOTAL ADDITIONS $ 25

SUB TOTAL $

TOTAL DEDUCTIONS $

REMARKS

TOTAL AMOUNT OF CONTRACT TO DATE $ 53178

WORK STILL TO FINISH (THIS DATE) . . . . . $ 21272

DUE CONTRACTOR TO DATE . . . . $ 31906

LESS RETAINAGE 10% . . . . $ 3191

TOTAL TO BE DRAWN (TO DATE) . . . . . $ 28715

CERTIFICATES PREVIOUSLY ISSUED . . . . . $ 18263

THIS CERTIFICATE . . . . $ 10452

$

This is to certify that all bills are paid for which previous certificates for payment were issued.

This certificate is based on the estimated amount of work completed in the period covered and any retainage shown is deducted therefrom.

This certificate is not negotiable, it is payable only to the payee named herein and its issuance, payment and acceptance are without prejudice to any rights of the Owner or Contractor under their contract.

ARCADIA BUILDING COMPANY CONTRACTOR

PER G. Framer DATE 2 OCT 1965

MARSHALL SHAPER ARCHITECT

By Marshall Shaper

of the "Completed to Date" entries is the total the contractor has earned, and the sum of the "Balance to Finish" entries shows the total value of work remaining to be done.

The contractor prepares his monthly application for payment in triplicate and sends all copies to the architect. The architect checks the application for correctness, basing his opinion on recent observations of progress at the site plus his knowledge of labor and materials costs. If he thinks some of the amounts are too high, or if there is defective work not yet corrected, he may do one of two things. He may disapprove the application and return it to the contractor explaining why. Or he may discuss the application with the contractor, who may agree to a revision of some of the amounts. The architect can then make pen and ink corrections, with his initials, on the application. In any case once the architect has decided how much you should pay for the month, he will prepare the certificate for payment as shown on page 246.

The entries on the certificate are self-explanatory except for the retainage and the contractor's signature. The size of the retainage will be stated in the Contract. There are two main reasons for retainage. (1) Some of the work that appears satisfactory at the time of payment may later prove to be unsatisfactory, in which case some of the retained money can be allocated to correct such work. (2) Toward the end of a construction project there are usually many small items of diverse work left to be done and numerous administrative details, all of which are important to you but a bother for the contractor. If you had by then paid the contractor, say, 98 percent of the Contract amount, he would probably be happy to kiss the final 2 percent goodbye if he could quit right then. If you have paid him only about 90 percent of the Contract amount, however, he will hardly be willing to sacrifice 10 percent of the Contract amount just to avoid the terminal nuisances.

It is noteworthy that a retainage of about 10 percent is about equal to the contractor's anticipated profits, so that withholding it will not deprive him of adequate working capital.

The architect prepares the certificate for payment in triplicate and sends it to the contractor along with the application for payment. The contractor now signs the architect's certificate in the lower left hand corner below the statement "This is to certify that all bills are paid for which previous certificates for payment were issued." The purpose of this signed statement is to give you some degree of protection against mechanics' liens. I will have more to say about liens in the next chapter.

After signing the certificate, the contractor will forward to you your copy of the application plus the certificate. If, and only if, both forms are in order, you are now obligated to pay the contractor the amount shown on the certificate.

SHOP DRAWINGS

You will be happy to learn that shop drawings are not your worry, nor are they much used in house construction. It may therefore not be necessary that you read this section, but if you do it will help round out your picture of the building industry and the architect's services.

Fabricators take information from the architect's drawings and specifications and use it to prepare their own drawings to be used in their own shops. The aim is convenience. Consider a cabinetry fabricator—a woodworking shop—that has a subcontract to build your kitchen cabinets. The architect's drawings will show, at medium scale, the kitchen with the cabinets in it. The shop drawings prepared by the fabricator, however, will show just the cabinets, with all extraneous surroundings omitted, at large scale. For the convenience of the shop carpenters, who must build the cabinets, the shop drawings will show the exact size of each piece of wood required. This information is not absent from the architect's drawings: It is just that to learn, for example, the width of a certain cupboard door, one might have to add up a series of dimensions, subtract another dimension, and divide the result by three. It is easier to have this arithmetic done by the fabricator's draftsman than to leave it to the carpenters in the shop.

In the architect's drawings there are some intentional omissions, and shop drawings have the additional purpose of remedying them. As the architect wants to give each member of the construction team as much latitude as possible, consistent with your interests, he avoids showing certain details. He may show the exterior appearance of cabinetry joints, for instance, and specify that they be "strong" (he will require a paragraph to define that word). If that is as far as the architect goes, the fabricator is free to work out what he thinks will be the best and cheapest way of cutting, notching, blocking, gluing, and nailing, to achieve the desired results. His decisions will appear on the shop drawings, which the architect will eventually review.

When the fabricator completes the shop drawings, he will print a few sets and send them to the contractor. The contractor should check them to make sure they show everything the fabricator is required to provide under the terms of his subcontract. If the contractor disapproves the shop drawings, he will send them back to the fabricator for revision. If the contractor approves the shop drawings, he will send them on to the architect for his review and approval. The architect should carefully check the shop drawings to insure that they correctly reflect the design embodied in the Contract Documents. Checking structural or reinforcing steel shop drawings for a $500,000 school may require about two days' work. If the architect discovers errors in the shop drawings, he will send them back to the fabricator for correction. When shop drawings are finally approved by the architect and contractor, everyone who needs copies will get a set, including the project representative if you have one.

In each trade division of the specifications the architect will state what shop drawings, if any, are required to be submitted for his approval. The bigger the job, the more shop drawings he will want. The twenty lineal feet of stair handrail in your house will not require shop drawings; the thousand lineal feet in a school will. On large jobs perhaps as much as 20 percent of the architect's activity during the construction period is devoted to checking shop drawings.

OWNER'S VISITS TO THE JOB

You will naturally visit the construction site from time to time and look over the work. As owner you are not restricted to sidewalk-superintending. You can walk right up and get in the way. You can engage the workmen in conversation, joke with the superintendent, and kid the architect. You can outline to all of them your suggestions for improving the work. Actually, however, behavior of this kind is not entirely desirable. When you visit the job there is a certain etiquette; there are one or two rules.

It is well to remember that you are the guest of the contractor. He is in charge at the site, and his authority entails a responsibility for the safety of persons. Although Article 13 of the General Conditions gives the architect right of access to the work, it says nothing about you. Of course, no contractor in his right mind would bar you from the project, but I suspect he would have a legal right to do so if your presence interfered with his work. When you visit the job, therefore, you should first inform the superintendent of your presence and listen respectfully to anything he has to say, such as "Please don't go downstairs. The concrete hasn't set yet." If he offers you a hard hat, wear it. As you wander around, keep out of the way of the workmen and don't unduly distract them by forcing them into long conversations about this one's lumbago, that one's missing fingers, and so forth. If you have questions, direct them to the superintendent, or better yet to your project representative, or best of all to the architect.

In view of the fact that the work is being performed under contract, perhaps the most important thing for you to remember is that any oral agreement you make with the contractor or his superintendent can be held to modify the Contract. This fact has widespread implications for governing your utterances at the construction site. You should never, for example, give orders to the contractor. If you want something changed, discuss it with the architect, letting him work out the most economical and efficient rearrangement with due regard to the investigation of side-effects. If you bypass the architect, the contractor may be tempted to take unfair advantage of your innocence, but even if he doesn't, you will produce confusion resulting in later mistakes, delay, extra cost, or all three. Nor should you ever tell the contractor that any part of the work is satisfactory. How do you know it is? Have you studied—and fully understood—all relevant parts of the drawings and specifications? If you say something is satisfactory, you just mean it looks right to you, but the contractor can hold that your approval means you accept the work as conforming to the Contract Documents. Judgment of this sort is what you pay the architect to exercise.

Besides not asking the contractor to make changes and not volunteering approval, you must avoid letting the contractor worm them out of you. He may be in a bind about something, pounce on you in the architect's absence, and prophesy delay or disaster unless you agree to something or other immediately. "Look here," says he, "if we don't put a nipple on the vent stack, all your sinks'll back up." You may feel like a fool if you refuse to agree, but the only correct thing to do is to call the architect, or instruct the contractor to call the architect. (That is one order you *can* give.) If the contractor declares that an emergency exists and there is no time to call the architect, direct the contractor's attention to Article 12 of the General Conditions. Emergencies are *very* rare.

If these cautions and strictures make you nervous at the prospect of visiting the job, you can relax if you will just remember that a sure-fire method of keeping out of trouble is to avoid statements and confine your remarks to questions. Questions can perfectly reveal your thoughts without committing you to them. For instance you might say "Isn't this wood terribly knotty and warped?" or perhaps "My! This brickwork is sloppy . . . isn't it?" or merely "Nipples? You don't say." Conducting yourself in this way will keep your foot out of your mouth, even if it will not necessarily endear you to the contractor.

It is best if your visits coincide with the architect's. You needn't guard your tongue with him, but you should avoid arguing or disagreeing with him in the contractor's or workmen's hearing. Otherwise you tend to undermine the architect's authority and reduce the construction team's respect for him, both of which complicate his job and diminish his effectiveness, which in turn harms you in the long run because he is your representative.

Enough of deportment. How does the building look? One of the things you may notice with dismay during the early stages of construction is that all the rooms look too small. This deceptive appearance is another example of the various phenomena of scale. Before the walls are finished, the eye is constrained to relate the size of the rooms to the size of all outdoors. The rooms are actually small only by comparison, but the eye takes this as evidence that they are absolutely small. After the walls are completed, and outdoors is visible only in segments through the windows, the illusion vanishes and things look "right."

When the finishes begin to go on—flooring, plaster, paint, and so forth —you will tend to scrutinize them with extraordinary care and detect many small flaws. When the novelty of these finishes wears off, many of the flaws will be unnoticeable unless you get in a tizzy over them in the first place. The architect will require the contractor to improve anything that is below the standards specified by the Contract Documents, but this improvement will still leave a few nicks and gouges that you will have to accept, along with a few things that are a trifle out-of-plumb or a hair out-of-square. The construction team can no more build a perfect building than an architect can produce a perfect set of drawings. Don't hesitate to point out flaws to the architect, but don't be surprised if he considers that some of them are too minor for correction, or actually within the quality standards of the Contract.

THE HIGH COST OF BEING IN A HURRY

If you hurried the architect through the preliminary design, you probably found it necessary to have him make quite a few changes to the design during preparation of working drawings and specifications. These changes will have entailed extra architectural fee. If you hurried the architect through preparation of the Contract Documents, you will probably find you want to make many design changes during construction. These

The Hauswirth living-dining area. The viewpoint of the camera differs from the viewpoint used for the interior perspective in Chapter 11. Note also some changes in the fireplace and furniture.

changes will entail not only an additional architectural fee but also extra construction costs. If you try to hurry the contractor through construction, you will pay for your haste. In the first place, if you insist on crash construction, the bidders will bid high because they must plan on overtime wages and less opportunity to negotiate for favorable materials prices. Liquidated-damages and penalty-bonus clauses, which are intended to speed construction, also result in higher bids. Increasing the number of carpenters or tile-setters or plasterers on the job will save time, but at the cost of decreased efficiency: They stumble over each other, which drives up the cost of their work. Rapid delivery of materials tends to cost more: Air mail is quicker, but first-class is cheaper. A partly loaded truck can depart earlier, but the freight cost per pound will be higher than if the truck were fully loaded. A project representative's presence is an excellent way to help expedite construction, but he too costs money.

Haste makes waste, as you may have heard. Also, time is money, but this old saw applies with a twist: It means here that the more time you allow, the more money you tend to save. Any step you take to make others perform faster than the rate they normally set for themselves will tend to raise the cost of what they do. I don't mean to imply that you should accept lethargy on the part of the people you hire, but you should be aware of the high cost of being in a hurry, and not commit yourself to such expense unless you are pretty sure the results will be worth it.

CONCLUSION

The construction process should be enjoyable: a mounting pleasure that reaches a climax when the building stands completed and you move in. If the building is personal, such as your own house, your tendency may be to commence the project in a logical frame of mind, but as time passes and the work advances, your rationality may diminish as your excitement increases. You then become subject not only to pleasant feelings but also to exaggerated disappointments over delays, small errors in design, and so forth. If problems arise, your emotional state may induce you to make unwise decisions. Therefore this chapter is designed to fortify you against letting shock get the better of you if serious problems come up during construction, and to help you remain dispassionate over trifles. The problems of construction can be solved if they are not falsely magnified by anxious owners.

Chapter 19

COMPLETION AND MOVING-IN

GRADUALLY the time comes when the percentage completion of all items on the application for payment grows into the high nineties. Shortly thereafter the architect will make an extra-thorough inspection of the entire job, in the course of which he will write down each item of work remaining to be done and every defect of workmanship requiring correction. His notes are called the *punch-list,* and it is the beginning of the finale.

When the contractor receives a copy of the punch-list he proceeds, with his subcontractors, to complete or correct all the work noted. Meanwhile other terminal events take place.

EQUIPMENT LITERATURE

The construction team should turn over to the architect all manufacturers' guarantees, as well as installation, operating, and maintenance instructions that "came in the box" with things like the furnace, bathroom exhaust fans, kitchen range, plumbing fixtures, and the rest of the products and equipment incorporated into the project. When the architect's collection of these papers is complete, he will turn it over to you. I recommend that you preserve all the items in a known, readily accessible location. Their potential future usefulness is obvious.

SHOP DRAWINGS

If you have a project representative, he should have a complete collection of shop drawings for the project. The shop drawings can be conveniently matched up with the other equipment literature and all filed in the same general location. If there is no project representative, the architect will turn over to you his collection (or duplicate collection) of shop drawings.

ROOFING BONDS

Low-slope roofs over 5,000 square feet in area may be bonded, along with their flashings. A twenty-year roofing (and flashing) bond is a bonding company's promise to pay the cost of repairs if leaks develop any time during the twenty years after completion. If such a bond is called for in the specifications, the contractor will buy it and turn it over to the architect for his approval. The architect will forward it to you, and you can stow it with the other papers described above. As neither small-area rooves nor shingled rooves are bonded, you cannot expect a bond for a house roof.

OPERATING INSTRUCTIONS

The specifications usually require that the contractor provide instructions for you, or your representative, on the operation and maintenance of equipment in the building. Generally this instruction will consist of an hour or two of lecture-discussion with the mechanical and electrical subcontractors' job foremen. It will probably be a good idea to take copious notes.

FINAL INSPECTION

When the contractor informs the architect that all items on the punch-list have been accomplished, the architect will conduct a final inspection of the job. You may accompany him if you like, and he will probably urge that you do. If any further unfinished work comes to light, it will be noted and the contractor informed. When all the work is determined to be satisfactorily completed, the architect will give you a written statement to that effect. The various one-year, two-year, five-year, etc., guarantee periods start from the date of this written statement.

The local building inspector may also have to make a final inspection before you can occupy the building, and he should by now have done so and issued an occupancy permit.

Don't forget to collect the keys. The contractor has them.

Now, although the physical work is done, and you can move in, some important paper work remains.

WAIVERS OF LIEN

Every subcontractor, contractor, supplier, and fabricator who worked on the job or furnished materials for it may have a potential claim on *you* if he was not paid by the contractor. The Contract, of course, requires the contractor to pay these other parties, but if for some reason (bankruptcy, dishonesty) he fails to pay them, then under the lien laws you may be on the hook for his debts. Therefore before you pay the contractor the final 10 percent retainage, the architect will require all parties with inchoate liens to submit waivers of lien, which are statements to the effect that the undersigned has received all payment due him for work on your project and he therefore relinquishes all claims against you. If any party refuses to sign a waiver of lien, you should seek your lawyer's advice. Chances are the correct procedure will be to deduct from the final payment to the contractor the amount of the refuser's claim, and put the money in escrow. The balance of the Contract amount can then be paid to the contractor.

FINAL PAYMENT

The contractor will submit his final application for payment when he believes his work is done. The architect will review it as usual, check the arithmetic, and if he is satisfied that the work is indeed complete, that equipment literature has been received, operating instructions given, roofing bond forwarded, and all waivers of lien submitted, the architect will issue the final certificate for payment. Thus end his basic services.

AS-BUILT DRAWINGS

A lot of small changes, and perhaps a few large ones, will have been made in the course of the work. A while back we widened a doorway and omitted a door. The water heater that we finally got straightened out was not installed exactly in the position shown on the drawings, and a number

of other things had their locations or sizes modified. The point where the house sewer leaves the building may differ from the point shown on the drawings.

Most, if not all of these revisions were scrawled in red pencil on the prints during the course of the work, but those prints are all tattered and unusable by now. For future reference it may be advisable to have correct drawings of the building as it was built. This is especially true if future remodeling or additions seem likely. As an extra service, the architect will revise his original drawings to incorporate the changes made during construction. He will give you as many sets of prints of the revised drawings as you wish, and will retain the originals in his files, or on microfilm, indefinitely, so that you can obtain additional sets if you ever need them. The cost of having as-built drawings for a medium-sized house will probably be on the order of a hundred dollars.

THE GUARANTEE PERIOD

Construction work is customarily guaranteed against defects of materials and workmanship for a period of one, sometimes two years from date of acceptance or completion. Equipment may come with a manufacturer's guarantee for an even longer period. If any defects appear during the guarantee period, you should call the contractor to come and remedy them. The contractor, of course, is not required to remedy without charge defects caused by your use of the premises or equipment. After the expiration of the contractor's guarantee period, defects in equipment having a longer guarantee period are a matter between you and the manufacturer or supplier.

Final satisfactory adjustment of the air-conditioning system will very likely take the full year. Only the most extravagant systems approach perfect balance for all seasons of the year, and your system will probably require tinkering every few months before the optimum settings of all dampers can be determined.

Just prior to the end of the guarantee period some owners recall the architect to make a thorough inspection of the building and note any defects the owner may not have discovered.

The Hauswirths and Shaper stood on the balcony watching the sun descend behind the grove. The air had an autumn bite. Harriet was about to go in and take the roast out of the oven. Shaper drained his cocktail glass and spoke hesitantly.

"This may be a dangerous question, but I'll ask it anyway. If you had it all to do over again, what changes would you make?"

"I don't know," said John, ". . . why do you ask?"

"Maybe I'll learn something that will help in the future. Maybe I'm just angling for compliments."

"Marshall, it's a lovely house," said Harriet. "Some of the doors still stick, of course, and you've simply got to get that man back to fish out the piece of plasterboard that fell into the duct to our bedroom before the cold weather sets in. And the light in Cheryl's room . . ."

"Harriet," interrupted John, "how's the roast?"

"Oh. I'd better look." She went in.

"Building a house is always nerve-wracking for the wife," said Shaper, nervously.

Later it rained. As Shaper went to his car water gushed noisily from the open metal spouts at the corners of the roof. They'll never have to clean out eaves troughs, he reminded himself, nor have clogged downspouts. As for the rest of the house, he knew it wasn't perfect, and perhaps the next one would be better. Still, he felt that although the Hauswirths' house naturally reflected the architect who conjured it up, nevertheless in every way that mattered it truly reflected the Hauswirths who called it forth, and that was as it should be.

GLOSSARY

Acoustics. Pertaining to the control of noise and sound in and around buildings.

Air Conditioning. Usually means summer-cooling, but should mean any and all of the following operations on air: heating, cooling, ventilating, humidifying, dehumidifying, and filtering.

Apron. Wood moulding up against the underside of a stool and against the wall.

Backfill. Fill installed to restore an excavated area to its original level.

Batten. Narrow strip used to cover a linear joint.

Bay. The space between columns or piers.

Beam. A structural member, horizontal or nearly so, supported at its ends by walls, columns, piers, or girders.

Bearing Wall. A wall that helps support the floor(s) and/or roof.

Blocking. Small pieces of material, usually wood, attached to structural members to position finish elements, such as curtain tracks, fascias, etc.

Bridging. Short, diagonal pieces paired in rows between joists or beams to help stiffen them by holding them upright.

Cantilever. A building element or that part of a structure which projects horizontally (or nearly so) beyond its support. An overhang. Example: stretch out your arm horizontally and it becomes a cantilever; if then you press your hand down on someone's shoulder, however, your arm ceases to be a cantilever (or ceases to cantilever, as the word is also a verb—transitive and intransitive).

Carriage. Strong, inclined members supporting a stair.

Casing. Mouldings covering the joint where an opening frame meets a wall.

Cement. A grayish or whitish powder that comes in a bag and is used in making concrete and mortar. Sometimes erroneously used to mean concrete.

Chimney. Supporting encasement for one or more flues.

Column. Vertical structural member; usually of wood, steel, or concrete; and relatively thin in cross section. See Pier, Post.

Concrete. A properly proportioned mixture of cement, sand, gravel, and as little water as practical, which hardens (sets-up) into a rocklike mass.

Conduit. A pipe, usually of metal, in which electric wires are encased for protection.

Contemporary. Existing at the same time, as "Most of the framers of the American Constitution were contemporary with Ludwig von Beethoven." Contemporary is often erroneously used to mean modern.

Convenience Outlet. See Outlet.

Coping. Watershed along the top of a parapet.

Cripple. Short piece of stud above or below an opening in a studwall.

Cut. To remove a layer of earth over a wide area with a bulldozer or scraper. See Excavate.

Deck. A continuous horizontal (or pitched, if a roof deck) surface; often of wood, sheet metal, or thin concrete; to which flooring or roofing will be applied.

Design. To originate or invent. An invention.

Dimension. Length expressed in conventional units such as feet and inches. A dimension line on an architectural drawing is a two-headed arrow with figures stating the length.

Draftsman. One who makes architectural or engineering drawings, under supervision, but with some discretion as to design.

Duct. A rectangular or circular pipe, of sheet metal or other material, for the conveyance of air.

Elevation. (1) A vertical distance above or below some reference, such as a floor, or the earth's surface. (2) A type of architectural drawing, see Chapter 11.

Esthetic. Pertaining to art.

Excavate. To dig a relatively deep hole or trench with a shovel or trencher.

Fascia. (Pronounced FAY-sha) (Plural: Fascias, Fasciae). Usually an upright, horizontally running board that covers the ends of roof rafters. Eaves.

Fill. Earth installed to raise the grade. To install fill.

Flashing. Thin sheet metal or plastic, installed at exterior joints where the conjunction of other materials is not naturally waterproof.

Flat (Roof). A misnomer. Like walls, most rooves are flat or composed of flat segments, and those who say "flat roof" usually refer to something better termed "level roof."

Floor. A composite of deck, subfloor, (underlayment) and flooring.

Flooring. Floor surfacing, chosen for durability, appearance, etc.

Flue. Smoke pipe. See Chimney.

Footing. Concrete pad placed on earth to carry a column or foundation wall.

Foundation. The supporting parts of a building, encased on both sides by, and resting on, the earth.

Frame. A set of linear members joined at their ends to form one or more polygons, usually rectangular. Doors fit into door frames, window sash fit into window frames, etc.

Framing. Building framework such as the combination of studwalls, rafters (or trusses), and joists of "frame" houses; or the columns and beams of other buildings.

Functional. Characterized by physical utility rather than by imitative, emotional, or whimsical content.

Furring. Strips attached to walls or structural framing to provide continuous, accurately positioned, points of attachment for finish surfacing of walls or ceilings.

Girder. A beam that supports the end(s) of other beam(s).

Grade. The level of the earth's surface. To alter the level of the earth's surface.

Grout. A kind of mortar placed on top of a footing to position a column base plate. To install grout.

Hardware. (Rough) anchor bolts, joist hangers, and other miscellaneous metal fittings that will be hidden by finishes. (Finish) Door knobs, hinges, cabinet pulls, and other fittings meant to be touched and/or seen.

Harmony. The relationship between members of a happy family; a pleasing juxtaposition of diverse elements.

Head. The horizontal upper member of a door or window frame.

Hipped (roof). A pitched roof whose segmentation results in a level eave line all around the building with no gables.

Home. (1) One's primary abode. (2) Real estate salesman's term for any house he is trying to sell you.

House. A building designed for human residence.

Jack. A shore of adjustable length. To adjust the length of a jack.

Jamb. A side member of a door or window frame.

Joist. A light beam.

Ledger. A board nailed to studs on which the ends of wood joists rest for support. A steel angle bolted to a wall, or anchored to upright steel framing, for the support of steel beams or joists.

Level. (1) Horizontal; at right angles to a radius of the earth. (2) A land surveyor's instrument consisting of a telescope with crosshairs that can be swung in a horizontal circle and is mounted on a tripod base. In conjunction with a graduated rod or pole a level is used to measure differences in elevation between points where the rod is stood. (3) A straight length of wood or metal containing glass tubes partially filled with liquid, which indicate, by the position of the bubble, whether the level is horizontal or vertical. Used by carpenters and masons to level and plumb their work. (4) To make level.

Light. One piece of glass in a window.

Lintel. A beam over an opening in a wall to carry the load of wall above in the absence of support from wall below.

Masonry. Bricks, concrete blocks, glass blocks, clay tiles, stones, or gypsum blocks, set in mortar, usually to form walls.

Modern. Of the present; new-fashioned; what the Parthenon was 2,500 years ago.

Mullion. A riblike piece of wood or metal that divides a window into smaller segments or lights.

N.I.C. "Not in Contract." A future element of a building, drawn for clarity, but not to be provided by the contractor.

Noise. Unwanted sound.

Nosing. The part of a tread that projects over the riser.

Outlet. (Electrical) A fitting where electric current is available. There is an outlet for each built-in electric light and electric appliance. A convenience outlet is one where the cord of a portable electric light or appliance can be plugged in.

Parapet. When a wall extends vertically above the level of the roof, the part of the wall higher than the roof is the parapet.

Partition. An interior, or "indoor," wall.

Peak. A point where three or more plane segments meet. See Ridge.

Pier. A vertical support that is relatively thick or wide, usually of stone or brick.

Pillar. Popular term for column.

Plate. The upper horizontal member of a studwall.

Plenum. A box of concrete or sheet metal large enough to serve as the junction between several ducts and the furnace.

Plumb. Vertical; at right angles to the horizon. To make vertical.

Post. A relatively short column, such as one that is less than a story in height.

Rafter. A wood beam that supports a roof deck and is pitched.

Retaining Wall. A concrete or masonry wall designed to hold earth at a steeper slope (up to vertical) than the natural slope (angle of repose).

Ridge. The highest line of intersection of the segments of a pitched roof; sometimes erroneously called a peak.

Riser. (1) The vertical piece of a step of a stair. (2) An essentially vertical pipe.

Roof. A composite of deck and roofing.

Roofing. A waterproof, durable roof surfacing, such as shingles, sheet metal, or layers of tarred felt mopped on with hot asphalt.

Sash. The movable part of a window. The sash contains the glass and is hinged to the window frame, which is installed immovably in the wall.

Sheathing. Plywood, wood boards, or composition board nailed as a continuous surfacing on the outer face of stud walls for rigidity, the attachment of some kinds of finish material, and to a minor degree for thermal insulation.

Shore. A temporary vertical support. To install such supports.

Sill. (1) Horizontal exterior member at bottom edge of a window, and pitched to shed water. A wood window sill that is part of the window frame often rests on a masonry window sill that is part of the wall. (2) The lower horizontal member of a stud wall. (3) Mud Sill: A plank laid on the ground as temporary footing for a shore.

Soffit. The exposed underside of a building element such as a moulding or roof overhang.

Stool. Horizontal interior member at bottom edge of a window, sometimes erroneously called a sill.

Stop. (1) A thin strip of wood, metal, or plastic that holds a piece of glass against its sash or frame. (2) A thin strip of wood or metal lining a door frame and against which the door impinges when closed.

Structure. (1) The relationship among the elements of something. (2) In buildings, the system of strong elements, such as beams and columns, whose purpose is the support of the building as a whole. The design and mathematical analysis of the strength of such systems is termed structural engineering. (3) By extension, loosely, a building as a whole.

Stud. One of numerous vertical structural wood or metal story-height members usually about 4 inches wide by about half as thick.

Studwall, Stud Wall. Most common house wall construction consisting of (usually) 2 x 4 studs spaced (usually) 16 inches on centers, joined at their lower ends by a 2 x 4 sill and at their upper ends by a double 2 x 4 plate.

Style. A set of coherent characteristics that distinguish an individual or group from other individuals or groups of the same kind.

Survey. A land, or topographical survey, is a map of a site showing all features that might prove relevant to design or construction decisions; including trees, earth slope, buried utility lines, boundaries, etc. (2) To make a survey.

Topographical. Of or pertaining to topography: the shape of the earth's surface plus other natural and man-made features.

Traditional. Long-established; customary.

Transit. A land surveyor's instrument consisting of a telescope with cross-hairs that can be swung in a vertical as well as a horizontal circle and that is mounted on a tripod base. It is used to measure the vertical or horizontal angle between sighted objects, for which purpose the transit embodies both vertical and horizontal azimuth circles graduated in degrees of arc. A transit can also be used as a level, but is slightly less accurate than instruments designed for leveling only.

Tread. The horizontal piece of a step of a stair.

Trim. Finish mouldings in the aggregate.

Vapor Barrier. A thin membrane, usually of plastic or paper, impenetrable by water vapor.

Veneer. (1) A thin layer of expensive wood glued to a stiff backing. (2) A relatively thin layer of brick (4 inches or one-brick thick) or stone used as a wall finish, as opposed to a thick layer(s) used as a bearing wall.

Vent. (1) An opening or duct for the escape of unwanted fumes. (2) A plumbing vent is a pipe that extends through the roof and is so connected to the plumbing system as to prevent differential pressures that might cause siphoning away of the water that lies in fixture traps to seal off sewer fumes.

Wall. (See Bearing Wall) (1) Strictly, an exterior wall. (2) Loosely, an exterior wall or a partition.

INDEX

INDEX*

* References in boldface indicate that an illustration appears on that page.